*For shelter dogs everywhere—
may you prosper and live long.*

SUCCESSFUL DOG ADOPTION

SUCCESSFUL DOG ADOPTION

SUE STERNBERG

HOWELL
BOOK
HOUSE

Howell Book House

Published by Wiley Publishing, Inc., Indianapolis, Indiana

All photographs by Sue Sternberg

For general information on our other products and services or to obtain technical support please contact our Customer Care Department within the U.S. at 800-762-2974, outside the U.S. at 317-572-3993 or fax 317-572-4002. For group sales call Wiley Customer Service at 800-225-5945.

Wiley also publishes its books in a variety of electronic formats. Some content that appears in print may not be available in electronic books.

Some material in this book originally appeared in a different form in the newsletter of the Association of Professional Dog Trainers in the Jan/Feb 2000 and Nov 2001 issues, and in *Great Dog Adoptions*, published by the Latham Foundation.

Library of Congress Cataloging-in-Publication Data:
Sternberg, Sue.
  Successful dog adoption / Sue Sternberg.
    p. cm.
  Includes index.
  ISBN 0-7645-3893-4 (alk. paper)
  Dogs. 2. Dog adoption. 3. Animal shelters. I. Title.

  SF427.S85 2003
  636.7'0832—dc21

                          2003009304

Manufactured in United States of America

10 9 8 7 6 5 4 3 2 1

Book design by Marie Kristine Parial-Leonardo
Cover design by Wendy Mount
Book production by Wiley Publishing, Inc. Composition Services

Contents

Chapter 1

So You Want to Adopt a Dog 1

What's Involved in Adopting a Dog? 2
Do You Think You're Ready, or Do You Know You're Ready? 2
Your Pre-Adoption Checklist 3
Take a Look at Your Own Lifestyle 9

Chapter 2

Where Do I Start? 13

On the Telephone 13
What to Look for in a Shelter 19

Chapter 3

Where Should I Go for My Dog? 21

What Kind of Shelter? 22
Regional Differences in Shelter Dogs 25
Rescue Groups 27
Internet Adoption 29
Attitudes about "Rescued" Dogs 40

Chapter 4

What Am I Really Looking For? 47

What Should I Expect from the Shelter? 47
What Is the Adoption Process Like? 49
Why Temperament Testing Is Vital 51
What Should I Worry about Most? 52

How Can I Avoid Dogs Who Bite?   53
What Being a "Fearful Dog" Means   58
Male or Female?   60
Are Puppies Clean Slates?   61
What if I Have Allergies?   63
What's the Best Age to Adopt?   64
To Pit Bull or Not to Pit Bull?   72
Breed Generalizations   74
The Ideal Temperament of a Family Dog   76
Safety Scan   76
Bite-O-Meter   82
The Importance of Selecting Carefully   89
Behavioral Rehabilitation Programs in Shelters   90

Chapter 5

How Do I Meet the Dogs?   93

What to Bring With You to the Shelter   93
What You Can Expect from the Dogs   94
Your Gender Matters   95
How Will the Dog Behave When Meeting Guests and Strangers?   96
Temperament Testing Shelter Dogs   99
Tests to Leave for the Pros   114
The Wrap-Up   137

Chapter 6

What Have I Done?   139

What Gender Is Your Dog?   141
Guessing the Age of a Dog   141
Guessing the Mix of Your Dog   146

Chapter 7

Basic Manners   151

Pledge for New Dog Adopters   151
When Should I Start Training?   153
What Kind of Training Class?   153
Housebreaking for Puppies and Adult Dogs   155
Male Dog Urine Marking   157
Cleaning Up the Spots   158

The Basic Sit   158

Coming When Called   160

What to Do if Your New Dog Gets Carsick   161

Helping Your Dog Stay Home Alone   162

Don't Be a Spectator   163

Extracurricular Activities   165

Chapter 8

When All Else Fails   175

Problem Behaviors and What to Do   176

If It Just Doesn't Work Out   181

What to Expect When Calling the Shelter   185

Special Considerations for Families with Young Children   186

Don't Go It Alone   191

Chapter 9

Adding Another Dog   193

Choosing a Compatible Companion for Your Resident Dog   195

Why Dog-Dog Aggression Matters for Everyone   196

The Dog-Dog Aggression Test   197

The Four Play Styles   212

Welcoming a Second Dog into Your Home and Your Heart   215

What Do Dogs Fight About?   217

Index   223

Chapter 1

So You Want to Adopt a Dog

This book is designed to guide you through the process of adopting a dog, and to help you to find that "right" dog. The right dog in your life is a sacred and unparalleled friend. The relationship between you and your dog will be more powerful than you can imagine, and more intensely rewarding than you will know until you actually do it. Adopting the right dog is likely to be the most gratifying thing you will ever do, and I would like you to find this exceptional dog at a shelter.

While I would like the animal shelter to be the premier place to obtain a dog, at the same time I recognize the truth that it can also be the worst. Animal shelters in the United States are filled with some of the very best and some of the very worst dogs. While thousands of absolutely wonderful, sweet family pet dogs are euthanized in shelters that do not have a lot of resources (or a lot of good adopters), the awful flip side is that thousands of aggressive and downright dangerous dogs are available for adoption to unsuspecting people, or are spinning interminably in their cages. Many shelters are run by well-meaning animal lovers who know little about dog behavior or temperament and can offer you little help in selecting the right dog.

I have dedicated my life to trying to make the shelter the best place for people to go to get a dog. That means replacing some of the pity and raw emotions shelter people use to make decisions on adoptions or euthanasia with a solid foundation of dog behavior and training knowledge. While I continue to work toward that goal within the shelter industry, I hope this book will help the general public successfully adopt safe, appropriate and wonderful dogs. I hope this book can serve as a guide so that if you do decide to go to the shelter, you're more likely to bring home a great companion and not a behaviorally disastrous dog.

My goal is to make life and death better and less random for dogs in shelters, and to make shelters safer and better for people visiting them. We need to educate people about the shelter world, and educate the shelter world about people. And educate everybody a little more about dogs.

With a boost of dog behavior knowledge and some tips on assessing temperament, this book will, hopefully, make your adoption experience a lifelong success. Living with a great dog is something no one should miss.

WHAT'S INVOLVED IN ADOPTING A DOG?

For first-time dog owners, your journey into life with a dog is about to begin. Your life is about to change forever. The people in your life will be different. Your schedule will change. Your activity level will go up. Your exercise routine will either begin or change for the better. It will become much harder to be depressed. There will now always be someone overjoyed to see you whenever you return home from work, and just as overjoyed to see you return to the room from a trip to the bathroom. There will, at last, be something substantial to vacuum up from your floors, as tumbleweeds of dog hair will form under your furniture daily.

For experienced dog owners, this may or may not be your first adoption experience. Either way, I want your next dog to be the best ever.

DO YOU THINK YOU'RE READY, OR DO YOU KNOW YOU'RE READY?

There are two basic kinds of people: There are people who readily admit to, want to and are ready to commit to joining the ranks of dog owners everywhere, and are choosing the shelter as their primary resource. For the others, becoming a new dog owner is the kind of thing that, the more they think about it, the more arduous or impossible it seems. The confines of their schedule and the demands and restrictions the dog will make on their life seem to exclude them from dog ownership. Or so they tell themselves. This group tells itself that the time is just not right. And, on the outside, they may act like they're not ready. They are the browsers, the many people who come to the shelter "just looking." But on the inside, they really are ready—*if* the right dog were to come along.

The truth is, it is never really the right time. It is never really convenient to bring a dog into your life. There will probably never be a time in your life when your schedule is free and open, you have plenty of time and feel completely prepared. The truth is, there really is nothing convenient, ever, about having a dog. But it is worth every inconvenience. I'm not trying to convince someone who really doesn't want a dog to go out and get one. But chances are if you are reading this book, you are at least secretly ready—ready somewhere deep down inside—and you would take the plunge if you visited your local animal shelter and met the right dog.

We see this group of people in the shelter as often as we see the group that is absolutely ready, know they are ready, are hot on the trail of the right dog and want that dog now. Today. For this weekend. These people choose the animal shelter because shelters are filled with ready-made dogs. You don't have to research a breed, locate a good and reputable breeder, wait for the bitch to be bred, wait for the puppies to be born, and then wait yet another eight to 12 weeks until they are ready to be sold. At the shelter the dogs are there in front of you, available for adoption in the here and now.

You can either aim for the "right time" in your life to get a dog or aim for the "right dog" in your life. My advice is to go for the right dog. That may mean you don't find the dog of your dreams on your first visit to the shelter. Also, depending on where you live, there may not be a lot of dogs to choose from. The pet overpopulation problem is, thankfully, not what it used to be in many parts of the country, and many shelters, especially the ones that do not make available for adoption aggressive or dangerous dogs, may have more empty kennels than occupied ones.

YOUR PRE-ADOPTION CHECKLIST

Listed below are some suggested mental and physical preparations you can make before you come home with a dog. Mostly, they are things to think about, so that you don't bring a dog home and have all these thoughts come rushing at you at once. There is enough to do and to think about and feel overwhelmed with in first few days you have a new dog, so it can be helpful to try to mull over these things at least once before the dog comes home with you.

Household Rules

Decide now on some household rules. These can be arbitrary at first if you have no particular rules in mind, or you may already know exactly what you will allow from your new dog. Either way, it is far better for your dog to enter a home where he senses many clear rules and regulations than to enter a chaotic situation where you try to implement the rules later on.

Even if you aren't by nature a rule-maker or rule-implementer, doing this with your new dog is a favor to him. Dogs love consistency, and they can relax when they understand the things you want and don't want right from the get-go. Dogs won't *judge* your rules; they will just start adhering to them as you insist. Your new dog is likely to be anxious and agitated in the first few days, and having you insist on some consistent rules will help him feel like he's making fewer mistakes and will give him a clear understanding of what is a mistake and what isn't.

When you're visiting an unfamiliar relative in a strange town, wouldn't you rather have your kin tell you up front please not to put your feet on the coffee table, please turn the heat down to 62° before going to bed, please feel free to eat anything in the refrigerator on all but the top shelf (which is food reserved for your diabetic uncle), etc., than to endure being yelled at and reprimanded for inadvertently doing all these things wrong? It is the difference between having the opportunity to get things right and feel good, and being left to get things wrong and get yelled at, feeling bad and confused without knowing what was right or wrong to start with.

It is much fairer to your dog to teach him what is acceptable and what is not. Some people don't have the personality type to have any preconceived rules in mind, and other people know automatically what they will tolerate and what they won't. Either type needs to set up a number of household rules and encourage, aid and reward the dog for getting them right, rather than starting off the relationship by yelling at him for getting it wrong, or worse, letting your new dog believe that in the absence of anyone with good leadership skills, he will make his own rules. You cannot really "build up" to getting your dog to listen to you, respect you and behave. The more a dog does what he wants and gets away with it, and the more you figure you'll let him settle in before dealing with that "pesky" behavior, the less likely your dog is to ever listen to you, do what you want or behave the way you want him to.

Teaching your dog how to sit, stay, lie down, come, stop barking and stop jumping up are easy enough. This sort of teaching should be accomplished using mostly reward-based training and positive reinforcement. These techniques are fast, fun and effective. But the *relationship* with your dog requires one of you to follow the lead of the other. Making sure, at the outset, that your new dog follows your lead is best accomplished the minute he walks across the threshold. And it is accomplished by setting rules, guidelines and limits, and being willing to firmly and immediately tell your new dog "no" if and when he needs it.

Your new dog needs no adjustment period for this. Quite the contrary. Don't think somehow your "poor" shelter dog has had a traumatic past and needs to be shown only love and kindness. Your new dog needs you to forget his past and start with his crisp new future—right now. He needs love, kindness and leadership. At best, when dogs are allowed to make all their own rules, they become anxious, agitated and have a difficult time settling down. These dogs tend to bark at any noise and end up becoming nuisance barkers woofing at every little bump in the night. Or they pace and pant in the house, never seeming to relax into a nap or even to lie down and relax. At worst, the dog who makes his own rules in the absence of any from you can behave more aggressively. Then your new dog may be experiencing a traumatic *present*, never mind his *past*.

More Things to Prepare

- Your new dog will not (initially, at least) be allowed up on your furniture or on your bed. This is a great example of a rule that is easy to implement at the start and then ease up on as things play out, but an extremely stubborn habit to break if you start out allowing it and decide later on to nix it.

- Your new dog will eat a high-quality dog food, twice a day, after the humans have dined, and will neither be fed from the table nor be allowed table scraps or snacks as you eat your own meals or snacks. (Leftovers and delicious human food, when you feel you must share it, should be set aside in a plastic zipper bag in the refrigerator and used for training purposes, during training sessions.) At first, every calorie should count for something; every morsel should be used as a reward for good behavior, or as a lure or reward when the dog is learning something new and desirable.

- Your new dog will be taught how to sit (see Chapter 7) or requested to sit (because chances are, your new dog already knows how to sit) at least 25 times a day, partly to practice having you give some commands and having your dog comply, but mostly so that at least 25 times a day you both can share the understanding and definition of at least one word in the human language. Soon, you will teach your dog many new words and behaviors, but sometimes at the beginning you will have just one word in common. Think of it as arriving in a foreign country, where you know just one word. No matter what the word, wouldn't it be a relief to hear someone use it with you in its proper context?

- You will have to decide on a good potty elimination area for your new dog *before* he comes home. If you live in the suburbs or the country, the area will likely be somewhere in your yard. If you dream of having a pristine lawn and want excrement only in the woods to the back of your property, spend the first few weeks reinforcing this with your new dog. This is the kind of thing that, if decided on beforehand, is easy and quick to teach your new dog, but is extremely time-consuming to try to implement after your dog has formed a habit of eliminating in a different area. If you live in the city, the best rule is to teach your dog to eliminate in the gutter directly outside your building (not on plants or on the sidewalk). Do NOT get into the habit of walking your dog all the way to the park to eliminate. Then you will be obliged to walk your dog all the way to the park in rain, snow or flu season.

- Take a tour around your own house, starting in any room. Get down to about the three-foot-high level and look over the entire room, scrutinizing every detail—electrical cords, outlets, carpet fringes, rare books on the bottom shelves, eyeglasses and eyeglass cases on coffee tables, pens, pencils on coffee tables, framed (metal, glass or plastic frames) photos, photo albums, anything made of wicker, any irreplaceable or expensive carpeting or rug that can be pulled up and stored away, any worn out or frayed corners of upholstery (too tempting for your dog to nibble), linoleum that is pulling up at its corners and molding that is bent or curled outward. All this must be repaired, moved or removed. Remove any and all pillows and throws from the furniture, and move into storage anything of sentimental or financial value that you would be devastated if it were gnawed on or worse, ruined with some unidentifiable fluid that came from your dog. Even after all this, Dr. Suzanne Hetts, a certified applied animal behaviorist in Denver, Colorado (who is also a dog trainer and adopter), likes to warn people that they need to expect to lose something of value when they bring a dog into their household. And she is right. Her own adopted Dalmatian chewed up and destroyed the only photograph she had left of her grandmother. Adopting a dog who is at least two years old greatly reduces your chances of having him destroy anything, because mature dogs seldom chew for reasons other than severe separation problems, which are relatively rare. The beauty

My dog, Hop Sing, caught shortly after having
dragged a potted houseplant onto the couch.

in adopting an adult or older dog is that once you have lived with him
for a few weeks and determine that he is not a chewer, you can quickly
return your home and its contents back to normal.

- A crate can be a good idea, although many people are reluctant to
  consider one. A crate is a portable dog kennel, sometimes made of
  plastic (like airline carriers) and sometimes made of metal wire. Many
  people gasp and shudder at the thought of a crate for their dog, especially for an adopted dog, feeling that it is yet another cage and the
  dog will feel like he has gone from one cage to another. Although I do
  believe crates are often over-recommended, I also know they are a god-
  send for some dogs and have saved many a strained relationship
  between dog and owner. Crates can be especially useful for young,
  robust dogs, puppies and adolescents at the peak of their chewing
  prowess. Crating is also useful for house-training because most dogs
  will not soil inside a crate. When your new dog arrives, after acclimat-
  ing him slowly to the crate (by placing treats in the back, placing a
  comfy blanket in it, feeding him his meals in it and giving him a
  peanut butter-stuffed hollow bone or toy only when he is confined in
  his new crate), confining him to a crate when you have to leave him

alone or cannot watch him can mean the difference between a house full of poop and pee and a dog who holds it until you arrive home to take him to his appropriate potty spot. Crates are almost a necessary resource in your car, because an unbelted, uncrated dog in a moving vehicle can become a missile during an accident and injure you from inside the car—not to mention the harm to your dog. There are seat-belt restraints made specifically for dogs riding in cars, and they can be useful. But, true confessions—I know not only the logic but the safety of what I've just said, but my five dogs ride as free as missiles in my car—and I worry (fruitlessly) each time I drive about what will happen to them if I have even a minor fender-bender.

- Look at your schedule over the next few weeks and re-schedule any dinner engagements away from home, or change them so that your friends are coming to your home and you are cooking for them (or ordering take-out). While you don't want to glue yourself to your home with your new dog, you don't want to schedule a full day's work *and* then dinner out—thereby leaving your new dog home alone for more than 10 hours. Remember, you have a responsibility at home now, and you will need to schedule time to come home, after being out for more than a few hours, to walk your dog.

- Seek out, *before you need them*, pet sitters, boarding kennels or other dog owners willing to swap dog-sitting or dog-walking services. There are times when emergencies come up, and you will suddenly need someone to go to your home and walk your dog. It's easier to do this research before you need help.

- There is no dire need to purchase items like dog bowls, grooming items and dog food *before* you actually bring home your new dog (you really won't know what your new dog will look like—how big or small, what type of coat, etc.), and you can buy all these items on your way home from the shelter. However, I do advise prepurchasing odor-neutralizing clean-up products and having them ready. The best product to have around to clean up any bodily fluids that may come from your dog (since you'll find out soon enough that many mysterious and hideous fluids do come out of dogs) is an enzymatic product—that is, one that uses enzyme action to neutralize the odor, not just cover it up. The first place you might meet these fluids are in your car on the way home from the shelter. I recommend buying a couple of gallons of odor-neutralizing liquid. Fill a few empty spray bottles and keep them in different rooms, plus one in the car.

- Buy many rolls of paper towels to have on hand, to go with your enzymatic cleaner. Place one roll in every room of your house, and one in the car.

- Check out and familiarize yourself with all the hiking trails, state parks, community parks, rail trails and bike paths in your area, and plan daily outings with your new dog. Not only is exploring these areas fun and interesting, but you'll appreciate the extra exercise and incentive for getting out and about that your new dog will provide. Dogs do best when they get at least one off-territory walk a day. Not only is the exercise and olfactory stimulation fun for them, but it can help keep them from getting too territorial about their own home and yard.

- Set your alarm clock for half an hour earlier in the morning. You'll need to get used to waking up earlier in the day to accommodate walking, playing with and feeding (and walking again) your new dog.

With all that said, the majority of adopters are actually surprised by how easy it is to have a dog. At our shelter we offer adopters a free six-week training course of their choice with every adoption (Puppy Kindergarten, Adolescent Manners, Introduction to Agility or Basic Manners), and many times the adopter will call back a week or so after bringing home their dog and say they don't know what course to sign up for because their dog doesn't seem to need any training. Mind you, these are invariably the adopters of adult dogs, or senior dogs, which might inspire more people to adopt these rather than puppies or adolescents.

I, personally, have never adopted a dog with whom I didn't initially have moments of panic and thoughts of, "Oh my, what have I done?" (and I've adopted 13 dogs over the years—not all at once!). And I have never regretted a single adoption. On the contrary, I feel blessed with the most wonderful dogs a person could ever have.

TAKE A LOOK AT YOUR OWN LIFESTYLE

- If you live with another person or other people, it will be important to look for a dog who is compatible with all the residents in the household.

- If you have children or might have children within the next five to 10 years, look for a dog who will do well in a home with young children, even if you have none yet. Nothing is more heartbreaking than to watch a couple have to give up their beloved companion dog because they have had a baby and the dog is aggressive toward children. If the card on the dog's cage or someone at the shelter recommends a home with no young children, anticipate your future and err on the side of safety.

- Do young children visit your home? How often? Then even if you do not have and do not plan to have children, you, too, will need to adopt a dog who is compatible with young children. A friend of mine is head of the dog training and behavior center at a large shelter. She and her staff are responsible for temperament testing all the dogs to see whether they should go up for adoption or be euthanized because of aggression. The importance of temperament testing and good match-making was underscored for her when her youngest daughter's piano teacher (a single, adult woman) adopted an adult Siberian Husky from her shelter. Each week, her daughter goes to the home of the piano teacher for a lesson, and now each week, a lovely Siberian Husky rests his head on her daughter's lap during the lesson. Imagine if the piano teacher had adopted a dog who was aggressive with children! Even though the piano teacher lives alone, children are in her life.

- Do you currently have other pets in your home? A cat? Another dog? A rodent or a bird? Then you will need help finding a dog who is compatible, as much as anyone can predict, with these species. A middle-aged couple came to our shelter looking to adopt a dog. Their only requirements, they said, were that the dog had to get along with chickens and not run away. They didn't care what their dog would look like or about size, age or gender. They lived on 70 unfenced acres in the middle of the Catskill Mountains and shared the property with another couple, who kept free-range chickens. Any dog they adopted would have to meet those requirements, to the best of anyone's predictions. The couple made a few trips to the shelter before we finally had a dog whose temperament tested as a possible match. We had a seven-month-old female dog who had very little predatory instinct (she was tested around large farm animals and cats, since we had no chickens to test her with—except for chicken in our refrigerators, which is not very helpful) and a very sociable and affectionate nature that would likely keep her from straying off when she was outside with her new owners. We phoned the couple to tell them we had found a possible match. They came, met, visited with and fell in love with Cedar Syrup, a young, chocolate-colored Pit Bull mix. Yes, Pit Bull mix. Although many of the bull breeds can be quite predatory, not all are, and the temperament test becomes the great, objective equalizer that judges each dog as an individual.

- What access will you and your dog have to aerobic exercise? Do you have a fenced-in yard? Do you have an unfenced yard? Will your dog be walked on a leash? Will you be depending on dog parks for the only off-leash exercise? Then it will be important to adopt a dog who plays well with other dogs. Are you sedentary or active by nature? Are your personal outlets for aerobic exercise ones that could include your dog? Membership at a gym will do your active Labrador Retriever mix no good, since you can't take your dog with you. If you mountain bike or hike or go for brisk walks or jog, these are exercise regimes that welcome an active dog. If you're a bit of a slug, you'll need a sluggish, low-key kind of dog to adopt. And remember, a fenced yard in itself does not exercise your dog. Most dogs who live in homes with fenced-in yards will not go outside and exercise on their own. Companion dogs want your companionship. If you let the dog out into your yard and you remain inside, your dog will sit at the doorway, staring dolefully and waiting for you to come out and play. And if you leave your dog in the yard while you go to work, he will likely spend most of his day sleeping. So no matter what your access to an exercise area for your new dog, include yourself in the plan.

- How much time away from home do you spend each day? The formula for how long a puppy can be happily left alone is to take their age in months and add one, up to eight months—at which point nine hours becomes the very top limit. For example, a four-month-old puppy can be left alone for up to five hours at a time, a two-month-old for three hours. These figures are for daytime, as most puppies older than eight to 10 weeks can last through the night. So if your work keeps you out of the house for seven hours (including your commute), you shouldn't adopt a puppy under the age of six months unless you can change your schedule or hire someone to come and visit with your puppy while you're away. This is not just for housebreaking. Puppies and dogs need human company. The longer they are isolated, the crazier they are when you return home, not just from lack of exercise or the need to eliminate, but because they have been lonely and need company.

Whatever your personal lifestyle, it will be enhanced by a dog. There is no other species out there like them. They'll burrow into your heart in surprising ways.

Chapter 2

Where Do I Start?

In the previous chapter, you started the process of adopting a dog by examining yourself, your lifestyle, your activities concerning physical exercise and your schedule. Now you need to figure out where to go for your dog.

Wherever you live, you will have many options in looking for a dog to adopt. Every community has its local shelter or animal control officer, at the very minimum, and if you have a telephone and access to the Internet, you will have way more options to choose from. It is a good idea to try to get a recommendation for a good shelter from a friend or acquaintance who has either had a successful adoption experience, or knows of someone who has. Word of mouth is very helpful.

ON THE TELEPHONE

- Call your local veterinarian's office and ask if they can recommend a good local animal shelter. Vets will be a good resource in your community for a referral, since they will most probably know what diseases may be prevalent in your area that you should watch out for, as well as which shelters have adopted out the least (and most) aggressive dogs.

- Look in the Yellow Pages under "animal shelters," "SPCAs" or "Humane Societies."

- Call your local police department (*not* the emergency number!) and ask for the phone number of your local dog or animal control officer.

- Call your town clerk or local town council for the telephone number of your local dog or animal control officer.

Realistically, once you have some phone numbers, you can expect to meet with a lot of answering machines, busy signals and delays in returned calls. While admittedly this is not great customer service, most shelters are under-staffed and very busy, and most dog or animal control officers only work part time and are often out on the road picking up stray dogs. Think like a terrier, and be persistent, relentless and stubborn in your pursuit of information. Reward the good behavior—having someone finally return your phone call—and ignore the bad behavior—not getting a prompt return call. Don't take it personally; please cut them some slack, and please don't confront the staff person who finally does return or eventually answer your phone call. (This non-confrontational technique will also work well with your dog.)

To put myself in the shoes of a novice dog owner looking to adopt, I phoned nine shelters, mostly in the Northeast but also in the Midwest, posing as a wife and mother of two young boys, five and 10 years old. The only information I gave was that I was calling for my family, inquiring about adopting our first dog. The only other inquiry I made was into how the dogs were temperament screened for biting.

I was personally familiar with all the shelters I called, either from having met many of the dogs they had adopted out or because I personally had visited the shelter. Of the nine shelters, I knew that two of them do what I consider to be very formal and thorough temperament testing, and do not put up for adoption any dog who shows aggression during the test. These shelters also knew of and made recommendations about which dogs would be suitable for a family with two young boys, and which dogs would not. In six of the nine shelters, I know that a majority of their population consists of aggressive dogs, and they do little or no temperament screening.

Of the nine, there were two that never answered the phone at all and had no answering machine. One of the shelters had a recording that said the number was not accepting incoming calls. Two shelters had a live person answering the phones, and the other four started with a recorded menu that gave very detailed and helpful information on all their adoption requirements and procedures, and then I was easily able to speak to a live person.

In terms of customer service, only two of the people answering the phones were friendly and seemed at all pleased to take my call. All the others sounded harried, had an impatient and disdainful tone in their voices, and were less interested in me and more interested in being overprotective of their dogs and puppies.

All the shelters clearly communicated their adoption guidelines, and thoroughly instructed me on what I needed to bring and what I should expect during the adoption process.

Almost all the shelters provided an extensive and generous health care package with the adoption: Almost all the dogs would go out already spayed or neutered, all had at least their first set of vaccinations, most of the shelters had performed a heartworm test so adopters would know up front if the dog tested positive (and not have to bring the dog home, fall in love and *then* find out he has heartworm), and most offered free, post-adoption veterinary care packages. So, for the most part, the consumer can expect some of the best health services available in the dog world from a shelter! You would spend 10 times the adoption fee to buy a dog from a pet store, have all the same health risks, and yet not receive any of the benefits you get with a dog adopted from the average shelter. You'll never get an already-neutered puppy from a pet store or from most breeders, and yet, in most shelters it will be done before you adopt, or you will be given a discount voucher.

One of the shelters had only one dog available for adoption. (This is good news for dogs, not as good news for adopters.) I was informed that the one dog was a puppy, part Pit Bull and part German Shepherd Dog, and that if I adopted the puppy, we would be required to take a mandatory dog obedience class. I asked if this was standard policy with all of their puppy adoptions or if this puppy in particular needed it. Before the shelter worker answered, she asked how old the children in the household were. When I told her I had two young sons, five and 10 years, she said emphatically, "Not this puppy." When I asked why, she said this puppy was "very nervous and mouthy." I was impressed, because that is a good reason not to adopt out a dog to a novice owner with young children. The next thing she said, however, was disappointing. When I asked what could happen if we did adopt such a puppy, she said, "Young children can be inappropriate with puppies," thereby implying that children ruin puppies.

Information to Get on the Phone

- Begin with: I am (we are) thinking of adopting a dog and want to find out more about the dogs in your shelter.

- What can you tell me about the different personalities of the dogs you have available for adoption?

- What kind of temperament or behavioral evaluation does your shelter do with the dogs before putting them up for adoption?

- Would I be more likely to get a good dog if I started out with a puppy?

It seems the shelters in which you are the most likely to find a safe and appropriate dog are the ones that will *restrict* you from certain dogs. While some people may feel insulted by this refusal (often because of the way the information is delivered) and take it personally, from my phone calls I found that the shelters in which you would most likely find the best and safest match for you and your family, the ones that effectively screen their dogs for aggression, are the ones that will tell you that you *should not* adopt certain dogs or puppies.

During the phone call, you should feel that the shelter starts out assuming you are a kind, caring person looking to adopt a dog (not a serial killer looking to practice on their animals . . .), and you should be treated as such.

The shelter should have a specific procedure for testing the temperament of their dogs in a variety of situations. Listen carefully to make sure you are not subtly being told that the responsibility to detect aggression or assess temperament is *your* job. A shelter should be willing and able to take responsibility for helping you find a great dog who has been thoroughly screened for aggression before becoming available to the public. Dogs can cause great harm. The shelter has to take responsibility for helping you find the safest and best pet.

Responses That Should Alarm You

- Avoid shelters that assume puppies are clean slates and will turn out as good or as bad as you raise them. When I called one shelter and asked what procedures they had in place to help make sure I didn't bring home to my children a biting dog, the woman on the phone told me that puppies under six months didn't and couldn't bite—anything like biting was "just teething and chewing."

- Stay away from shelters that use the observable ways the dogs act in their kennels as their only form of temperament evaluating. You may to have to sift through a higher percentage of aggressive dogs to find an appropriate one. At the shelter I mentioned above, the person I spoke to then told me that with dogs six months and older, the kennel staff will know which ones "are the sweeties and which ones are a little nippy." I asked how they could tell this, and she told me they were able to tell by how the dogs acted in the kennels. While it is useful to observe and record the dogs' behavior in the kennels, this is not nearly enough to determine their true temperament and how they might act in a home.

- Avoid shelters that subtly or not so subtly blame you or hold you responsible for the temperament and behavior of the dog. The onus of recognizing aggression should not be on you, the adopter. One of the shelters I called told me to just "use your better judgment" when I asked what to look for when bringing my children in to see the dogs. A shelter cannot expect you—the adopter—to somehow innately know how to select a safe dog. That would be like sending you into a blood bank to look at and spend time with all the samples and then, for your upcoming transfusion, "use your better judgment" in trying to select the blood least likely to carry the AIDS virus. You're not a hematologist. In looking for the safest blood for your own transfusion, you expect the blood bank to have experts who use a proven method of screening for common transmittable and dangerous diseases. You would hope the blood bank wouldn't use "the way a donor looks" or the donor's assurance that they are healthy as the screening process. Aggression in dogs can be just as insidious, and requires a knowledgeable staff of experts to help you get the best and safest companion. I know I probably sound like the voice of doom, and I want this book to inspire you to get a dog at a shelter, but at the same time, there is a very serious side to this.

- Avoid shelters that use the past behavioral history from the previous owner as their primary or only guide for determining a dog's temperament.

Are Kids Allowed?

One of the shelters claimed that their insurance did not allow children in the adoption kennels. If a shelter's adoption wards are not separate from their stray dog or holding pens, and the adoptable dogs are mixed in with the quarantined dogs or legal court case dogs, then it indeed is safer to prohibit young children from entering these kennels. But if the adoption kennels are separated from the other wards and all the dogs in the ward are available for adoption, then there should be no reason for a shelter to restrict visiting, supervised children from going in there.

While that shelter may indeed have such an insurance policy, it is not the norm. And while it certainly can be an increased risk to have children in the adoption wards, I wonder if that shelter may have had enough visiting children who were bitten that their insurance carrier will no longer allow it, or they are using the insurance excuse as a way to keep children out of the kennels since their dogs are such a risk. I do know that shelter has hundreds of dogs, most of them seriously aggressive. Many of these dogs have bitten before, some have bitten volunteers or staff, and some have been adopted out and bitten and returned, only to be adopted out again and again. So perhaps a good conclusion to draw is that if a shelter prohibits children in their adoption kennels, then it's best to look elsewhere—even if you don't have kids. If these kinds of dogs are available for adoption and they get adopted at some point, they will certainly encounter children somewhere in life. And if the liability of having them near young children is too much for the shelter to assume, then the liability is also too much for you and your family to assume.

Questions from the Shelter

You might be asked questions about your family, household and situation, or you might be informed of the shelter's policies, requirements and procedures for adopting. At the strictest end of the spectrum, you can expect a shelter to ask you to bring two forms of identification and residency, such as a photo driver's license, a phone bill, etc. You may be required to arrive with every single member of your household, —your entire family or your roommate(s). You may need to provide a reference, someone who can be called and reached while you are at the shelter or a veterinary referral (difficult to provide if you've never owned a pet before . . .).

Some shelters will allow you to come in and look at the dogs, but will require a home visit before approving the actual adoption. Home visits can serve two functions:

1. Many shelters use them to find out if you were dishonest on your application in any way—for instance, you really do not have a fenced yard when you said you did, or you have many carcasses strewn about your lawn and in your basement, despite your glowing references and seemingly wholesome appearance.

2. A shelter worker comes by to help you dog/puppy proof your home, to sit you down in a nondistracting environment to give you some behavioral or training advice, or to look for potential hazards in your home or yard.

I have, more often than not, seen a proportionate relationship between the thoroughness of a shelter's home visit and a lack of good temperament screening in their dogs. In other words, the more thoroughly they check you out to make sure you have a "good home," the more likely it is that the dog you are allowed to adopt has not been well evaluated. If you are going to be so thoroughly screened, make sure you inquire about how well the shelter knows the dogs; their experience with aggression; their policies regarding dogs who bite, snap or growl; how often a dog has been returned; how much information they get from the former owner if a dog is returned for any reason; and so on.

Most shelters want to know that your decision to adopt is well thought out, that you are aware of the responsibility you are getting yourself into, that you are ready to put some work into the relationship, and that above all, you are committed. We have found at our shelter that most people coming in to adopt will rise to the commitment and responsibility, if they're given a safe and loving dog, and the right dog for them. An animal shelter should always be just as concerned about what harm their dog could do to you or your family as they are about what harm you could do to their dogs.

Of course, before hanging up, don't forget to get driving directions to the shelter and the hours they are open. Ask what is the latest time you can arrive so there will be enough time to complete the adoption procedures.

WHAT TO LOOK FOR IN A SHELTER

I'll start by saying that the criteria for selecting a shelter always depend on where you live and on the resources available to you. That said, it's important to keep in mind that shelters inherit their physical facilities, and it takes years and usually a professional fund-raiser to acquire the funds for a capital campaign to renovate or build a new facility. Don't judge a shelter by its cover; judge the shelter by its people, how you are treated, how the dogs are treated. An animal shelter should be a place that treats dogs humanely and humans equally humanely. To say you love the animals but not the people is to admit to a basic lack of respect for all life.

For me, in all my travels to hundreds of different shelters, once I connect with a certain dog—he or she gives me "that look" and I fall in love—nothing else matters. All other considerations are secondary: financial concerns, geographical logistics, convenience, my schedule, etc. When you lose your heart to a dog in a shelter, nothing else matters. But if you haven't lost your heart yet—if you haven't yet seen and fallen in love with your dream dog—then for you, starting with a pleasant overall experience is certainly nicer than being treated badly. You really have two choices in pursuing a shelter adoption: The first is to seek out a great dog no matter what the shelter looks like, no matter how the staff might treat you or make you feel. The second is to seek out a great shelter, putting the priority on a pleasant and supportive overall adoption experience. Really, neither choice is the "right" one; neither choice is the "better" one. In an ideal world, all shelters would be located in convenient neighborhoods, look and smell modern and welcoming, be staffed with people who like people as much as they like animals, have a keen knowledge of dog behavior and temperament, care as much for the health and well-being of your family as they do the dogs in their shelter, and be filled with highly adoptable, safe and friendly family pets. (Or perhaps the ideal world would have *no* shelter, but would be a world where no dog was homeless or unwanted, no dog needed to be caged, and there was just the right number of dogs and puppies for just the right number of responsible people. Then animal shelters would be educational and resource centers to help build a more humane world. But we're not yet in the ideal world.)

Don't think just because a shelter is a no-kill facility that there aren't any aggressive dogs there, and don't only choose to go to a no-kill shelter because it's "so sad" or "too difficult" to go to a place that euthanizes dogs. Euthanasia happens to dogs whether it is done at the facility you choose or not.

No matter what, you need to be prepared to lose your heart and fall in love, and then be able (with the help of this book) to convert into an all-business, Spock-logical person to objectively assess your dog for safety and compatibility.

Chapter 3

Where Should I Go for My Dog?

There are many different types of animal shelters. "Animal shelter" is sort of the generic term for Humane Society, Society for the Prevention of Cruelty to Animals (SPCA), Animal Care and Control, Dog Control or any private shelter with a unique name. The phrase we used to use, "dog pound," is now considered a derogatory term for an animal care and control facility.

By definition, an animal control facility is responsible for picking up stray dogs and/or cats for their town or county. They usually have dog control (dogs only) or animal control (dogs, cats, sometimes wildlife) officers who respond to phone calls about free-roaming lost or found dogs. Most times, these facilities also accept pets surrendered by their owners. Some only take in lost or stray animals.

Sometimes, in small rural towns, the dog control facility consists of a couple of chain-link kennels set up behind the highway department or behind the town dump. These counties have no centralized animal control facility, usually just a single hired person to work part time and take care of unwanted or stray dogs in the kennels.

Every town and each state has its own legal holding period for stray animals. It usually ranges from 48 hours (as in New York City) to 14 days. Animals are held for a given period to allow their owners time to find and claim them.

WHAT KIND OF SHELTER?

There are many private shelters that have contracts with local government to house, hold and care for the stray dogs in their communities. Other private shelters only accept owner-surrendered animals. An "open admission" or "full access" facility is one that accepts any animals who arrive, adoptable or not. Some open admission shelters have animal control contracts, others don't. Some privately run shelters only accept those dogs they consider adoptable, and turn away dogs who may be difficult to place or unadoptable by that shelter's standards. These shelters are called "limited admission" or "limited access" facilities. Some limited admission shelters restrict incoming dogs to those they consider adoptable, but also euthanize when necessary (such as when an animal is ill, suffering or aggressive). These facilities may also be called "low kill."

Some limited admission shelters euthanize unadoptable dogs; others are called "no kill," which is a trickier term to define, because it can mean different things to different shelters. Sometimes a no-kill shelter doesn't euthanize at all, or only in cases of extreme physical suffering. They are willing to keep all of the dogs forever, so the adoptable dogs live there for as long as it takes to find them homes, and the unadoptable dogs basically live there until they die of natural causes. Other no-kill shelters will euthanize dogs who turn out to be aggressive or unadoptable, but use the term "no-kill" to reflect their policy of finding homes for all their adoptable dogs without any time limits. Still other no-kill shelters send their behaviorally unadoptable dogs out to "sanctuaries," and do no euthanasia on site themselves. What is a sanctuary? A sanctuary is a no-kill shelter.

Within the shelter industry, the term "no-kill" has not been clearly defined. The current definitions used by no-kill shelters are that "euthanasia" refers to the humane killing of animals who are suffering or in pain, and "kill" refers to killing animals because the shelter has run out of time, money or space. In other words, "killing" means putting animals to death because there are too many; "euthanizing" means putting animals to death to spare them physical pain and suffering—and, depending on whom you ask, killing of animals deemed behaviorally unadoptable or dangerous.

A no-kill policy at an animal shelter can mean many things. Some no-kill shelters do not kill the dogs in their facility, and they restrict the new ones they accept to nonaggressive dogs with no history of aggression. They assess incoming dogs and interview owners carefully, have a waiting list (often months long) to get in (a new dog has to wait for a current dog to be adopted out to make space for him), and turn away dogs with problems or dogs whom they consider unadoptable. The dogs who are turned away usually end up going to a local open admission facility (one that accepts any and all incoming dogs), where they get euthanized. Very often, the open admission shelter ends up resenting their local no-kill facility, not only because funding is much easier to obtain for shelters that call themselves no-kill, but also because this arrangement usually dumps all or most of the responsibility for euthanasia onto their facility. This "kill" facility is usually less popular in their community, since everyone knows they euthanize lots of dogs. In fact, they often end up euthanizing a high percentage of their incoming dogs, since the most adoptable dogs go to the no-kill facility, and the least adoptable and unadoptable dogs all end up at the open admission shelter—which must always make more room by euthanizing dogs.

A no-kill shelter really can't have an open admission policy. It must limit its intake if it wants to adopt out animals and not kill them; otherwise the no-kill shelter will be filled to capacity within a week or two, because the number of dogs coming in is greater than the number of dogs adopted out. The behaviorally adoptable dogs get adopted more quickly than the problem or unadoptable dogs, so the shelter gradually clogs up with the problem or unadoptable dogs (unless they're sent away to sanctuaries or euthanized) and the population of adoptable dogs gets smaller and smaller. Many dogs who start out as behaviorally adoptable dogs will, over time, deteriorate in the shelter/kennel environment, becoming less and less adoptable with each passing day. Eventually, in worst-case scenarios, all the behaviorally adoptable dogs will have been adopted, and all the cages will be filled with unadoptable dogs. The more aggressive, "kennel crazy" unadoptable dogs there are, the quicker the behaviorally adoptable dogs deteriorate because of the heightened state of arousal and aggression in the kennels, until they're all lunging at the front of their cages.

In reality, all shelters are responsible for the euthanasia of dogs in their communities, despite what they call themselves or others. Turning away unadoptable dogs, or turning away dogs when a shelter is full, does not spare the lives of these dogs. It merely puts off the inevitable, or forces another shelter to do the deed. It's unfair to call one death "euthanasia" and another death "killing"—unfair to the shelters that are still overwhelmed by the sheer volume of incoming dogs, and are under-funded and without resources. Nobody in the shelter field *wants* to kill animals.

The problem within the shelter world is really not with the terminology. The biggest problem is the confusion stemming from the lack of standardization of what is considered behaviorally adoptable, what is considered trainable (with the right resources), and what is considered unadoptable. Some shelters re-home known biters and aggressive dogs. Other shelters deem aggressive dogs and biters unadoptable and euthanize them. Still other shelters have no idea

This photo was taken at a shelter in Hawaii. The soft-eyed,
sweet-looking dog on the left caught my eye.

which dogs are dangerous and which are good-natured, and adopt out as well
as euthanize both groups pretty much at random.

All of this is to clarify some of the behind-the-scenes issues for you, so that
what kind of *shelter* you want to patronize will become less important than what
kinds of *dogs* you are likely to find there. In the end, you're only looking for *one*
dog, *your* dog, and that "right" dog for you could be waiting in any shelter.

You are no more or less likely to find "better" dogs in a no-kill facility than
you are in an open admission or animal care and control facility. I have trav-
eled the country visiting many shelters, and I can tell you that there are good
no-kill shelters and bad ones, and good open admission shelters and bad ones.
There are small, very poor shelters with dilapidated buildings that are run by
friendly, caring, knowledgeable staff and volunteers, with lots of wonderful
dogs who are clean and exceptionally well cared for. There are huge, multi-
million-dollar new facilities that have staff and volunteers with highly aggressive dogs waiting for adoption in sterile, empty kennels—kennels with no
bedding, no toys, no stimulation.

This book will help you adopt the right dog for you, regardless of the policies or quality of the shelter you visit. It will also include a section for those of
you who are willing to travel farther and search wider than most dog adopters
traditionally do.

REGIONAL DIFFERENCES IN SHELTER DOGS

The population of dogs is vastly different depending on where in the country you visit a shelter. The differences seem to boil down to whether the shelter is in an urban area or a rural area. The shelters in just about every large city across the country, whether on the East Coast, West Coast, Midwest or South, tend to be filled with a combination of macho and muscle breeds such as Pit Bull Terriers and Pit Bull mixes, Rottweilers and Rottweiler mixes, Chow Chows and Chow mixes, and a blend of all these. The dogs tend to be very dominant, often dominant aggressive, and frequently come from fighting dog stock or guard dog stock. Litters of puppies are rare, except for the occasional litter of Pit Bulls or Pit Bull mixes. Not infrequently, a single, slightly older puppy comes in either as a stray or surrendered by the owner, usually (but not always) with serious aggression problems. Since puppies are scarce, they tend to get adopted very quickly.

In some rural parts of the country, the dog populations are very different. In the rural South (Virginia, South Carolina, Tennessee, etc.), the rural Central and Southern Plains states, the rural Midwest and the rural West, the population of dogs coming into shelters consists of many young, sweet-tempered, soft dogs and puppies. "Soft" dogs are usually people-oriented, ears-back, squinty-eyed, low-tail-wagging dogs who need and adore humans. Soft dogs are not pushy or assertive with their human families, nor are they determined to get what they want by use of aggression or physical strength. These soft dogs are primarily the progeny of unwanted or stray farm dogs, hunting dogs, hound dogs and back-country family dogs. Spay and neuter education has not been as effective in reaching the more remote parts of these communities, and many people cannot afford veterinary services.

It is the "failed" working dogs who often end up abandoned: the herding dogs who were too soft on stock and too soft to properly work the farm, the hound dogs who preferred to stay with the hunter rather than run with the pack after a raccoon or bear, the gun-shy gun dogs. Often these failed-instinct dogs have soft, mushy, sweet temperaments. Unfortunately, many of these dogs are dying needlessly due to contagious diseases such as distemper, parvovirus or upper respiratory infections that can have an entire shelter sick and coughing within days. Many are euthanized from just plain old being one of too many.

Litters of puppies in shelters, more so than adolescents, adults or singleton puppies, are markers of true pet overpopulation. Shelters with many whole litters or nursing mothers with puppies are most likely experiencing true overpopulation in their community. Shelters with mostly adolescent or adult dogs, or with the occasional single puppy, are probably experiencing more of a surplus of problem dogs—dogs who became unwanted due to difficulties with their temperament or behavior.

One shelter I was visiting in rural Virginia on a day in July had 11 separate litters of puppies, not one of whom were Pit Bull or Rottweiler mixes. This is practically *unheard of* in urban areas, and especially in the Northeastern and mid-Atlantic states.

At my shelter in a rural part of the Northeast, two separate litters recently came in, and some of the puppies were growling aggressively at humans by the age of three weeks. These puppies were in no way scared or defensive. These puppies were bold. They would turn to face you and look directly into your eyes if you tried to make them do anything they didn't want to do—for instance, pick them up, carry them, hold them longer than they cared for or push them out of their food pan. Yet in the rural regions of the United States there is a surplus of great dogs and puppies who are dying needlessly due to real pet over-population.

I have a theory for why this might be the case. In urban areas, spay and neuter education has effectively reached the dog-owning public, and virtually all family pets and companion animals are spayed or neutered. The majority of surplus dogs in our big cities consist of fighting dogs, macho and muscle breeds, drug guarding and area guard dogs, and junkyard dogs. These are dogs who belong to street kids and tough guys, who may know about spaying and neutering but lack the incentive and intention to do it. Breeding their Pit Bulls is an easy way to make some money and get more fighting dogs—which all the other kids want. The reasons they have heard to recommend spaying and neutering don't apply to them. Many of these dogs are bred, but few produce good family pets.

With our successful spay/neuter campaign perhaps what we have done is educate the educable. Anyone who takes their dog or puppy to a veterinarian will, in almost all cases, be educated about the benefits of spaying and neutering. We have, for the most part, successfully spayed and neutered the family pet dogs. Think about it. Think of every great family dog you know. Is the dog neutered or spayed?

What does all this mean for you? It means if you live in a big city, you may have to sift through a higher percentage of dogs to find adoptable ones, while if you live in a rural area outside the Northeast, you may have many more adoptable dogs to choose from. Some shelters partner with other shelters and form a funnel from the overcrowded, poorer shelters out to the larger facilities with more time and resources, and usually, fewer adoptable dogs. Usually the facilities with more resources are in urban or suburban areas and have many more adopters coming to adopt a dog than do the more rural and less well-funded facilities. Some shelters partner together to even out the balance and save more dogs.

This kind of partnership can be controversial within the shelter world, since other local facilities or rescue groups that are taking in only local dogs may think all the shelters in their area should be working to help all of their local dogs, before branching out to help "immigrant" dogs. This problem is further aggravated when some shelters that import dogs from other areas do not themselves accept returns. In other words, if a shelter imports a litter of puppies that get adopted out locally, and one of the puppies is aggressive and the owners cannot keep it, they will contact the original shelter to return the dog. If that original shelter won't take the dog back, that dog ends up being surrendered to a different local facility, and that shelter now carries the financial and emotional burden of taking in what should be the other shelter's responsibility.

When partnership programs work well, more good dogs get adopted, less good dogs get euthanized, and the glut of adopters in areas with few family pet dogs available for adoption have more dogs to adopt. When these partnerships work miserably, more dogs are brought in (many of them puppies), they are adopted out before being spayed or neutered, some don't get spayed or neutered at all, and they breed more dogs. And if the shelter that originally imported the dogs won't accept their dogs back or is a limited admission facility and is full, they are, in essence, making more dogs, causing more problems and accepting no responsibility.

A wonderful dog is a wonderful dog. It shouldn't matter what shelter in what part of the country the dog ends up in. If we can share resources and save the wonderful dogs, it should be done.

RESCUE GROUPS

Another place to get a dog is from a rescue group. There are many privately run purebred and mixed breed rescue groups to choose from. Rescue groups are usually made up of dedicated volunteers who do not have a specific physical facility (a shelter), but who network with one another to take in, foster and adopt out dogs—usually of one particular breed—who might otherwise end up homeless. Many rescue groups also take in non-purebreds, sometimes only terriers, or only hounds or small dogs. These dogs are usually thoroughly checked by a veterinarian and often get cared for in someone's home. The benefits to this are that the foster person or foster family can get to know the dog well—to see how he gets along with cats, other dogs, and in the house.

In an ideal world, a rescue group is a core of dedicated people—some experts in their breed, some just caring and generous volunteers. The dogs are carefully health screened and appropriately taken care of. If the rescue group specializes in a particular breed, the adopter reaps the rewards of being in contact with a group of people with extensive knowledge about the character, instincts and traits particular to the breed, who can offer better education for the interested adopter on the compatibility of that breed, and also lots of post-adoption support and hand-holding. Purebred rescue groups also enable people who are interested in a particular breed to adopt a dog rather than buy one—a wholesome sentiment.

In the not-so-ideal world, a rescue group is a core of animal "humaniacs"—crazy dog people, driven by raw emotion, with no solid knowledge of dog behavior. These fringe groups often rescue any dog, without regard for temperament or aggression, and have little knowledge of behavior or training. These well-meaning volunteers believe not only that all aggression must be a product of prior abuse, but that with enough love and obedience training, all dogs can be saved.

Somewhere in between is what you are likely to encounter. Breed rescue groups are a great resource for you if you are interested in one particular breed, and it is well worth it to call them, fill out the paperwork, get approved to adopt and then be called when a dog becomes available. Purebred puppies are scarce, purebred adolescents or adults are the norm.

Breed rescue groups can also be particularly useful if you or someone in your family has allergies and you need a dog with a more hypo-allergenic coat. No breed is truly "nonshedding," but certain breeds sometimes don't trigger allergies in usually allergic people. Generally, these are the curly-coated or long-coated breeds: Poodles, Bichons Frises, Portuguese Water Dogs, Soft Coated Wheaten Terriers. Not all these breeds offer the same protection for individual allergies, but that is also the beauty of a breed rescue group—you would be able to spend a few hours in the home of someone with several representatives of the breed, and find out not only whether you like the personality of the breed, but whether or not their coat triggers your allergies.

Purebred rescue groups can also keep you aware of health problems particular to your breed, and answer a lot of ongoing, detailed questions about your new dog.

It is important for you to know that there can be a paradox created by a good breed rescue group: These rescue groups usually consist of experts in the breed and highly experienced dog people who are, by nature and experience, excellent dog handlers. So one of these experts may be the person who fosters the dog you ultimately are interested in. This breed rescue expert may keep the dog in his or her home for even a few months and experience no behavior or aggression problems whatsoever. However, after *you* adopt the dog, his behavior and temperament may, in some cases, seem to change drastically. While the breed rescue caretaker experienced only an obedient dog, you may experience (usually after a honeymoon period) a holy terror. You might experience a dog with a significant temperament and aggression problem, while the rescue group saw no hint of those issues. This is *not* because you are ruining the dog or mishandling the dog or are "too soft" on the dog, or any other excuse someone may accuse you of. It is because of that paradox I just mentioned. The breed rescue person usually has several dogs, and often the foster dog is crated for moderate periods of time and let out less frequently than the average single dog. When the dog does come out of his crate, he is handled and cared for by a professional. This foster caretaker will, without even realizing it, inhibit and interrupt sequences of bad behaviors—to the point where they won't even know the dog has these potential problems—because their own handling is so proficient.

Unfortunately, more often than not, the adopter is blamed for the dog's bad behavior, since no one saw it before. And to the adopter, it may feel as if someone lied to them or hid the information about how aggressive or dominant the dog actually was. Neither is necessarily the case. The dog is simply experiencing a different environment, and will show his true self when he is the center of attention and among unfamiliar people who are equally unfamiliar with dogs.

The problem with a rescue group with this kind of attitude is that the dogs can do no wrong, and the owners are to blame for any and all problems. If you are going to adopt a dog through a purebred rescue group, look for a group of people who will be supportive and encouraging and informative for new owners, not antagonistic and blaming. And there is no blanket "right" or "wrong" breed for new or inexperienced dog owners. Within any breed, from the most dominant to the most submissive, there are individual dogs who would be appropriate and inappropriate for new or inexperienced dog owners. It is the job of a knowledgeable rescue person to evaluate the individual temperament of each dog, and try to pair him with the desires and capabilities of each individual adopter.

INTERNET ADOPTION

Starting your search for a dog on the Internet can be a great idea. There are many web sites that make "shopping" for a dog truly easy and accessible. It's a great way to gather the majority of information you will need (adoption policies, pre-adoption requirements, directions to a shelter) before you visit the actual facility. Most Internet adoption ads have photographs of the available dogs, and usually accompanying personality descriptions. Photographs can shoot Cupid's arrow through your screen and into your heart. Many people make strong emotional connections with a dog they find on the Internet because of the photograph.

The Internet is also a very efficient way of searching for a particular breed or breed mix. A few years ago at my shelter, a number of purebred Great Pyrenees adults and puppies were surrendered to us by a local breeder. When we posted them on our web site, we had calls from people hours away who were willing to take a day's drive (if we would put a hold on the dog) to come and adopt. The beauty of the Internet in this situation is that adopters who have researched a particular breed and want that type of dog can be immediately hooked up with available dogs. And the dogs benefit because they are not randomly adopted out to people who just happened upon them while visiting the shelter and who may not be aware of certain characteristics (grooming requirements, health problems and so on) particular to that breed. Because of the Internet, these dogs get adopted by people who are very prepared for what they are getting, and these are usually very successful adoptions.

Using the Internet gives you a virtual tour through the shelter's kennels, as well, to see how many dogs catch your eye as potential matches before you decide to make a long drive to the actual facility.

Interpreting Adoption Ads

The Internet has been a great boon to the shelter world. Advertising dogs on the Internet has increased adoptions for any facility that has a web site. The caliber of adopters is also excellent. The adopters who contact shelters through the Internet tend to be educated and have thoroughly thought out what they want in their next dog. Often they are attracted by a particular breed or breed mix, or have fallen in love with the photo of a dog on the Internet. Adopters will go to great lengths to adopt a dog they have fallen in love with over the Internet.

The advertisements that begin on page 32 are excerpts from real Internet adoption sites. Because of the huge emotional investment rescue people (and adopters) have in their dogs, I thought it would be useful to look more closely at these descriptions, and to point out some important details for you to think about. I would like to help you decode some of the many euphemisms for serious, sometimes even dangerous, temperament and behavior problems in the dogs being advertised.

Remember, the people describing these dogs on the Internet are seldom behavior experts. They are not professional dog trainers. They are not experienced temperament evaluators. They are usually highly emotional rescuers who believe that with enough love, training and compassion, any dog can find the right home and be a good dog. Often, they believe that as long as an aggressive dog is not placed in a home with young children, everything will either be okay, or it's just not as serious if anyone other than a young child (like a teenager or adult) gets bitten and scarred.

There are five important issues to watch out for when you are reading an Internet ad:

1. Many of the ads contain roundabout ways of describing and, at the same time, hiding the dog's behavior problems or aggressiveness. There are some catch phrases that can clue you in to a potentially problematic dog. No adoption ad will come right out and say, "Jake is a large, dominant aggressive dog who has threatened staff members here at the shelter, and been adopted out three times and returned each time for biting. If you would like to bring a large, scary and biting dog into your home, Jake is the right dog for you." A euphemistic ad might read, "Jake is a big, beautiful guy who, due to his large size, would do better in a home without young children. Jake is real smart and we know with some dog obedience classes would be an A+ student. Jake just needs a highly experienced owner who will give him the chance he deserves to live with someone who will show him that they love him and won't give up on him."

2. Watch out for euphemisms for breed type and purebreds—how many ways can you describe a Pit Bull Terrier without actually saying or even implying "Pit Bull"? If the dog is a good dog and is also a Pit Bull, then call him a Pit Bull. Adopters will either be open to any dog, regardless of breed reputation, or they will want to avoid certain breeds. That is the decision of the adopter, and should not be influenced with creative breed descriptions. Beware all "Labrador Retriever–Boxer mixes," "Dalmatian mixes" (usually piebald, or white and black Pit Bulls), "Pharaoh Hound mixes" (often red Pit Bulls with red noses) and the terrier mixes that conjure up images of Benji.

3. Beware of ads that tell a sad story about the horrific abuse or neglect the dog suffered in the hands of cruel abusers, and that are clearly designed to convince readers to adopt the dog based on pity alone.

Although his blue eyes are beautiful, this dog shows a wide-open,
hard expression, with no softness or overt signs of friendliness.
It is his *lack* of greeting that is disturbing.

4. Watch out for ads that make the reader feel so guilty about how many
    other people have passed by the particular dog and how long that dog
    has been waiting to get adopted, that the reader is motivated to adopt
    the dog just to get him out.

5. Beware of ads that pressure the reader into adopting by threatening to
    euthanize the dog, or implying that "his time is up."

Ice

Our first sample ad is for a purebred Siberian Husky named Ice. His photo is a
head shot, and he is indeed pretty—solid white with ice blue eyes. He is facing
the camera and offers a direct, hard stare. His description is brief, but telling.

"Ice is a 2.5-year-old neutered male Siberian Husky. Active and very intelligent. Prefer to place in adults-only, experienced dog-owning home as the only
pet."

"Adults-only," "experienced dog-owning home" and "as the only pet" may
all be trying to cover up a dog who has bitten and harmed another dog, and
one who was also possibly pushy and aggressive with previous adopters or volunteers at the shelter. If a rescue person lists a dog as for "adults only," there is

probably some serious problem with the dog. Recommending an "experienced dog-owning home" is also a euphemism for wanting someone with the capabilities of a professional dog trainer, but without the broad knowledge of aggression (since anyone who knows dogs wouldn't take on such an aggressive dog), which means the dog probably has a history of biting. Topping the ad off with "as the only pet" clearly suggests a dog who is aggressive with other dogs and with cats.

The ad also describes Ice as "active and very intelligent." But note that nowhere is there any reference to sociable or affectionate behavior. Active and very intelligent are actually two adjectives that are not so desirable in a pet dog. Intelligence and trainability have nothing to do with each other. In fact, it is much easier to train a less intelligent dog, and much more difficult to live with a highly intelligent one. Especially a highly intelligent and active dog who bites.

Charlie

Charlie has been advertised on the Internet for *years*. I found him while trolling through adoption sites a few years back. He is obviously still available for adoption, and I'm sure he's getting more and more aggressive the more time he spends in a cage.

His description says, "Charlie is a challenge." How bad must he really be for a rescue group to admit he is a challenge? "His large size (100 lbs.) and beautiful looks attract would-be adopters, but Charlie has lost two homes." Lost them where? Misplaced them, like a pair of eyeglasses? "This is because he is not well trained" (blame a human!) "and is dominant with women. He plays roughly and is mischievous like a puppy, and would definitely benefit from positive reinforcement training. Abused as a puppy, Charlie has a hard time trusting people—he needs a dog savvy owner, preferably male. Because of his size we would not place him in a home with children. A home in the suburbs or country with a fenced-in yard would be ideal." Or perhaps a federal penitentiary? "Experienced dog people only."

To describe a 100-pound dog as "mischievous like a puppy" is to infer that his level of aggression and his violent behavior are innocuous and silly. Describing his two experiences of getting adopted and returned ("Charlie has lost two homes. This is because he is not well trained") puts the blame on those owners, and suggests that if people weren't so darned lazy and uncommitted, this dog would be OK.

The ad for Charlie is like listing an Uzi machine gun for sale on eBay, and describing the weapon like this: "This beautiful Uzi would do best in a home with no human targets, as it has been known to go off on its own, probably due to prior mishandling from its former owner." A 100-pound biting dog, especially one who has been kenneled in a shelter environment for a few years, is not a dog I would want in my neighborhood.

Peggy Sue

"Peggy Sue was born 4/93 and she is a very pretty black and tan female spayed Shepherd. She has a very pretty face, and is friendly and well behaved. She loves to go for long walks and to be petted. While Peggy Sue definitely does not like other animals, she is smart and affectionate and would be very devoted and protective of her special person. We think a single woman would be delighted to have a loyal friend like Peggy Sue as a companion and devoted friend, and that Peggy Sue would make a fine pet."

This ad is one giant euphemism for a seriously aggressive dog. Peggy Sue's description is that of a dog who directs her aggression toward strangers. A stranger is defined as everyone in the world, until Peggy Sue gets to know him or her. "Very devoted and protective of her special person. We think a single woman . . ." Dogs who direct their aggression toward strangers, either on the street or in the home, are almost always worse with men. What the ad tries to downplay is that Peggy Sue lunges at and tries to bite, or has possibly bitten, men. Luckily, only 49 percent of the population is men!

Many people believe that this kind of behavior arises because a man abused these dogs. In all likelihood, most dogs who are aggressive with strangers, whether it is based on a fear response or an aggressive one, were not abused by anyone. They are simply that way. These dogs react more toward men for several reasons. First, approaching men are usually larger and have deeper voices—and these are, to all animals, more of a threat. Men, in general, tend to greet with a more direct and frontal body posture; they approach with direct eye contact, and face fully front. To a dog who is either scared of or aggressive with strangers, this posture is more threatening than a relaxed body orientation, glancing eye contact and a higher pitched voice—which is, in general, how women greet.

For example, when the average guy is introduced to another guy, he will most likely move directly toward the person he was supposed to meet, with an outstretched hand, leaning forward and offering direct eye contact. "Johnson here, Doug Johnson, nice to meet you." It is the rare woman who strides forward directly to the person, looks them right in the eye and pumps their hand with a very firm grip. Peggy Sue would probably be just as happy to go after her.

Bridget

"Bridget is a small (35–40 lbs.), black, mixed-breed dog born in 1995. She was once extremely shy, but with the help of volunteers who took her on walks and gave her extra attention, she has come out of her shell. She is a quiet, gentle dog and would be perfect for someone with a quiet, gentle lifestyle."

Bridget has been in that shelter for more than four years. If she's perfect for someone with a quiet, gentle lifestyle, then is it humane to keep her alive for four years in what she would therefore consider to be hell? Loud barking, excitement and arousal every day? Has it been any favor to Bridget to subject her to a cacophonous, over-stimulating, frustrating and highly arousing living situation, day in and day out? And for how much longer? Until she dies a natural death? Will she be adopted out in a year?

What is the best choice for a dog that fearful, whom volunteers have spent over four years helping to become less shy? (Of course, she has only been trained in that environment—she has not been away from the shelter and she will, in all likelihood, be just as shy in any other environment.) The volunteers didn't actually help her with her shyness—they just watched as she slowly got used to them and the environment within and directly outside the shelter.

A dog as shy as Bridget, after spending four years in a cage, could stand little chance of *not* being a fear biter. She has spent four years lunging at the front of her cage, at any stranger who happens by. All that lunging and cage aggression adds up to a lot of what Bridget considers successful practice. Successful, in that she has learned that when she feels trapped and sees an approaching stranger, if she is afraid and wants him to go away, she can lunge and charge aggressively and he will go away. When Bridget gets into a home, the first person who knocks on the door or rings the doorbell will most likely get bitten.

Magic

"Magic was born 10/97 and is a very handsome back and white male Dalmatian mix. He is very sweet, playful and affectionate and lively. He's strong, active and loves to run and play. He's cheerful and friendly and full of pep and energy, and just loves to kiss people and to be petted, but he does not like other animals. If you like to play and have a lot of fun, Magic's for you!"

Magic, from his photo, looks to be a purebred Pit Bull (remember what I said about Dalmatian mixes), and has been at his shelter for more than four years. "Full of pep and energy," "playful," "energetic," "lively," "strong, active and loves to play" are often euphemisms *not* for a silly, goofy playful dog, but rather an aroused, easily stimulated dog who probably uses his body and strength to overcome and overwhelm humans. My guess is that Magic is a dangerous and dominant aggressive dog. He is so confident, so self-assured that he never displays any overt aggression; his aggressiveness is not born out of fear, but power.

Never underestimate the seriousness of a dog (especially a dog who is large, athletic, strong and powerful) who "doesn't get along with other animals." Shelters always insert this as if it's no big deal. It can be a huge deal. If Magic gets placed in an urban environment, let's say New York City, he will encounter other dogs each and every time he goes out for a walk. If he lunges and tries to fight or hurt other dogs, each walk will be a nightmare, and will give Pit Bulls the bad name they cannot shake. His only possibility for off-leash exercise in New York City is at public dog runs, for which Magic would be ineligible, since he could attack and possibly maul or kill another dog.

If Magic were to be placed in a suburban home, one can only hope his backyard (if indeed he has one and that it is securely fenced) doesn't abut any other backyards with dogs. He could then fence fight daily, practicing his aggressiveness with other dogs and making him that much worse with every encounter. If Magic gets to go off-territory for a walk, perhaps once a day (which one would hope—off-territory walks are enjoyable and stimulating, and healthy for his behavioral as well as physical health), he will most certainly encounter other dogs in suburbia, and then the walk will be a nightmare. Dogs are everywhere. While some dogs are high-ranking with other dogs, and would do best with another subordinate dog in the home, these types can often still live harmoniously in a home with the *right* dog. But a dog who seeks out, intends to and would cause harm if he could reach another dog is a menace in society.

And if Magic gets placed in a rural home, once again the dilemma of a fence continues. But if there is no fenced yard (many people in very remote areas with a lot of land do not fence in their properties), Magic will never be able to go outside except on a leash and collar, or tied up outside with little or no chance for aerobic exercise.

Fred

"Fred was born 8/91 and is one of our sweet seniors living at the shelter. He is a tan and black male neutered Shepherd mix. He is a little shy at first, but then he warms up quickly and he is playful, affectionate and loving, a gentle, sweet well-behaved dog that loves to go for walks and never pulls. He would make a fine and loving pet. Please, let's give him the chance to know what it's like to have a home of his own and someone to love him. He deserves a chance to be free and to play and to have a family that loves him. Please come to the shelter and adopt Fred. He should not have to grow up and spend his entire life in a shelter."

This adoption description points the finger of blame for Fred's state on the adopting public, is if, for whatever selfish reason, we pass him by for other, perhaps younger dogs. Dogs who linger for months (or years) at a shelter are usually not "sweet" or "loving." Truly sweet and loving dogs get adopted fairly quickly, since they usually offer a soft expression and a pleading kind of eye contact when potential adopters pass—not a hard or blank stare. In all likelihood, Fred appears aloof, unconnected or serious when people pass him in his kennel. If the shelter staff and volunteers believe "he should not have to grow up and spend his entire life in a shelter," well, he already has. He's been there more than 10 years. If they truly believe this is no life for Fred, they should do something about it. It is Fred who is living a daily hell. By feeling sorry for Fred, the shelter has let him go on suffering for *10 years*, and heaven knows how much longer he will have to suffer, to avoid an enemy called euthanasia that I'm sure, to Fred, would not seem like such an enemy.

Annie

"Hi! My name is Annie and I am a very pretty, loving, happy spayed female red and white Pit Bull mix born in 1996. I need a new home. It has to be 100 percent safe and secure since I am an expert escape artist. I need a home with a highly experienced dog owner who can train me. I need a home where I can get lots of love and attention. Can you give me a perfect permanent home?"

There is a lot more to this ad than meets the eye. Needing a "highly experienced dog owner who can train me" is often a euphemism for such a difficult and problematic dog that she should live with a professional dog trainer. Then to add to that the dog is an "expert escape artist" is to acknowledge that this potentially dangerous dog is apt to get loose in the neighborhood. This is a huge liability. Being an "expert escape artist" usually means that a traditional six-foot fence is not adequate, because the dog can either scale it or clear it (Pit Bulls are incredibly athletic and are often difficult to contain with traditional fences if they don't want to stay confined). The severe restrictions on the type of adopter needed for Annie suggest that she may end up living out her life in a shelter.

Bonnie

"Bonnie was rescued by the humane law enforcement department of our local shelter. When taken from her owner she was emaciated. Her owner was arrested for animal cruelty. Bonnie has been boarded for one year while waiting for a home. She loves people. She was in obedience training for two months and is housebroken as well. Bonnie is not fond of other animals."

Which caretaker is more inhumane? An owner who underfed their dog, or a rescue organization who incarcerated this Pit Bull in a boarding kennel for over a year? Which situation is worse for the dog? It's a toss-up. Neither is particularly humane, nor should it be more humane just because a rescue organization is involved. How long would you, as a pet owner, board your own dog in a kennel before you would worry about the stress levels of long-term kenneling? In fact, most dog owners don't feel comfortable boarding their pets in a kennel for even a weekend.

This is not to say there is anything inherently wrong with boarding kennels. When run well, they are safe, efficient housing for dogs when owners are away from home for short periods. They are, however, not humane or comforting places to house dogs for more than a couple of weeks. To keep a dog in a boarding kennel for one year because she was rescued from someone who was inhumane or cruel does not make it OK, even though one person is labeled neglectful while the other feels self-righteous about what they have done. Was the dog underfed due to lack of basic care education? Would it have been possible to educate the previous owner? How much would it have cost to offer or donate high-quality dog food if finances were tough and the owner didn't have the funds to properly buy food for his dog? How much would it have taken to spend a little time, not punishing or blaming or judging the previous owner, but coaching or assisting him to be a better care-giver for this dog? Probably less time and cost than a year in a boarding kennel.

Zulu

"This beautiful 2 year old, 65 lb. American Staffordshire Terrier was a victim of one of the worst cases of neglect. Zulu's owner basically locked this beautiful boy up in an abandoned house, feeding and visiting him only once every couple of months. Nevertheless, this special boy somehow managed to survive the loneliness and lack of food and is doing just great with his newfound freedom. We're proud to report that Zulu is making great strides in our Socialization kindergarten. While he's no A+ student (yet!), we definitely give him an A+ for effort! In due time, and with the right loving person, we are confident that this neutered boy will flourish into the smart, loyal and affectionate dog he was destined to be."

It is important to remember that isolation, no matter for how long, does not make or create an aloof or asocial dog. It is the unfortunate truth that a dog who is neglected or ignored, if he was sociable and affectionate to begin with, will remain sociable and affectionate, just biding his time until he finally gets to be in close contact with people again. An aloof, antisocial and aggressive dog who is neglected or ignored will remain aloof, antisocial and aggressive, and often, these temperament qualities were the very cause of the neglect or isolation. This is hard to hear, because we somehow feel better assuming it is cruel, heartless humans who cause dogs to end up problematic, not the other way around.

Sporty

"A couple of weeks ago this 'Petey' look-alike came into the sanctuary's life. I would say this baby came through our doors, but that was something that he didn't . . . he was too hurt. This little boy had been abused. So badly abused that he needed immediate surgery. It seemed that somebody thought it would be fun to torture an innocent dog and this loving creature was the one they found. Although Sporty is a tough looking little beefcake, it didn't deter the cruel hearts of this abuser(s?), who proceeded to cause such trauma to his rear area that he was unable to make a bowel movement because of the amazing amount of tissue damage. Since becoming a sanctuary dog, he has undergone surgery twice to try and fix the damage. For all the pain that he has obviously gone through (as well as the swelling and tubes and bleeding), he was so full of happiness and life . . . so full of love . . . it was impossible to get him to stop wagging his tail while we tried to take his picture!!! We will never know the details of what happened to this poor dog, but we do know that it was by a human's touch that he has been on the verge of death for the last two weeks, and yet it is a human's touch that is what he craves most. Sporty is a special needs dog. He is incontinent."

Who wouldn't want a full-grown Pit Bull who will leave fecal deposits all over the house? This ad really is searching for someone to adopt this incontinent dog out of pity, which is not a healthy way to begin a long-term relationship.

Tammy

Sometimes the most promising dogs on the Internet are usually described sparingly and simply. Tammy is a good example.

"Australian cattle dog mix. Tammy is about 1 year old. She's a friendly red heeler mix."

And that's all the ad says. Most of the dogs listed on that shelter's web site are similarly described. This usually at least lets you know that no one is using euphemisms for problem behaviors. Tammy may have problem behaviors, but at least they are not obvious to the shelter staff and thus covered up with words.

My favorite way to "shop" the Internet for a good prospect is to access all the shelters in the rural Southern states (Mississippi, Alabama, Kentucky,

Tennessee, South Carolina), seek out the open-admission facilities (most of them are animal care and control shelters) and scan for shelters with lots of young dogs with little time left. I scan for shelters filled predominantly with young (under a year), mostly herding mixes (Border Collie mixes, Cattle Dog mixes—also called Heelers—Australian Shepherd mixes, Collie mixes) or Sporting Group type mixes (Pointer mixes, spaniel mixes, retriever mixes, set-ter mixes) or scenthound mixes (any of the Coonhound mixes or Beagle, Basset Hound, or Dachshund mixes). High-volume shelters with a high turnover of dogs—from euthanasia or adoptions—tend to have the best and most adoptable dogs and puppies around. Sometimes these shelters have little money, few resources and few adopters (because they are in remote areas), but they do have caring, inspired hard-working staff doing grueling jobs with little support. These communities are still experiencing true pet overpopulation, and have many sweet farm dogs and "failed" working dogs who are great family pets or produce litters of great family pets; their shelters are overflowing with this surplus. Unfortunately, it is the urban area shelters and most shelters in the Northeast that have the largest number of people interested in adopting. The greatest obstacle to bringing these wonderful dogs and wonderful adopters together is geographical distance.

The Internet can provide the access, and I encourage interested adopters to search out dogs in these distant, rural states and then call them and inquire about out-of-state adoptions. Many shelters will allow out-of-state adoptions. It can be worth the time and effort of freeing up your schedule to take a trip down South, spend some time visiting a few shelters, find your once-in-a-lifetime dog, and remain long enough to complete the necessary vaccinations or sterilization prior to adoption. People think nothing of driving two days to get to a good purebred dog breeder to buy and bring home their new puppy. Why should it be any less worthwhile to travel far and wide to seek out the future greatest dog in your life?

ATTITUDES ABOUT "RESCUED" DOGS

I once had a conversation with an instructor at a dog training camp in which I was enrolled. This instructor bred Rottweilers. Because I arrived at her class with a mixed-breed dog, I suppose she assumed I had "rescued" the dog. Or maybe the instructor knew my involvement in the animal shelter world. For whatever reason, she began a conversation about "rescue."

She said that she, too, had a "rescue dog"—a puppy she had bred a year ago whom she knew immediately was a problem puppy. She said that from the start the puppy had been mouthy and growly and downright aggressive. She said that she knew she would probably get this puppy back, and indeed, the buyer kept this particular puppy for only a few weeks before returning her. The breeder sighed and told me she kept the puppy—after all, what else could she do?—and then went on to describe the horrible temperament of this dog: aggressive to her, very aggressive and tending to lunge at strangers. Yes, she continued, this was her little rescue, since the dog has so many behavior problems.

I was stunned. To her, "rescue" was synonymous with "problem." To her, a rescue dog was automatically a difficult dog. I hate the term "rescue dog." First of all, technically, a "rescue dog" is a search and rescue dog—the kind of dog who finds lost children and searches the rubble after earthquakes. Second, I may have adopted or found my dogs, but I don't refer to them as "rescues." I don't cut my dogs any extra slack for having been adopted or found. I don't blame every training or performance or behavioral problem on something that may have happened to the dog before I got him.

Of course, it took some time for me to realize this point. When I was 19 years old I "rescued" a red Doberman Pinscher. For the first few months, every time I grasped her face to kiss her, she yelped and bolted backward. I contacted a professional trainer for advice, and I remember blathering on and on during our initial telephone conversation about how I had rescued her and how I assumed because of this panicky behavior that she most probably had been abused. The trainer listened politely, then completely disregarded all my excuses about former abuse and simply suggested ways to get my dog over the problem. Her advice was simple (although I felt at first it was rather unsympathetic) and effective: She told me to ignore my dog whenever she acted like that, and it worked. It worked because, in all honesty, I doubt this dog had been abused. But if she had, the advice would probably still have worked, because this dog was unused to sudden bursts of affectionate display, whether she had come from the perfect upbringing or an inhumane one. The truth was, she was yelping not because of cruel treatment received in her former home, but because I was approaching her in a manner she found, at first, threatening.

I was teaching a retrieve training clinic a few years ago for dogs competing in obedience, and in the later part of the day I was specifically working on more advanced retrieving issues with dogs who could already retrieve. A woman with a Standard Poodle came up in front of the group to work on trying to get her Poodle (who was currently showing in American Kennel Club obedience competitions) not to roll the dumbbell in his mouth when presenting the dumbbell during the sit in front exercise in competitive obedience. My first question to her was whether the dog already had her Companion Dog

Excellent degree (CDX, the second level of obedience titles), since I wanted to gauge the extent of the problem.

"Oh, heavens no," she replied. "This is a rescue dog!"

To me, that response was as irrelevant as if she had answered, "I enjoy Grape Nuts for breakfast." When I asked her what that had to do with the fact that he hadn't yet earned his CDX, she said he was having problems with retrieving and also not paying attention to her in the obedience ring. I wondered if perhaps the previous owner had beaten the dog with a dumbbell when he peed on the rug. Or maybe, I thought, the dog had been abandoned and left to starve in an obedience trial ring. If only this woman could have purchased this dog from a reputable breeder at the age of eight weeks, after a very promising puppy aptitude test score, and raised this puppy "just right," the dog would be retrieving reliably and would not only have his CDX, but probably an Obedience Trial Championship.

Actually, the advantages of adopting a dog are that you can really see what you are getting. Adopting an adolescent or adult dog is a great way to see the dog partially or fully developed (both physically and mentally). Assessing the dog's orthopedics is much easier—not just by looking him over, but because you can have the dog X-rayed if good structure is paramount to the goals you have for this dog. Temperament is clearly apparent, as well. The fearful dog reveals himself more overtly as an adolescent or adult dog than as a puppy. Certainly size and appearance are no surprise when you adopt an adolescent or adult dog.

Adopting or taking in a stray puppy is also an option. It's a crapshoot as well, as is (although to a lesser extent) buying a purebred puppy from a reputable breeder. When you buy a purebred puppy, you do stand a better chance of researching and reaping some benefits from meeting the parents of the puppy, studying lineage, selecting only from breeders who home-raise and go out of their way to expose their puppies from birth on to novel stimuli and handling. But just as often, the ignorant family whose dog accidentally had a litter quite successfully socializes those puppies. With no regard (due to lack of knowledge) for immunity or disease exposure, or safety, their puppies often are out and about, manhandled by kids, exposed to rowdy friends and neighbors and, by the time the adopter meets them, these puppies have clearly survived and are downright friendly. Now, I admit there are just as many poorly raised and socialized litters that end up in shelters or as strays—litters "bred" by people who allow the dam to have her puppies under a pick-up truck, don't handle the pups at all, and then dump them. But for every poorly raised litter that ends up in a shelter, there is a poorly raised purebred litter from a not-so-reputable but well-known show dog line.

It's funny. We have had countless mothers and their litters come through my shelter. A few very late-term pregnant strays have even whelped in our shelter. I can say that the temperament of the mothers seems to have no relation to the temperament of the puppies. The unstable mothers have often produced the most stable and wonderful puppies. The nicest mothers have had litters of growly or dominant aggressive puppies.

I have met countless hand-shy dogs with no prior history of physical abuse (unless teeny tiny bad people had beaten the fetuses in utero). I have met dogs of all ages who come into the shelter from convicted animal abusers. Sweet, trusting, gregarious dogs whose owners either confessed to kicking and beating their dogs or were captured on film, or witnessed by passers-by; dogs who are not hand shy or foot shy, with no fear issues, no aggression issues whatsoever, whose drunk and violent owners kicked them down the stairs or neglected them in backyards or chained them outside for years.

Good and bad dogs, confident and fearful dogs, aggressive and affable dogs come from shelters as often as they come from reputable breeders, are as often found as strays as they are found in pet shops. "Rescuing" isn't an excuse for poor temperament, behavior problems, fear responses or unsuccessful performance. "Rescuing," or adopting, is a choice. The "rescuer" or adopter chooses to partner with a particular dog, a choice that moves forward from that moment on. The only objective, whether or not there are behavior, temperament or motivation problems, is to move forward, begin working with the dog, and begin the fun and challenge of training.

Too many dog trainers I know say things like, "I would rather start with a puppy instead of rescuing because I don't want to have to iron out any issues before getting down to competitive sports training." Why assume there are issues? Why not evaluate the available dogs and select a dog without issues? And aren't there more issues stalling training when you choose a puppy? Housetraining, leash training, mouthing, not to mention their tender growing bones that cannot begin earnest jumping and impact activities until the dog is mature.

Why should adopting or "rescuing" refer only to big-hearted people taking on a long-term project, a problematic dog?

A few years ago, my shelter received an urgent phone call from a local rescue group. They had been involved in a cruelty case in which a white German Shepherd Dog, chained outside her whole life, was left behind in the backyard when the owners moved away and almost starved to death. Because our facility can give more personal attention to the dogs and more training, the group wanted to send this German Shepherd Dog to us—for care, rehabilitation, nursing, and ultimately, to adopt her out. We accepted.

The dog who arrived a few days later was a robust, outgoing, cheerful, tennis-ball-loving purebred white German Shepherd Dog. She was friendly, relaxed and remarkably heavy for a "starved" dog. Now I'm not certain whether the rescue group put all the weight on her, or whether when she was rescued she was much thinner (but hardly emaciated) and the rescue group had fed her amply. But for sure, there was nothing pathetic about this dog. On the contrary, she was lovely—an outstanding temperament and highly adoptable without any further help.

The rescue group had promised, when they dropped her off, to help us find a good home, advertise her plight and send potential adopters our way. Within a few days, we did, indeed, receive a phone call from an interested woman referred by the rescue group. The woman had heard about the plight of this dog, was appalled by what humans could do to helpless creatures, and could provide this dog a good and permanent home. And a good home it was: a huge fenced-in yard, another dog to play with, people around almost all day, no financial concerns whatsoever.

We had the dog out in the front yard of our shelter the next day when this woman arrived to meet her. She had made all sorts of preparations for the dog—she bought high-quality calorie-dense food and nutritional supplements, and she had arranged to halt all visitors and loud activities in her home for the next few weeks.

There was visible surprise and disappointment on her face when she arrived. In fact, when we handed her the tennis ball, she looked down at the dog and asked if this was actually the dog she had come to see. Finally, she mustered a comment about the dog being thin, and left without adopting the dog. She clearly didn't want a happy and optimistic dog in her life. She wanted to rescue something. (We eventually adopted the dog out, without a story attached to her, to a wonderful shepherd-loving, active couple.)

This woman's goal was to save a needy, helpless animal. And that's one of my goals way down deep inside as well, or I wouldn't run a shelter. But my bigger goal is to make everyone happy—the dogs who come to me, the people who come to me. My goal is that people will come to the shelter for the same reasons people go to a reputable breeder: *to get their dream dog.*

Why should the animal shelter be a place only big-hearted people come to?

Dogs live in the moment, in the present. It is, of course, what we love the most about them—they are as happy and thrilled to see us when we step out of the bathroom as they are when we come home from a business trip. They love us as much when we are in a crabby mood as they do when we are playing with them in the yard. An owner can have as much of a training or performance problem with a sound, well-socialized dog purchased as a puppy from a great breeder as they can with a found dog or adopted dog or "rescued" dog. Because it's not about the dog—it's about poor or improper training, or training that's not thorough enough. A dog is only pathetic or pitiful or a victim if he is treated as such.

Chapter 4

What Am I Really Looking For?

A great many shelter workers and volunteers go about their work believing or continuing to try to convince themselves that all the dogs in their care are not aggressive. But, although this may sound gloomy or pessimistic, I still think it is safer to go into a shelter assuming every dog is aggressive unless proven good-natured, as opposed to assuming every dog is good-natured until proven aggressive.

How does a caged dog respond differently from one who is in a home? While it is most difficult to evaluate the true personality and temperament of a dog while he is in a cage, there are very predictable responses that you *can* expect from a caged dog. Once you learn what responses to look for, you should be able to find the right dog at the shelter.

WHAT SHOULD I EXPECT FROM THE SHELTER?

There are many things you can do for yourself to find and choose the right dog, but there are more things you should expect the shelter to do for you. Some shelters rely very heavily on a thorough screening and matchmaking process. Other shelters won't ask anything about you, and will allow you to just go in and choose.

Some shelters spend hours interviewing prospective adopters. Meeting the criteria for adoption can be a challenge in itself for many adopters. In many shelters, the public is not allowed to go into the kennels and look at the available dogs until they have filled out the adoption paperwork. Sometimes, you have to pass muster and meet all the criteria before you are allowed to even take "a quick peek." One shelter I know of realized they were seriously limiting their adoptions with their rigorous screening process and strict requirements when a board member applied to adopt a dog, was screened and then rejected for not having the required fenced-in yard! That shelter had a meeting and revamped their requirements, realizing that a fenced-in yard was irrelevant to whether or not the dog would get enough exercise or his owners would adhere to a leash law.

While you should appreciate a shelter that cares enough about its dogs and its adopters to take the time to thoroughly screen you, you shouldn't have to tolerate something that feels more like an inquisition and a criminal background check in order to adopt a good dog. Thankfully, the trend today at many shelters is toward more open adoption procedures. This means that the once rather severe adoption screening process is being replaced by a less formal screening that is more educational than punitive or restrictive. This enables the shelter to better work with adopters to help them realize their realistic needs and desires in a dog, and to explain and educate them about basic care and training issues.

This problem in finding the right balance between interviewing and interrogating adopters was emphasized for me a few years ago while traveling to a conference. The person sitting next to me on the plane asked me about my profession, and we began talking about dogs. He told me that a few years ago he, his wife, and their six-year-old son went to their local shelter to adopt a dog, and came home with a wonderful Basset Hound mix. This man described his adoption experience rather neutrally: His family encountered no obstacles or hindrance in adopting, but also received no educational advice. They simply filled out the obligatory adoption forms and were shown into the kennels. It was by sheer luck that they ended up with a good dog who was safe with their young son, and that the dog ended up with a novice family able to provide a good, safe home. This was the first pet anyone in the family had ever had, and they were enjoying the experience so much that they went back to their local shelter to add a cat to their household. At the shelter they filled out the brief cat adoption form and gave it to the adoption counselor. They were stunned to find out they would not be allowed to adopt a cat. The man told me his family felt humiliated and confused. And worse, he had absolutely no idea why he and his family were rejected for a cat adoption.

As it turns out (the man had phoned the shelter later to get an explanation), there was a question on the application that asked whether the cat would ever be allowed outdoors. Never having owned a cat before, he figured the best way to keep a cat is to allow it some access to the outdoors—just like a dog. But the shelter would only adopt out cats to people who planned to keep them indoors, since indoor-only cats tend to live longer (no deaths from being hit by a car or injuries from fights with other animals, and they are less likely to contract communicable feline diseases). While there are a good many reasons to keep a cat indoors, this family had never owned a cat and had no idea what the ideal was. They fully intended to care for their new cat properly and safely, and just needed someone to tell them the best way to go about it. It wasn't the shelter's policy that was a problem, but the fact that they kept the policy a secret and did not use it as an educational opportunity. As a consequence, the family left the shelter that day, mortified. Worse, they never adopted a cat.

In a survey done at a shelter in the Midwest a few years ago, the researchers followed up on everyone that the shelter had black-listed or refused to adopt to in the course of the previous year. They found that a stunning 95 percent of the people they called had simply gone out and obtained a pet elsewhere. The people had adopted animals anyway, but the original shelter had missed out on the chance to explain how to take care of their pets in the best possible way.

Hence the movement toward a more open adoption process, where the role of the shelter is as much to educate and inform prospective adopters about proper pet care and training as it is to interview and screen them for the best match. Needless to say, not only more animals get good homes this way, but shelters are then also in the position of being a resource in their community to help everyone become the best possible pet owner—which is, after all, the goal.

WHAT IS THE ADOPTION PROCESS LIKE?

At the very *least*, you can expect to receive no assistance and just be given access to the dogs in the kennels. If you have the money to pay for the adoption and you are 18 years or older, you can adopt a dog. At the very *most*, you can be interviewed in person at the facility or rescue group, fill out numerous forms, and then await a representative to come to your home for an inspection and further discussion. Sometimes a home visit is a way for the shelter to flush out any discrepancies between what your home and yard are really like and what you said on your application. *Do you really have a fenced yard? Are you worthy of a dog?*

Thankfully, most shelters or rescue groups want to do a pre-approval home visit to help you safeguard and dog-proof the house and yard, to have the time to sit down with you and further discuss your needs and desires, and to help find exactly the right match for your lifestyle.

The most common procedure you can expect is to be asked to fill out some forms or sit down with an adoption counselor before being allowed into the kennels to view the dogs. You should be prepared to bring with you to the interview proof of identification, age and residency. The shelter will most likely want to find out if you rent or own your home, and, if you rent, you will be asked if pets are allowed and if you have informed your landlord about your intention to bring a dog home. Even if you live in a "pets allowed" residence, it is a good idea to let the landlord know ahead of time, especially if you find out there are actually some restrictions—you may be allowed to adopt a dog but it must not weigh more than 25 pounds, for instance, or your landlord may love almost all dogs, but be prejudiced against Pit Bulls and Pit Bull types. If that is the case, and you have your heart set on a Pit Bull type, this is a good chance to sit down with your landlord and educate him or her on the myths about the breed. Or, if you had no particular breed in mind, you can choose to avoid Pit Bull-type dogs to keep peace with your landlord.

Having worked in various shelters my entire adult life, I have experienced the shelter side of the adoption screening requirements and procedures. For the last nine years at my own shelter, we have boiled our adoption process down to what seem to be the essentials, and have come up with a good formula. We have found that most people come to the shelter just wanting "to look." At most of the other shelters I worked at, we would not allow just casual "look-ers." We would allow only prescreened and pre-approved people in to see the dogs. I am not really quite sure why we made this restriction. I think we didn't want "our dogs" to get unnecessarily aroused by a visit unless someone was really ready to commit.

The truth is, we have found that for the average person, the process of adopting is less about planning, preparation, goals and recommendations, and more about *falling in love*. At my shelter, we have found that anyone ready to stop by the shelter "just to look" has, somewhere deep inside of them, been contemplating adopting a dog, and, although they may not admit out loud that they are ready to take the plunge, they stop by the shelter knowing that if they find the right dog (that is, fall in love) that day, they will indeed adopt.

So ideally, a shelter should welcome you for a sneak preview, or accompany you into the kennels while extracting from you, on the fly, the bare essentials of what your needs are and which dog might be the best match for you.

WHY TEMPERAMENT TESTING IS VITAL

A family adopting a dog from a shelter that implements no formal temperament testing procedure is equivalent to that family walking into a shop filled with guns of all sizes, shapes and makes. The family peruses the aisles, looking at all the different makes and models, and then agrees on one particular handgun. They proceed to the front counter and tell a clerk they would like to see that particular gun outside its bin. The clerk smiles approvingly and remarks on how that particular gun is a staff favorite, and that generally speaking, Smith and Wesson/Colt 45 mixes make great family guns and are usually not dangerous with young children.

The clerk brings out the gun and guides the family into a small room, where they are left alone for about 15 minutes with the gun. It seems fine. It doesn't go off. It allows the children to handle it; it's pretty and shiny and well kept, probably somebody's faithful handgun. Maybe they were moving and couldn't keep it.

The family tells the clerk that they have made their decision; they'll buy the gun. The proper forms are filled out, and then the gun shop takes down the family's vital information and they are given a barrage of papers describing various aspects of gun maintenance, cruelty to guns, sterilizing guns, what to do if

Aggression in dogs is not to be taken lightly.

they lose their gun, where they can go to gun school to learn more about the gun, etc. There are so many papers, and the family is so excited about the real thing, that the papers get shuffled away in the trunk of the car while the new gun is placed ever-so-lovingly between the kids in the back seat so they can't argue the whole way home about who gets to play with the gun first.

And there you go. You have no idea if the gun is loaded. You have no idea if the gun is cocked. Is there a safety lock? Is it engaged? Does it just shoot a white flag that reads "Bang!" or does it shoot real live ammunition? How many bullets are in it?

A dog can be just as deadly. While I think dogs bring much more pleasure than a gun ever can, they can both produce the same horrifying harm.

WHAT SHOULD I WORRY ABOUT MOST?

Coming from the viewpoint of a trainer and behaviorist, I think you should be most worried about adopting an aggressive dog. Many people think the worst problem they could bring home is a dog who isn't, or can't be, trained to eliminate outside, and they fear most a dog who constantly has "accidents" in the house. From a trainer's viewpoint, that problem is small and very fixable. A biting dog, on the other hand, is not a small problem and is virtually incurable.

More professional dog trainers and behaviorists are hired, and more dogs are given up for, housebreaking problems than for aggression. This is not because people are shallow and care more about their carpets than their dogs, or because people like to be abused and to live with a violent dog. It is because the dog who is not housebroken will exhibit his problem several times a day, while the aggressive dog may only flair up once every few months, or even less. And the more serious the aggressiveness in the dog, the less often he is likely to have an aggressive episode, so this dog might go for a year or two before even showing he has a behavior problem, while the most un-housetrained dog could have problems every hour. And it's usually the *frequency* of Bad Dog: Good Dog incidents, rather than the *severity* of the problem, that predicts whether a person will try to work through a dog behavior problem.

Dog trainers and professional behaviorists are delighted to get a client who complains of a housebreaking problem or straining at the leash or destructiveness. These are training problems, and are *easy* for a good pro to work through and solve. But it's a trainer or behaviorist's nightmare to be hired by an owner with an aggression problem, because aggressiveness is a temperament problem, not a training problem, and is virtually incurable—only, at best, manageable.

BEHAVIOR PROBLEMS ON THE SCALE OF SEVERITY

	Toward Humans	Toward Other Dogs
More severe	Biting	Biting
	Snapping	Snapping
	Growling or snarling	Lunging
	Straining hard when your dog sees another dog on the street	
	Separation anxiety or panic responses when left alone	
	Thunderstorm phobia	
Less severe	Housebreaking	

BEHAVIOR PROBLEMS ON THE SCALE OF FREQUENCY

	Housebreaking
More frequent	Vocalizing or destructiveness when left alone
	Pulling or straining at the leash
	Jumping up
Less frequent	Biting

HOW CAN I AVOID DOGS WHO BITE?

An aggressive dog is *not*, despite what TV and your imagination and Stephen King would like you to believe, a slathering, snarling, vicious beast. Sometimes the most dangerous dog will, especially in a kennel or shelter situation, appear perfectly friendly, even to experienced shelter staff.

"Bad" people do not create "bad" dogs. Aggressiveness in dogs isn't caused by permissive people allowing their spoiled dogs to run amuck. Aggression is a component of a dog's temperament, and temperament is mostly what a dog is born with. This is absolutely not to say that training, socialization and clearly setting limits are not worthwhile. Indeed, they are vital to the health, sanity and appropriate behavior of pet dogs. But certain aggressive traits and tendencies are dug in deep, and can only be slightly modified or improved with continual behavior modification, training and vigilance.

Aggression is not "curable"; it cannot be dissolved with love, kindness and understanding. Aggression is rarely significantly influenced by traditional obedience training. A seriously aggressive dog can quite easily be trained to sit, lie down, stay, come and heel, but that will not change his thresholds for biting or his impulses toward violence. Obedience training is helpful for training *in* desired behaviors, but it does little to train *out* unsafe behaviors.

I think there was one episode of *Star Trek Voyager* in which a violent criminal alien was "cured" of his aggressive and violent tendencies. This was because the holographic doctor located a defect in the alien's DNA and was able to miraculously fix it, leaving a kind, compassionate and gentle being in his place. Much as I'd like to have the good doctor around in real life, we can't use the skills of a television future world to miraculously convert aggressive dogs into kind and gentle family pets. There is no superhuman dog trainer or behaviorist who can magically take the aggression out of an aggressive dog. The best outcome to hope for is lifelong management of the dog's problems. Aggression requires management for life.

"But 95 Percent of the Time They're Fine"

The truly aggressive dog is not easy to recognize. People who live with an aggressive dog rarely experience a biting episode. Ask anyone who is living with an aggressive dog, and they will inevitably tell you that "95 percent of the time, they're fine." In fact, their dog *is* usually a great dog 95 percent of the time, and aggressive only a small percentage of the time. People will live with, interact with and meet many very aggressive dogs and have no idea—they'll think the dogs are perfectly friendly. In fact, the more dangerous the dog is, often the more difficult it is to recognize the aggression. The truly aggressive dog has little to no fear component to his temperament. Without much (or any) fearful behaviors, the dog offers little display, few obvious warnings and is virtually unrecognizable to the average person as a dangerous dog. The aggressive dog will often look excited, playful, youthful or just happy to see you.

An aggressive dog does not bite or even try to bite every single person he encounters. Recently, a woman adopted a large, adult Pit Bull mix from a shelter. The dog had been in that facility for a year. The woman had him for six weeks with no apparent problems, except one afternoon her neighbor, a 75-year-old woman, came to visit. The dog launched himself at the neighbor, attacked her face, and by the time the owner fought the dog off (sustaining her own bites and damage), and before emergency medical services could get there, the 75-year-old neighbor bled to death from her wounds.

This dog *killed* a human being. The newspaper reports described neighbors as disbelieving and stunned—how could this dog have attacked someone like that when just hours before a neighborhood boy was petting the same dog? The shelter staff who housed the dog for a year reported observing no aggression from the dog. Newspaper reports concluded that the dog must have suddenly "snapped" or "turned." The idea was that a dog who is really so dangerous must surely appear savage and ferocious all the time, with all people.

I assure you that in a formal temperament test that dog would not have tested as good-natured. Evaluated with a formal temperament test, the severe aggressive tendencies in this dog could and would have been identified. A truly dangerous dog should not get to the point where he kills a human to indicate that he *might* kill a human. A truly dangerous dog, to a dog behavior expert, indicates he could kill a human with many other signs and behaviors—highly recognizable to a professional, subtle for the average person.

At our shelter, a family came in to surrender their one-and-a-half-year-old Boxer named Bingo. It was a heartbreaking situation—this family had been involved in a serious automobile accident, and they were all injured, the father the most seriously. They were now recovering at home, but the father was still fairly incapacitated. Apparently he had a long recovery ahead of him. The family felt it was too overwhelming for them to take care of Bingo. He was surrendered reluctantly, with many emotions, the wife sobbing. They had had Bingo since he was a puppy. The whole family adored him. He was very well taken care of, neutered, healthy, housebroken. Mostly they could not stop singing his praises as a family dog—how much he loved the boys, how he was so good with them, loved playing with them forever. We informed them anyway of our policy about incoming dogs: Despite the fact that he didn't appear to have any aggression issues whatsoever, we allow all incoming dogs a few days to adjust to the shelter environment and then do a thorough temperament assessment. If the dog passes, he will be made available for adoption; if he fails (for aggression), he will not be made available for adoption. We allow the owner to sign over the dog with two choices. The first is that they can leave the dog's fate up to us, choose not to follow up and find out what really happened, but instead leave and hope for the best. At our shelter we euthanize dogs if we do not feel it is safe to adopt them out. The second choice is that they can be called if the dog fails the temperament test, at which point they are given 24 hours to come and take their dog back (they can do what they wish—contact a private rescue group, try to place the dog privately, see if a relative or friend will take the dog or keep him). The second option is what this family chose.

Everyone at the shelter felt sorry for Bingo's family, and sorry for Bingo. He seemed like a nice dog, and the family was emphatic about how wonderful he had been with their two sons. We kept Bingo up front in the main office for awhile before sending him back to the kennels. A volunteer with a young son who had been on a waiting list for a Boxer was at the shelter that day. Within minutes of interacting with Bingo, the dog growled and snapped at the volunteer's son. This was a shock.

After allowing Bingo to settle into the kennel situation and acclimate more to the shelter environment, we temperament tested him. He was asocial, independent, confident, alert. He failed the temperament test in the first two minutes, and tried to bite me just for petting him too long. It was surprising behavior from such a beloved family pet. I called the owners and spoke with the mother. She was astounded and couldn't believe I found their dog to be aggressive. I questioned her carefully about Bingo's behavior with her sons, since I couldn't imagine such a dominant-aggressive and aloof dog "playing for hours with" and "never getting enough of" the boys. I asked the mother to describe what Bingo did with her sons that made them all believe he was so great with them. She described how Bingo would be restrained outside in their yard on his cable runner, and the boys would be playing in the yard and Bingo would jump and leap and bark and strain to get to the boys. He had a history of playing very roughly with the boys, and had sometimes "accidentally" bruised their arms. He was always wagging his tail and always seemed happy and excited and playful.

All the behaviors Bingo exhibited in his home were dominant, aroused, aggressive behaviors misinterpreted as playful ones. Because Bingo is young and so dominant, he feels unthreatened by the children. He sees them and treats them as toys, not humans, and his frustration and over-stimulation at trying to get at them were misinterpreted as excitement in wanting to *be* with them.

In the early years of running a shelter, we would rely heavily on the previous owner's information about the dog. If a dog was surrendered by his owner for valid reasons beyond their control, and not for problem behaviors, we would skip the formal temperament test and make the dog immediately available for adoption. We felt fairly confident in re-homing surrendered dogs who had been raised with children (and had no biting incidents) with new adoptive families with children. We actually felt most comfortable placing surrendered dogs (if they had a clean history with young children) with families that had young children—certainly more comfortable than placing stray dogs who had unknown backgrounds with families with young children. Surely, we thought, these family-raised dogs with such a stellar history with young children must be safe to re-home, without formally temperament testing them, until we realized too many of these owner-surrendered dogs with supposed clean histories of living with children were being returned for aggression. The temperament test is the most accurate predictor of future safety and success in a home.

For people surrendering their dog, euthanasia is the most feared outcome. Most people who surrender their dog, especially if they believe the dog to be a great companion, do not expect him to test as unadoptable or to have such a potential for biting that the shelter will not assume the emotional and financial liability for re-homing him. The average pet owner does not recognize or know how to categorize aggression. A professional knows. A dog can seem perfectly "fine" in the home, maybe has had an occasional incident—a growl, or a "nip," even perhaps a bite. The average person sees all the good in the dog—who is, they always say, 95 percent good—and assumes that the occasional "5 percent bad" is due to a lack of training or because the dog was provoked. The dog professional, however, can see the dog's true nature and his potential for biting again.

The risk for severe aggressive episodes in re-homed dogs are greater than with the original owner, since the original owner usually raised the dog from puppyhood and formed their relationship early on, when the puppy was adorable, vulnerable and not scary. Raising the dog from puppyhood means they get to know him while he is still nonthreatening. The owners will, consciously or unconsciously, have learned to maneuver around the dog's subtle threats and warnings while their little puppy matures. They will have learned to adjust their own actions to avoid the triggers that set off their dog. They learn this while the dog is still a baby—cute and young and small and forgivable and seemingly not aggressive. And they usually do this without even knowing they are doing it.

By the time the puppy matures into adolescence or adulthood, the owners rarely see any recognizable sign of aggression, or even threats, since they work around the dog's moods. For instance, if, at an early age, he mouthed, snapped or bit his owner's wrist when the owner held him by the collar to make him do something he did not want to do (like get off the sofa, get out of the flowerbed, etc.), the owners have learned to avoid the problem while the puppy is not causing any harm and is not really frightening them, and thus they believe (even if they continue to see mild flare-ups) that the dog will not and does not bite. They simply no longer grab the dog by the collar, or make the dog get out of the flowerbed—they know better. But if that adult dog is re-homed and the new owner takes the dog by the collar (a very common action when you're living with a dog), the dog does and will bite their wrist, and hard, because these new owners had no idea, saw no warning, were not able to recognize the dog's intentions, and therefore the dog had to go further than he ever did with his previous owners. Now the dog is mature and not such a cute little puppy. The dog is no longer "mouthing" or "nipping" or "playing roughly"—he is biting.

This is also why relying solely on the history from the previous home is not always reliable. It is not that the previous owners were lying or were keeping secrets about their dog during their surrender interview; it is that the owners simply did not understand how to interpret or predict their dog's temperament or behavior.

WHAT BEING A "FEARFUL DOG" MEANS

There are really two kinds of shyness. Dogs of the first kind are noise-shy or are easily spooked or frightened by objects in the environment. Sometimes the dog is frightened or panicked by the appearance of a lone garbage bag on the sidewalk during a nightly walk. Or the dog bolts to the end of the leash when a car backfires. Or, as one of my friends recently told me about her huge, seven-month-old mixed-breed puppy, the dog and she were in the living room and her husband was around the corner in the kitchen. He popped the cork from a wine bottle, making a loud noise, and it was three weeks before the dog would even set foot into the kitchen. This dog is not fearful or shy with people (friends *or* strangers) at all. He is just sensitive sometimes around things or noises in his environment.

Some dogs are confident in the countryside and panicked in the city. Many dogs are fearful of gunshots, backfiring cars, thunderstorms and fireworks. I know someone whose dog is afraid of rawhide bones. Rarely, if ever, is aggression associated with this type of fearful dog.

Big problems can arise with a dog who has rather severe panic responses to thunderstorms. Some dogs shake, tremble and hide during thunderstorms, or pace and pant. Other dogs panic. The panicked dog can destroy a house or injure himself in a desperate attempt to escape, crashing through glass windows, scratching at a door so furiously to get out that he bloodies his paws and toenails, not to mention destroying the door.

The other type of fearful dog is afraid of people. This type of fearfulness can cause more serious problems and needs to be considered before adoption. This temperament problem tends to manifest itself in response to new and unfamiliar people. The dog who is fearful of people will, usually quite quickly, get used to and bond heavily with his owner and the owner's friends, but remain afraid of all new people. Problems can arise while meeting and greeting these unfamiliar people. Dogs who are afraid of strangers often perceive approaching strangers as threats. At the front door or when encountering passersby on the streets, these fearful dogs may growl, back away and growl, growl and freeze, growl and snap, lunge forward or, eventually, lunge and strike out and bite.

The development of this temperament problem is not at its final stage until the dog has matured, usually around the age of three or four. So it is premature to meet a young dog who is fearful of strangers and say the dog is shy but doesn't bite. This is one temperament issue that is really difficult to predict with any certainty, since, even with the most vigilant owner who trains their dog every day, the most critical element to raising and training an innately fearful dog comes during his encounters with strangers, and controlling the

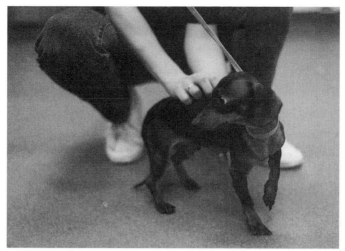

This little Dachshund is quite fearful. Small dogs can find the shelter experience even more frightening than larger dogs. This dog is facing away from the woman about to pick him up, and looks back at the hands on his back; he is quite uncomfortable and tense. Note the whites of his eyes and his stiff movements.

behavior of strangers is impossible. The fearful dog may respond fine with one pizza delivery person but bark and nip at the next. Some of this depends on the physical characteristics of the visitor; some of this depends on whether or not the visitor faces the dog directly, or ignores the dog; some of this depends on whether the visitor makes direct eye contact or concentrates only on the owner; some of this depends on whether the visitor leans forward and tries to make friends with the dog or ignores the dog; and much more.

A dog who is fearful of strangers (that is, pretty much everyone but the owner), depending on his age and his interactions with and experiences meeting new people, can develop into what people call a fear biter. A dog who spooks when an umbrella is popped open hardly bites at that moment. But a dog who is afraid of an approaching stranger is likely to bite if he feels cornered or trapped.

Many owners believe that since their dog is not afraid of them and would never bite (and has never tried to bite) them, the dog won't bite anyone. Remember, it is not that simple. Here are a few general rules to follow when assessing fearful dogs in a shelter:

- If you're looking to adopt a dog who is skittish around loud noises or sudden movement, ask yourself how chaotic your household and lifestyle is. With mildly skittish dogs, sometimes the more hectic and unpredictable the world they live in, the better they do, because they just learn to acclimate. This would work particularly well with younger dogs, when the window of opportunity for socialization is greatest. With very skittish dogs, a quiet or calmer, more routine household and lifestyle would be best. If that's what you can provide, great; if not, think about adopting a different dog.

- If you live in the city and the fearful dog has been raised in the suburbs or countryside, it may be risky to adopt. You might try asking the shelter if you could be allowed to foster this dog and try things out (in all fairness to the dog and you).

- If you're looking to adopt a dog who seems to be shy with people, there a few things to consider. Absolutely avoid adopting any dog who is actively lunging or barking and growling at the front of his kennel, no matter how nice the dog seems once he's out. This behavior will haunt you at home. It is not just a cage-related problem; this is a skeleton in the behavioral closet.

- If you are thinking of adopting a dog who is a little shy, look for the most affectionate and cuddly one—a general, helpful tip is that the more sociable the dog is, and the faster he can recover from his fear and make friends (fast means within two seconds), the less likely he is to become a fear biter.

MALE OR FEMALE?

I grew up with all female dogs. My parents always chose a female, but I'm not sure why. Perhaps they believed female dogs were more affectionate, or easier. Everyone has his or her own (usually strong) opinion about which gender makes a better companion.

I don't think you should limit your selection based on gender. Not at all. Look at each dog as an individual. Neutering (which is mandatory at most shelters) will take care of any negative affects you may be concerned about (whether your male dog will lift his leg in the house or garden, whether your female dog will go into a bloody heat cycle, and so on). And in terms of affection, gentleness, dominance levels and desire to roam or run away, *none* of these behaviors is decided by gender. They are all related to general, individual temperament—and that I can help you assess, regardless of breed tendencies or gender. So don't limit your options.

ARE PUPPIES CLEAN SLATES?

Many people mistakenly believe that by starting with a puppy, especially a puppy from a "reputable" breeder, with proper socialization and training you will be assured a good dog.

The British trainer Barbara Woodhouse promoted this idea in an indirect way, with the title and theme of her book, *No Bad Dogs*. Woodhouse implied that there are no bad dogs, only bad owners. I often overhear conversations between nonprofessional, regular dog people about Pit Bulls. The conversation always follows the same thread: It's only bad people who ruin Pit Bulls. All Pit Bulls are good dogs, but some are "made bad" by unscrupulous people. The truth is, there are good dogs with bad people, bad dogs with bad people, good dogs with good people, and certainly, bad dogs with good people. It is the goal of the shelter to match good dogs with good people, help bad people become better caregivers, and prevent bad dogs from ending up with good people.

So many trainers and shelter people seem encouraged when they find serious aggressive behaviors in young puppies, as opposed to adult dogs. The notion, I suppose, is that he's a puppy, and more malleable, and there are still many months in which to train and work with him, socialize him and mold him into a good dog. Unfortunately, this is not true.

The opposite is true—if you have a mature dog with a serious aggression problem, the truth is that he is not likely to improve much, or get much worse. And with certain mild behavior and temperament issues in puppies under six months (such as lack of socialization to the environment, some people, noises and other anomalies), there is, biologically, still a window of opportunity to get these puppies out and about and offer them multiple pleasant experiences to acclimate them gently to things in life they are worried about or unused to. For some puppies under six months who have problems being either afraid or unsure, or who play inappropriately (too roughly, or without boundaries), there is a window of opportunity at this age to train them to be more appropriate with other dogs, by carefully crafting playmates and play groups that will teach the problem puppy during each interaction and boost the puppy's dog-dog social development. But overt aggression problems in young puppies are quite serious, and generally cannot be fixed.

At one no-kill facility near me, I asked the shelter manager if she believed the aggressive dogs that her shelter refuses should be euthanized. She strongly agreed. Proudly then, she said that when owners try to surrender their biting dogs to her shelter, she looks them in the face and says, "You ruined him, *you* kill him."

Is it that easy to ruin a dog? Are all dogs basically good, until they are "ruined" somehow by teasing or lack of socialization or lack of training?

When given a choice, or when the parents are known, I would certainly increase my odds of getting a good-natured puppy by selecting one bred from nonaggressive parents. But I do not believe that either way you can be assured of a good, nonaggressive adult dog. Imagine that your sister has a baby, your first nephew. When he is three weeks old, your sister invites you over to meet the baby. When you arrive, he is sleeping in his crib, swathed in baby blue blankets with colorful clown mobiles dangling above his crib. "Sssshhhh," your sister says as you both enter the nursery. "The baby is sleeping." You tiptoe over to the crib, lean over, peek in. "Oh, he's so beautif—"you are interrupted when the baby whips out a switchblade from behind the bumper mattress, flicks it open, presses the blade against your throat and whispers, "Get the hell out of my crib, jerk."

Do you turn to your sister, smile and say, "Well, not to worry, he's young, and with the right schools and teachers, he'll be right as rain. There's plenty of time to raise him right"?

No. You would be extremely worried—more so, actually, than if her son had done this when he was 19 and home from college. And yet, with puppies, the younger the puppy with the serious aggression problem, the more hopeful is the rescue person.

A six-week-old fluffy, black and tan mixed-breed puppy was surrendered to my shelter. We named her Mary, and I remember picking her up, holding her up to my face and giving her a kiss on the nose. Slowly she turned her face to directly face mine (the size difference being equivalent to a Japanese actor looking into the face of Godzilla), looked me directly in the eye and, holding her gaze, lurched forward with a full offensive snarl, and snapped at my nose. Some people, including professionals, may think someone caused that behavior in the puppy, either through improper socialization, lack of socialization or abuse. How? A dog starts learning anywhere from three weeks and older. If Mary's aggressive behavior was learned or caused by the hand of a human, exactly what could have been done, or what could have been left out *in three weeks* to create this kind of aggression in this puppy?

The first thing a trainer usually suggests is *more* socialization. More? Mary showed an inordinate amount of chutzpah, an overabundance of confidence and courage toward strangers and strange environments. In fact, she had a creepy air of confidence and arrogance in the shelter—a lack of vulnerability and awkwardness usually present in normal puppies. Getting her out to expose her to more things and people would have been the last thing she needed, and would probably have increased her dominance.

What if someone abused Mary to make her this way? Maybe they struck her, beat her or kicked her. But she was neither hand nor foot shy, to say the least. Then maybe they teased her. Maybe they taunted her with food and then took it away at the last minute. Would that make her bold and offensively aggressive? Also, really, what is teasing to a dog? Isn't every meal, every snack in front of the television set, when they poise their noses centimeters away from the outer edge of your food and you *don't* give them any—isn't that teasing? And yet it happens every day. As you aim each forkful from your plate to your mouth, how does the dog know you're not in some way offering the forkful to him, and then not allowing him to have it as you swallow it down? And besides, when tested, Mary didn't overtly guard her food bowl. She stood over it, tail up, stance wide, and when I moved toward it she merely thrust her shoulder between me and the bowl. When a puppy barely six weeks old and weighing five pounds confronts a biped who stands 10 times her height, owns the territory, is familiar with the territory and produced and was responsible for delivering the food, that's an incredibly adult maneuver.

I can't come up with any way that Mary the puppy could have started out as a reasonable, friendly, normal and sociable puppy, and in three weeks somehow was converted into a monster. I believe she was mostly born that way—nature over nurture. These puppies are not puppies. There is nothing puppyish about them. Physically, they are agile, muscular, adept at balance and quick movements, and do not have the typical, clumsy, thick way young puppies have. These nonpuppies (or whatever you want to call them) need no time to learn about or get used to stairs or other novelties. Like seasoned adults, they just do it. Some of these puppies even have the bulky muscling and round, hard legs and shoulders that sexually and hormonally mature adult dogs do.

WHAT IF I HAVE ALLERGIES?

There are some good adoption options for people with allergies to dogs, or allergies to *some* dogs. People are not exactly allergic to the dog's haircoat, but rather their dander. Still, heavy shedders tend to aggravate allergies, while low-shedding dogs do so less often. Some sensitive people experience skin rashes from the coats of some breeds with very short, fine coats, such as the Shar-Pei or Pointers, particularly when they handle the dogs' muzzles. Breeds with undercoats (like all the northern breeds—such as Siberian Huskies and Alaskan Malamutes—and also German Shepherd Dogs, Welsh Corgis and other breeds) tend to be heavy shedders, and are often unsuitable for people with allergies.

Some of the short-coated breeds and some surprise breeds happen to be heavy shedders as well, although people often don't realize it. These include Pugs, Dalmatians and Golden Retrievers. Heavy shedders may also seem unappealing to people who have an aversion to vacuuming or to seeing tiny tumbleweeds of dog hair blow across their living room floor. But my advice is to always fall in love first, and then worry about the hair. Vacuuming becomes a less-dreaded chore when the cause is something you love so much.

Breeds with curly coats or hair that requires clipping or professional grooming are often good choices for allergic people. These breeds and breed types can include the Poodles (Toy, Miniature and Standard), the Bichons Frises, the Portuguese Water Dogs, Irish Water Spaniels, and many of the terriers and terrier mixes. A breed rescue group for any of these breeds can not only provide you with a dog to adopt, but can also be a resource to help you find out if indeed the breed's dander triggers your allergies. Many breed rescue folks are happy to invite you to visit their home for few hours, spending plenty of time breathing in an enclosed space with several representatives of the breed. Breed rescue people also like to have a chance to get to know you better, discuss the habits and instincts particular to their breed, and get a good feel for the personality of a dog who would best suit you and your situation.

If you have allergies, many shelters will give you a "day pass" for a dog, or allow a foster or trial adoption, since there is no reliable way to tell whether or not a particular dog will trigger a particular person's allergies until they spend time together. If a shelter cannot arrange for either a day pass or a trial adoption, you may ask if there is a small room where you could spend an hour or so with the dog you are interested in. When you are in this room, really massage your fingers into the coat of the dog, against the grain of the hair, and then pat the dog lightly to release the dander. (Remember, it is the dander that triggers allergic responses, not the actual hair.) The only problem with this is that the room, since it is part of the shelter, is likely to have the dander and dead skin cells of a hundred other dogs in there, too. But it is better than nothing. And no one should be deprived of the joys of living with a dog because they are allergic to some hair types.

WHAT'S THE BEST AGE TO ADOPT?

I have divided dogs into age categories so you can best understand how dogs develop and how they are likely to act in any particular age group. I hope this will help you assess which age might be most appropriate for you and your lifestyle.

Puppies: Seven weeks to 20 weeks

While dogs don't fully mature until they are three to four years of age, I consider a true puppy to be five months and under. After five months, I consider that puppy to be an adolescent.

If you are adopting a puppy in this age category, you can count on being with your dog during his cutest phase. Take a thousand photographs. Really! You'll appreciate them to no end later on. Those of us who have dogs adopted *after* puppyhood relentlessly and fruitlessly pursue the what-did-our-dog-look-like-as-a-puppy dream. So, most importantly, if you are going to adopt a puppy, make sure you have a fully loaded camera and lots of extra film.

At this age you can have the most influence on your dog's temperament. The puppy's critical socialization period is up until 16 weeks, so if you have adopted a puppy in this age category, you can reap the most behavioral benefits if you put the time and work into getting him socialized. Socializing a puppy means more than just passively taking him places and letting people come up and pet him. If you choose to adopt a puppy, or one simply steals your heart at the shelter, you'll need to ask yourself some critical questions:

1. Am I home enough to be able to properly housetrain my puppy? (A seven- to nine-week-old puppy will need to go out and eliminate every three hours during the day.)

2. Are my work hours too long to properly provide company, physical exercise, playtime and mental stimulation? (Calculate one hour for every month of your puppy's age, than add one. So a three-month-old puppy can regularly be left alone for four hours.)

3. Do I have young children in my home who require my constant attention and are already making me crazy?

4. Do I look forward to being awakened each day at dawn (weekends included) and supervising my puppy during every waking moment we are together, until he can hold his bladder and bowels and eliminate in the designated area?

5. Did I know that the real and scientific reason for "puppy breath" is *worms*?

Puppies are indeed adorable and irresistible. If you fall in love with one at the shelter, then by all means, adopt one. But don't adopt a puppy just because you think that it's the only way to "raise him right," or the only way to develop a strong bond. Quite frankly, other people raise most puppies really well, and

This sweet-looking, soft-eyed red and white mixed breed
looks to be about four months old. At four months, puppies
are approximately half the bulk they'll be as adults.

often even housebreak them for you and reinforce for them that humans are great. When that's the case, you can adopt that particular dog at any stage of his life (even if he is 15 years old) and he will still bond to you heartily, readily, deeply. Dogs are quite resilient and can be re-homed at any age better than our egos would like to believe.

Adopting a puppy *before* the age of seven weeks is generally a big mistake. Developmentally, puppies are not ready to leave their littermates or their mother until they are seven weeks old. For a few years at my own shelter, we were temperament testing and adopting out puppies as early as six weeks of age, until we found that too many of these puppies grew up and behaved much more dominantly and aggressively (with humans and, usually, dogs) than their temperament tests originally showed. Too many of these puppies under the age of seven weeks were being returned for aggression and/or significant dominant behaviors. We have no way to determine if the dominance and aggression developed because the puppies were leaving their littermates and mother (if there was one around) too early, or if the temperament test is not accurate at such an early developmental age. So now we hold all puppies until they are a minimum of seven weeks old, at which time they are temperament tested; then, if not they're aggressive, they are placed.

We have noticed that six-week-old puppies can appear very placid and easy to handle, when, a week later, they are much more lively and responsive. By seven weeks, puppies seem to readily show their true temperaments, and we can more accurately determine how dominant or dominant aggressive (or not) they are.

If you already have a resident dog at home, it is best not to adopt from this age category because, this being your puppy's critical socialization period, your puppy may tend to bond more closely with your resident dog than with you or your family. Left together, another dog will certainly provide good company and entertainment for your puppy and help keep him from getting lonely or bored, but the older dog can also teach him that playing is more fun and frequent with his own species than with a human. This doesn't always happen, but it's impossible to predict which puppies it will happen with. The tendency for most owners is to keep the puppy with the adult dog, and the tendency for most dogs and puppies is to play together. Play is extremely fun, and extremely tiring. This makes life for the owners easier. Satisfied and tired puppies are a cinch to live with. But at the same time the owner loses any status as the one in the household who is most fun to be with and learn from.

Adopting a dog who is five months or older (assuming he was raised believing that humans are more fun) allows you more freedom to let your adult dog and your new puppy spend more time together, since even if they play and have fun, the puppy has already spent his critical period developing his strongest bond with humans, and will usually retain that.

If you have a resident dog and you happen to fall in love with a puppy at the shelter, you can still adopt the puppy. You'll just need to work a little harder than people without a resident dog. See Chapter 7 for advice on what you need to do.

Resist the temptation to adopt two puppies at the same time, whether they are from the same litter or not. Sometimes it is so hard to choose between two puppies you have narrowed it down to. Or there may be only two puppies left, and it feels almost cruel to pick one and leave the other all alone. Or you may imagine that while you are at work, your two puppies could play and keep each other company and therefore be happier. There are many reasons why you need to resist this temptation.

The two puppies will play with one another, and the most common thing to come out of it is that their play will get rougher and more and more intense as the weeks progress. They will enjoy playing with each other to the possible exclusion of playing much (or at all) with people. Gradually, an owner can lose control over both puppies, and be unable to interrupt their play, or stop them and ask them to settle down. Eventually, the dogs will need to be crated or separated to get them to stop playing, since as soon as they are together, they start playing.

John Rogerson, a brilliant trainer and behaviorist from England, supposes that because their play gets rough, and because they play so much and become familiar with each other, when either puppy has to meet a strange or new dog, he will greet the new dog with the only style of play he knows. It will probably be rough and too casual for the new dog, who is expecting to be greeted more cautiously—which is the way most new dogs greet one another. If the new dog finds the puppy too inappropriate in his greeting, he might growl or snarl, and then the puppy is horrified. The puppy wonders, "Why did this new dog get so aggressive when all I wanted to do was to say hello?" If this surprising response from new dogs happens more than once, the puppy may then develop the idea that dogs (except for his littermate) are unpredictable and aggressive, and it is better to start out being aggressive to them.

Another issue that commonly comes up when two puppies are raised together is that one can become more and more of a bully, while the other becomes more and more inhibited, even shy in new situations. Usually by the time the puppies are about six months old, one ends up snapping or showing some aggressive tendencies toward people or dogs. More often than not, owners end up giving one puppy away after a few months of trying to raise them together.

On the other hand, many people have quite successfully raised two puppies together. Those who are most successful at it seem to spend a tremendous amount of time playing and training and interacting with each puppy separately. Each puppy is given his own private time with the owner to play or go for walks or go to training class. The puppies' playtime is limited and is heavily supervised; the owner interrupts, stops the play, makes both puppies lie down or sit and stay for a minute, and then releases them to play again together, thereby always remaining master of the game.

So the most success is to be had when the owner basically spends double the time raising and training two puppies at one time, with limited amounts of free play for the pups. For many, this defeats the original purpose of getting a second puppy to provide a companion and playmate for the other puppy.

Adolescence: Five months to 18 months

This is my personal favorite age for a dog to be adopted. The adolescent dog hides nothing: His personality, his physical beauty and flaws are there for all to see. By six or seven months, the dog's basic adult size (minus at most a couple of inches and a few pounds) presents itself. Adolescent dogs, even if they're not fully housebroken, can at least hold their bladder and bowels all day long. They can be left home alone for longer periods than young puppies, making them a better choice for the working owner.

This Basset Hound–English Springer Spaniel mix is approximately six months old. He shows a soft eye and a sweet expression, and is leaning into the people petting him, which shows friendliness.

They will, however, also make you tear your hair out. There is a reason why so many dogs who end up in shelters are adolescents. They are most difficult at this age. Even if you've started out with a young puppy, and trained and trained him, by the time he hits adolescence he still seems to forget everything he ever learned. Adolescent dogs, like adolescent humans, test authority and limits. They can be rebellious, or try to see how far they can push you. They're big, giant puppies now, and if they decide to chew on your furniture, you're likely to find your entire couch destroyed, not just one corner of it. I lost three queen-size mattresses during my one large, mixed-breed dog's endless adolescence. Why I bothered to replace them while she was still young, I don't know.

And then one day, they just grow out of it. You will wake up one morning and realize you haven't yelled at your dog in weeks. You realize nothing in the house has been destroyed in months. You realize your dog has been coming promptly, on the first command when you call him. He has quietly grown up while you weren't looking.

This is the age at which vigorous aerobic exercise and training classes are essential. This is the age that needs the most tending to. It is, again, a great age to adopt—the dog has many years ahead of him but still enough puppy qualities to satisfy the mothering urge. And if you're willing to put the extra time and effort into staying on top of the adolescent dog, you may not even notice his less-than-desirable "teenage" behaviors.

Adulthood: One and a half to five years

This age category is an excellent choice for the adopter who wants more of a ready-made dog. The adult dog is almost always done with destructive chewing and is usually quickly housebroken—if he isn't already there. Adult dogs still have many good years left, but have also left adolescence and all the hassles that come with that age.

Maturity: Five to eight years

This is a great age category from which to adopt. These dogs have much to offer, and so often they are already housebroken and trained, since no one would have kept an unhousebroken dog for eight years! Very few mature dogs are surrendered due to behavior problems, since any problem serious enough for someone to give up on a dog would not have been tolerated for so many years. The mature dog is done developing most of his behaviors, and has been for a few years, so these dogs rarely come to you with behavioral surprises, either. Even more than with dogs from the adult age category, mature dogs usually need little in the way of training or fine tuning. They almost always arrive as ready-made, perfect pets.

Despite all that, this is the age category (perhaps even more so than the seniors) in which the shelter has the most trouble convincing adopters to take dogs. People may be put off by the fact that the dog is seven years old, and worry if will he live a long enough life with them. At least when you adopt a senior dog, you do not do so with the expectation that the dog will live another 10 years. But with mature dogs, people are wary of adopting and falling in love, then losing their dog too soon to some illness or age-related disease.

Seniors: Eight and older

One of the great secrets of the dog world is how gratifying it is to adopt a senior dog. I adopted my first dog as an adult (I was 18 years old) when he was eight and a half years old. He was half Newfoundland and half Golden Retriever. He died 18 months later of metastatic cancer. His death was also the first dog death

I experienced as an adult, and I was devastated. But I wouldn't have traded that year and a half for anything on earth. He was a once-in-a-lifetime dog (since him, I've had four other once-in-a-lifetime dogs...), and I wouldn't have cared if he had only lived three months. The time I had with him was worth it; I adored him.

I don't want to suggest that adopting a senior dog means you're soon to be heartbroken because the dog is probably at death's door. One of my subsequent dogs was a Doberman Pinscher who had been hit by a car and was in rough shape. She was an adult—four or five years old at best, and more likely a little older. I had her for *years*, and I never said she was any older. Every time someone asked how old she was, my answer was perpetually "four or five years old." She never aged. And it's easy to have a dog who doesn't age at all when you adopt: Since you don't know his birthday, there is no momentous annual date when he gets a year older.

The beauty of senior dogs is that they usually come as complete and perfect packages—they are almost always housebroken, whether or not they've ever even lived indoors. A dog who has spent his life as an outside dog is usually so used to only eliminating on outdoor surfaces that he does not have accidents in the home, even when he moves indoors. And usually no one keeps an unhousebroken dog until maturity, so most senior adoptees are quite clean in their new homes. Senior dogs don't chew up your belongings, need huge

This harlequin Great Dane–black Labrador Retriever mix lived to be almost 14 years old. She was as sweet and kind at 13 as she was the day she was born.

amounts of exercise, or need that much entertaining when you get home from work after being at the office for 10 hours.

TO PIT BULL OR NOT TO PIT BULL?

It seems that people generally believe Pit Bulls are made mean by bad people, and that the basic Pit Bull is as good as any other dog—it's just that a lot of unscrupulous folks raise them wrong and train them to bite and kill. Still, almost no one will adopt a Pit Bull, even a puppy.

The myths about many specific breeds abound: All Pit Bulls are scary. All Labrador Retrievers are good with children. But I have met just about as many mean and scary Labrador Retrievers as I have mean and scary Pit Bulls. I have met more American Cocker Spaniels and English Springer Spaniels who have bitten and put people in the hospital than I have Pit Bulls.

The problem is that *when* a Pit Bull is bad, he is really bad. While perhaps more Cocker Spaniels have problems with biting than do Pit Bulls, I have never met a Cocker Spaniel who has killed anyone. Cocker Spaniels don't go that far. When I was growing up, the Irish Setter was the "bad" breed. Then the St. Bernard went bad. And never, ever did you hear about these breeds killing children or adults, or mauling the elderly. On the other hand, an aggressive Pit Bull is a formidable dog. A Pit Bull, even a small one, is athletic and strong. Physically speaking, he is capable of doing way more damage than the average Golden Retriever. The style in which a Pit Bull fights (with humans or dogs) is quite different from the style in which other breeds fight. When you have a Pit Bull who wants to bite (again, humans or dogs), over 100 years of selective breeding have enhanced the Pit Bull's ability to trigger or "ignite." Many Pit Bulls can instantly become aroused, and remain at the peak of arousal, basically until either the Pit Bull dies or his opponent dies. The Pit Bull was bred with a never-give-up trait; to fight with another dog to the death. Most other breeds are slower to arouse, do not get as highly aroused, and give it up more quickly. Combine the arousal with aggression, and you can get a Pit Bull who fights to the death. That may sound dramatic, but it's true—as true as the fact that not all Pit Bulls are easily aroused, and not all Pit Bulls are aggressive with either humans or other animals.

Probably one of the scariest questions I was ever asked was from someone who had been a Pit Bull rescue official for years. She came to me during a break at a conference and asked, "So, have you met any Pit Bulls that aren't aggressive with other dogs?" You see, the implication is that *every* Pit Bull she has placed has been aggressive with other dogs, but because that was what the breed was originally bred for, she cuts them slack. And I find that unacceptable. I don't care what the breed was originally bred to do—if the behavior is unacceptable or dangerous in society, then it is simply so, whether the behavior is instinctual or not. I don't think a person whose dog has been mauled by another dog cares whether the offending dog was a Pit Bull doing what the dog "was originally bred to do" or a Labrador Retriever bred to retrieve a bird. It's the aggressive behavior itself that is the critical problem.

You would expect to find more Pit Bulls who are aggressive to other dogs than Labradors, just as you might find more Border Collies able to gather a flock or sheep than Labrador Retrievers, because their original breeding was for those purposes. But it does not mean that all dogs can do, or are good at, what they were originally bred for.

A few years back, a four-month-old Pit Bull puppy was surrendered to our shelter. Not only because he was a Pit Bull, but also because he was mostly black, this dog remained at the shelter for 14 months before he was adopted. Fourteen months is a disturbing amount of time for a dog to be in a shelter. (Statistically, black dogs in shelters are least likely to get adopted. No one knows why for sure, but the prevailing theory is that black dogs have dark faces, and in under-lit shelter kennels and dark cages, their expression is very difficult to see and it hinders the ability of adopters to connect with them.) He had a lovely temperament with people and other animals, and was particularly super with other dogs. He could get almost any dog to play with him.

We spent a lot of time and energy with this Pit Bull, because he was a great dog and we wanted to make sure he didn't deteriorate behaviorally or emotionally during his stay at the shelter. While he was with us, I used him as my "therapeutic" dog when working with private clients and their dog-aggressive dogs. Our Pit Bull was skilled at making fearful and undersocialized dogs more comfortable until they could play, and also at indicating to me which dogs had really serious aggression problems and intended to do harm. He was finally adopted by a woman who ran a doggie day-care center. She brought him to work with her every day, and used him to test new dogs' compatibility with other dogs, to see if they were safe to come to day care and play with all the other dogs. She took great pleasure in the responses from dog owners in learning that it was a Pit Bull who would judge how aggressive or playful their own dogs were. He ended up being an ambassador for the breed. Later, he went on to train and certify as a FEMA search and rescue dog.

You can adopt an individual Pit Bull who has no aggressive tendencies toward other dogs, because there are many out there. And you should refuse to adopt an individual Pit Bull who does have aggressive tendencies toward other dogs, because these tendencies are a liability and a disaster waiting to happen.

There are great Pit Bulls and bad Pit Bulls, puppies and adults, from fighting stock and from top breeders. Each Pit Bull deserves to be treated and temperament tested as an individual dog.

BREED GENERALIZATIONS

The beauty of going to a shelter and adopting a dog, purebred or mixed, is that you have the chance to adopt a dog with all the characteristics you desire in an unlikely package. Don't assume that all Labrador or Golden Retrievers and their mixes are good with kids, and don't assume that all Chow Chows and Pit Bulls and their mixes are aggressive. Don't assume that all Border Collies and Border Collie mixes will need a lot of exercise or a "job to do." Don't assume that all terriers are dominant and busy and active.

I have a friend from high school who finally, a few years ago, decided he was ready to get his very first dog. Danny called to inform me that his friends had all advised him to buy a yellow Labrador Retriever puppy from a breeder. Their advice was to get a Labrador because they are congenial, easy and friendly, and to start with a puppy so he could make sure and "raise it right." I asked him to write me a list of all the qualities he wanted in a dog, describing everything in detail, except the physical characteristics.

Don't assume all Pit Bulls are bad, and don't assume all Golden Retrievers are good. This is a fearful-aggressive Golden Retriever. Note her retreating stance and gross threat display, which tells you she feels defensive and wants you to go away.

I called him back a week later and asked Danny if he had ever seen the movie *Mad Max, Road Warrior*. He said he hadn't. I suggested he rent it, and then tell me if he thought he could live with a dog who looked like the dog in the movie. The dog in the movie is an Australian Cattle Dog, or a Queensland Heeler, also called a Blue Heeler. We had a three-year-old male Cattle Dog in our shelter who fit every attribute my friend hoped for, plus, I knew, a few extra good points that I thought Danny would benefit from. The dog was an adult and housebroken, patient, not destructive, content when left alone for long hours. These extras would make him an excellent choice for an anthropology graduate student with long library hours and lots of traveling back and forth to rural, mountainous Latin America.

Danny liked the look of the breed, and I told him this particular dog had everything he wished for except one thing—this dog wouldn't fetch a Frisbee. He agreed to come out that weekend and look at the dog. Danny lived in Chicago, and the shelter is in upstate New York.

I received an e-mail that Saturday morning from a fellow shelter worker in Chicago who was socializing with some of her shelter friends at a bar downtown that Friday night. They met a guy at the bar who was proudly sharing the upcoming adoption of his very first dog. The shelter folks were all intrigued, and asked him what kind of dog he was about to adopt. He boasted about getting an adult male Australian Cattle Dog. Then he was crushed as the shelter group pounced on him and confronted him about how inappropriate an adult male Australian Cattle Dog could be for a first-time dog owner. And they were right—if this dog had acted anything like the typical adult male Australian Cattle Dog. But temperament tested as an individual, this dog was the perfect choice for a first-time owner, and a perfect fit for Danny. It came out pretty quickly that he was going to New York to get his dog, and then they all realized they knew me and trusted that Danny would be getting the right dog.

And he did. He drove the 18 hours to meet Mel (now Dingo), and it was love at first sight. Since he was going hiking later that weekend, and I knew by his wish list that he wanted an off-leash hiking companion, I did advise him to keep his dog on a long leash for at least three weeks, until the dog got used to him and learned to come reliably when called. I called to check up on them a few days later, and Danny informed me that not only was Dingo already a great off-leash hiking companion, but was a great Frisbee retrieving dog as well.

The moral is that the right dog is simply the right dog, no matter what the breed or breed mix.

THE IDEAL TEMPERAMENT OF A FAMILY DOG

What characteristics must a family pet have?

- The ideal family dog should be friendly to adults and children.

- The ideal family dog should be playful, but not too easily or aggressively aroused.

- The ideal family dog should have low levels of aggressiveness.

- The ideal family dog should have a high threshold for biting.

- The ideal family dog should be congenial with other animals.

A man e-mailed my shelter to inquire about adopting a dog for his nine-year-old daughter, Eliza. I asked the girl to write me a description of her "dream dog," so that I could try to match her with a compatible dog. She e-mailed me herself, and her document was called "Eliza Dog." It read:

Active but not insane.
Very happy and jolly and peaceful.
Floppy.
I do not want a dog who is always an angel. Barking is part of a dog.

I think that is a great general description for the ideal dog—for anyone.

In this next section I am going to try to help you adopt your dream dog by narrowing down your choices to the safest and least-likely-to-be-aggressive dogs. Use the Safety SCAN and the Bite-o-Meter when you are at the shelter and observing dogs. You can do this while you are watching the dogs in the kennels, or when you are visiting with a dog in a get-acquainted area. The more observations you make, the better you can put together all the pieces of the behavioral puzzle for the dog you are looking to adopt.

If you have young children in the home, or just want to be as sure as you can be about the safety and good nature of your next dog, the Safety SCAN and the Bite-o-Meter will help you know when to seek the advice of a professional behavior expert or dog trainer whom you can hire to come in and further check out the dog. The Safety SCAN and the Bite-o-Meter can point out potential aggression problems, before you adopt, in a dog whom you may already really like.

SAFETY SCAN

I use the acronym SCAN to represent four risk factors in unknown dogs. The more SCAN observations you red flag in a dog, the higher the risk not only of aggressiveness, but of severe aggression.

It is helpful to have a logical, Spock-like approach to interacting with unknown dogs. Hesitation when meeting and greeting unknown dogs is wise. We have such an immediate emotional response with dogs that often we put ourselves at risk. We fall in love so quickly that we throw caution aside and do with unfamiliar dogs what we would comfortably do with our own dogs, or familiar dogs. Often these things are intrusive, invasive or come across as threatening to a dog who does not know you.

Thus, it is useful to have a little rule to keep your brain just before your heart when you're with dogs. SCAN is an acronym for four observations to make before you lose your heart. It will help you assess your risk factors in the interaction you are about to have. It can help you decide (just as Captain Kirk benefits from having Mr. Spock counsel him on an emotional issue, such as an alluring alien woman with aphrodisiac tears). The Safety SCAN can tell you if you should bend down and get to eye level with this dog, if you should put your face in this dog's face, if you should hug this dog. And it can answer the question, "Would this dog be safe to adopt if I have young children?"

S = Sexually Mature and Sexually Intact

Ask yourself or the person with the dog, "Is this dog over a year or under a year?" The older and more mature a dog is, the more damage he could inflict, *if* he were to get aggressive. Although a dog doesn't reach maturity until he is three or four years old, I use one year as the marker, since it is usually around a year when a dog will start to bite, and starts to break skin. You're safer around dogs under a year, since they are usually—*if* at all aggressive—inexperienced. Because of their inexperience, they make threat displays and give inhibited bites (where they don't bite down hard) more often than actual bites.

The neutering of dogs is important as well. Simply put, testosterone can exaggerate aggression. Therefore, an intact male dog, especially a sexually *mature* intact male, *if* aggressive, can pose more of a danger to you than a neutered male.

I would rather approach and pet a neutered male dog than a sexually intact male dog. More serious bites to humans are from intact male dogs than any other type of dog. That's not to say that all sexually intact male dogs are going to bite, but rather that the bite is likely to be worse from an intact male than from a neutered dog.

Spayed female dogs are actually likely to have more testosterone than intact female dogs, since estrogens (present in intact females) compete with any testosterone. But with female dogs, the testosterone rule is overshadowed by the fact that if a female dog is sexually intact and has noticeable and protruding or hanging nipples, she is more of a risk to handle because in all likelihood, she has gone into heat every six months, for an average of three to four weeks. Most owners do not keep their female dog in the house, on the furniture, or allow her to sleep in the bed with the kids while she is bleeding on and staining everything. Most owners keep their bitches who are in season in the garage, or outside in a pen or even tied in the backyard (not that that keeps them from getting bred). So for those three to four weeks out of every six months, that female sexually mature and sexually intact dog has been kept rather separate from the family and at arm's length from the intimacy of home life. What this can mean for you is that she is likely to be less used to close contact and intimate handling, has been less likely to have been incorporated into regular household life, and therefore may be more intolerant of these things once she is adopted into a home. She also can pose more of a risk during routine handling, as she may not be used to it.

C = Cautious

Ask yourself, does this dog seem wary, suspicious or cautious with either the environment or with you or other people? When stressed, our thresholds for aggression are lowered. Imagine not getting a good night's sleep because you stayed up late trying to meet a deadline that you were not able to meet. You are up every hour worrying, then sleep through your alarm clock, wake up late, commute to work, get stuck in traffic. You arrive at work, head for the coffee machine, and someone good-naturedly teases you about being late—and you snap at them (or "take their head off," as we say figuratively).

Although the stressors are different, all animals respond to stress, and the more stress they (or we) are feeling, the lower their thresholds are for aggression.

Signs of cautiousness include:

- The dog will appear inhibited in his movements.

- The dog will not be relaxed.

- The dog's tail may be tucked, or carried stiffly.

- The dog's body will not be freely moving or wiggling.

- Cautious dogs will often appear calm or quiet when really they are frozen in position.

- Because dogs who are cautious often don't move their bodies freely, when turning their heads to investigate a noise the whites of their eyes will show dramatically. Since they are not moving their necks, they will look more with their eyes, which is why the whites keep appearing.

This English Springer Spaniel is slightly fearful. Note his furtive, sideways look and the visible whites of his eyes. He does not show freely-moving, relaxed friendliness, and there is no greeting display. He is cautious. This could indicate future aggression problems in a home.

A dog who moves himself away from you with furtive, backward glances and tries to hide away from you in a corner, or behind you, or behind or under some object, is cautious. These dogs should not be approached. If a dog is actively avoiding you or scared of you, you could be at risk if you proceed in engaging with him.

A = Arousal

Arousal is perhaps the most important characteristic to look for and carefully observe, because it is so often mistaken for friendliness. The dog who is aroused can *look* so friendly and happy, when in reality he is aroused. Being aroused lowers thresholds for all types of aggression.

Signs of arousal in dogs include:

- Being quite active and seeming "playful"

- Appearing very stimulated or overstimulated

- Appearing very excited

- Being sexually aroused (male dogs, even neutered ones, may get an erection)

- Panting and leaping and jumping all over the place

- Using his mouth to play with you

Although there is a sexual component to arousal in a dog, arousal in itself is not always sexual. The aggressive dog who is aroused and overstimulated, one who only appears friendly but actually isn't, becomes much more dangerous than a calmer, less aroused, less stimulated aggressive dog. I don't mean to say that that all aroused dogs are aggressive. It's just that if they are aggressive, they are potentially more dangerous.

In the shelter it is easy to make excuses for aroused dogs. They seem so friendly, so "untrained" and they "just need exercise after being cooped up in that cage." The state of arousal can so mimic a happy, friendly dog if you don't know what to look for. Here's all you have to remember: A dog can't just *look* friendly; he must *act* friendly.

Some dogs become aroused too easily and cannot calm themselves down quickly. We call them "zero to a hundred" dogs. They can be provoked at the drop of a hat, and then they spiral upward, getting more and more stimulated with no stimulant. Other dogs are in a constant state of arousal. People often call these types of dogs "hyper" or "high-strung," or describe them as having a lot of "nervous energy." These are all euphemisms for aroused.

Some dogs are fairly calm until you give them any attention or physical touch, and then they get more aroused—maybe not highly aroused, but moderately. Other dogs are fairly calm until you give them any attention or physical touch, and then they get even calmer, more settled. Friendliness and non-aggressiveness being equal, the dog who is easier to live with, train and have around young children would be the dog who is calmed by touch and attention, not the one who is stimulated by it.

Arousal prepares the body for action. All animals need some level of arousal to function and get out of bed in the morning. The ability to become aroused, take some sort of action, even if it is no action, and then calm back down again is a necessary trait. Pet dogs, good companion dogs, can be aroused when necessary, but not constantly (like the neighbor's Yorkshire Terrier who alarm barks and charges the front door each and every time he hears a noise). They look to a human for further information, and then either investigate or ignore the stimulant, settling right back down to their pre-aroused state. But those dogs who are aroused too sharply, too suddenly, to the point where they can't respond appropriately, are the ones whom even nature has no use for.

Difficult dogs arouse too easily, at everything, anything, all noises, any rise in emotion. They go "over the top" when someone rings the doorbell—they get frantic, practically hysterical, and cannot respond appropriately, cannot even be easily interrupted. In this peak of arousal, many dogs find the only way to calm back down is to bite, or "unload." People who have more than one dog, one of whom is easily aroused, will often complain that when someone rings the doorbell, the aroused dog turns and attacks the other dog(s). These types of dogs are very hard to live with and manage.

A great example of arousal is from an episode of *Star Trek: The Next Generation*. Captain Picard and Data (an android commander) are off the ship, and the rest of the crew contracts a retrovirus, one that affects their DNA. The entire crew quickly starts de-evolving into much more primitive beings. When the Captain and Data return to the ship, they find that the ship's counselor, Deanna Troi, is an amphibious creature living at the bottom of her bathtub. The Klingon security chief, Worf, has degenerated into a monstrous predator, on the loose and looking to kill. Other crew members are found all over the ship, in their quarters, at their stations, as lizards, protoplasmic blobs and primordial creatures de-evolved into either predator or prey. Data remains uninfected, since he is an android, but Captain Picard is now infected. He and Data try to find a cure for the virus before the Captain also becomes incapacitated. There is a scene in which Captain Picard is leaning over his computer console, intent on his work, when all of a sudden he straightens up, tenses and checks suspiciously behind him. Nothing is there, but it's a brilliant moment and an example the way arousal often expresses itself in animals. It is such a simple moment of alertness and readiness, almost fear, and so uncharacteristic of Captain Picard, who is normally a confident, dependable, secure and competent leader. The first symptom of his de-evolution is his heightened state of arousal. Arousal has made Picard more jittery, jumpy, excitable, stimulated and less capable of reason. Arousal lowers the aggression threshold.

Kramer (on the TV show *Seinfeld*) is aroused; Jerry Seinfeld is not. Kramer enters a room by skidding in—sliding to a halt, his hair up, his brow furrowed, his eyebrows taut, the whites of his eyes showing. Kramer over-reacts instead of responding. Like Kramer, the dog who is constantly aroused, or very easily aroused, makes for a difficult companion.

Learn by comparing a few dogs. Keep in mind that dogs who have been in their shelter and kenneled for one month or longer can *all* be highly aroused, so you may have no "normal" canine behavior to compare to.

N = No Need for Humans

The more people-loving your dog is, the higher and stronger his threshold is likely to be for aggressiveness. You need a dog with high sociability and affection. The more a dog likes people, wants to be with people, needs people, the more willing that dog will be to accept all kinds of handling and control, strange new people and different looking people. The more people-loving your dog is, the bigger the buffer zone of love and affection there is to chip away at before your dog resorts to aggression to get you to stop making him do something he doesn't want to do, such as having his nails clipped, or having a tick pulled off, or being hugged for too long by a child or adult, or being pulled by the collar to get him off a particular piece of furniture.

The more sociable and affectionate your dog is, the less likely he is to bite a friend or neighbor who comes onto your property or into your home, and the less likely you are to incur a lawsuit. The more affectionate and loving your dog is, the more joy and return you'll get from the relationship.

A dog who has no need for humans will think nothing of biting humans when and if he wants to.

BITE-O-METER

I received a phone message one day about a year ago. It was the voice of a distraught mother (there were kids in the background making kiddie noises) who said she needed some behavioral advice, because her dog had just bitten her. She had been bitten on the hand one time, quite hard, and he left puncture wounds. Specifically, she wanted advice on how to manage him. I liked immediately that she understood that with biting, management is as good as it gets, and that she had no false hopes for a "cure." I called her back. She had a 16-month-old Rottweiler, a "sweetheart," the "love of her life." She and her family had had him since he was eight weeks old. They had never had any problems with him. She had no idea what happened, where this bite came from, why, all of a sudden, he bit her. She promised that he had never, ever bitten before. She couldn't imagine what got into him.

I asked if he had ever growled before. "Oh, all the time," she replied. "But I always thought that meant he wasn't going to bite—that if he growled but didn't bite, he wouldn't."

Growling is a warning. It means, "If you don't stop what you're doing to me, I will bite you." Sometimes it means, "You are annoying me, but I am still a young dog. Now I only growl, but when I reach maturity, I will bite. I am warning you."

That Rottweiler growled whenever someone went near him when he was eating. He growled when he had a bone or a toy and anyone tried to approach. He growled sometimes when he was hugged. Sometimes he would allow hugging. Sometimes he wouldn't. He sometimes growled when petted. Sometimes he would request petting by nudging his owners, and then he wouldn't growl. Sometimes he requested petting but then would growl when he'd had enough.

And although the mother firmly believed the dog was not aggressive and had never bitten, upon further questioning I realized he actually had. Once, without opening his mouth, he had leapt up and used his muzzle to punch the face of the oldest daughter, giving her a bloody nose. This was when the daughter had tried to hug him when he wasn't in the mood. A muzzle punch is called a closed-mouth bite. But it is a bite, and the dog's intent is to do damage, to harm, to use violence to control human behavior.

What is the very first warning sign that a dog may be aggressive and should not be adopted? Usually, people think of snarling or growling. But there are important warning signs well before the snarl or the growl. A dog gives many warning signs that suggest he is on the path to biting.

A dog who does not initiate an affectionate, sociable interaction lasting more than two seconds at a time is potentially showing the first signs of being aggressive. This may be a dog who is very excited, one who looks happy and is jumping all over you or mouthing your hands. But ask yourself, "Is this dog sustaining any touching, licking, nuzzling or gentle, gooey jumping up, for a full two seconds or longer?" If not, and if everything the dog does is fleeting or hyper or lasts only for the briefest instant—consider this dog unsociable and therefore at much higher risk of being an aggressive dog in a home.

Remember, when evaluating a dog in a shelter, you are not at a friend's house, visiting with them and their dog—one who has greeted you at the front door and now is lying down by the hearth. That dog may not always be sociable with you, but it doesn't matter. With a shelter dog, or one you are looking to adopt, choosing a dog who is highly affectionate and sociable over one who is not greatly increases your chances of adopting a good-natured and safe dog. Remember, too, that an aggressive dog rarely walks up to you with a sign that reads, "I am a biter." An aggressive dog is unlikely to be a raging beast, straining on his leash, curling his lip and chomping his jaws. An aggressive dog will tell you in much more subtle ways that he is not a good choice for a companion.

Please understand that for each behavior described as a signal of potential aggression in a shelter dog, there are casual, if not meaningless, other reasons why the dog might look that way. But unless you are a professional dog trainer (and even then...) or have hired one to accompany you at the shelter, err on the side of caution.

Number One on the Bite-O-Meter

Lack of sustained sociability
Disinterest
Aloofness
More interested in the environment than in people

Sociability and affection act as a buffer against aggressiveness. The more a dog loves petting, touch, praise, eye contact and loving, human attention, the more armor he has to get him through the less desirable (but perfectly normal, common and humane) times when a human inevitably makes him do something he doesn't want to do (for example, groom or brush him, accidentally bump into him while he's sleeping or resting, or move him while he is eating).

The dog who merely *tolerates* petting, praise and affection will have no buffer. If he doesn't enjoy petting or touch that feels good, why would he tolerate handling that is uncomfortable or unpleasant? He won't. His aggression threshold lurks right below the surface at every moment, during every interaction.

A genuine show of affection from this woman to her dog. If this dog didn't love physical touch, affectionate displays and close contact, this woman could be bitten. Call me anthropomorphic, but I think both dog and woman love one another.

The same holds true for the fearful dog. A dog who is afraid of strangers (strangers are the most likely targets for aggression from fearful dogs) and lacks sociability (the desire to be petted, praised or give and receive affection), if cornered by an approaching big, scary (but benevolent) stranger, has no reason to tolerate the guy. Why wouldn't he bite, just to chase the stranger away? Why would the fear-aggressive dog "hope for a new friend" as the stranger gets closer? Humans can't intrinsically offer enough of a reward to make the fearful dog hold back his fear aggression.

On the other hand, the fearful dog who loves, seeks out, cannot get enough love, affection, praise and petting from family and familiar people, can at least see a light at the end of the tunnel. For this dog, the big, scary approaching stranger *could* offer something pleasant, could end up as a friend, could ultimately provide something pleasurable.

Number Two on the Bite-O-Meter
Dilated pupils

Arousal and dominance quite often go hand in hand, and these dogs will have big round pupils. They may be reflecting light and look like marbles. Usually dogs with dilated pupils also have a "hard" expression, which is characterized by wide, round, open eyes, sometimes even bulging a bit. They may have a furrowed brow (wrinkly and tense in the place just over the dog's eyes). And you may notice all this because the aroused and dominant dog may jump up and visit your face frequently, and look into your eyes with his own big pupils and wide eyes.

Quite often these dogs are also panting and seem excited or hyper. The panting may make them appear to be happy. Quite often these dogs are also wagging their tails a lot, and that, too, may make them appear happy. And they might actually be happy—but make a note and take seriously any signs of dilated pupils or a hard expression in a shelter dog you are interested in. These clues may indicate you will need to bring in the help of a dog behavior expert or a dog trainer to further evaluate the dog you are interested in, to make sure, to the best of everyone's ability, that he will be a safe dog.

The problem with making this kind of observation is that to be aware of the size of a dog's pupils, you must look directly into the dog's eyes. To a dog (or any other animal, for that matter), a sustained, direct stare can be interpreted as either a threat or a challenge, both of which can trigger aggression. But don't worry; there are ways to observe a dog's eyes without directly confronting him.

The trick to avoiding staring directly into the dog's eyes is to look at his eyes when he looking at something besides you, and also to look at the dog

This Rottweiler is quite aggressive. Note his wide, round, open eyes (that's why they look white to the camera), his dilated pupils, his direct stare, frontal body stance and high tail jutting out and visible behind the top of his head (indicating his dead-on frontal confrontation). This is a confident, aroused and dangerous dog.

from the side. From a distance or at an angle, dilated pupils will make the dog's eyes look like Darth Vader's—black upon black upon black. Also, from an angle, dilated pupils will cause the dog's eyes to look dark bluish, the iris will not be readily distinguishable, and you should be able to see the light reflecting back, thus making the eye look like a dark blue marble or a green and black swirly marble.

Look at all the other dogs' eyes as well. Are they all dilated or reflecting light back? Urban shelters tend to have more dominant and aroused dogs and puppies than rural shelters. So if you find yourself in an urban facility and *most* of the dogs' pupils seem dilated, you are probably making an accurate observation. If you find yourself in a rural shelter and most of the dogs' pupils seem normally constricted, again, you are probably making an accurate observation.

Number Three on the Bite-O-Meter

Seeing the whites of a dog's eyes, for brief moments but frequently in a short space of time

Human eyes are oval, so the whites of our eyes are always visible. Dogs' eyes are round and their irises take up almost the entire visible area of the eye. When you see frequent flashing of the whites or corners of a dog's eyes, it can indicate that he is uncomfortable in some way—either worried and therefore not freely moving his head and neck, or irritated and tight with tension. (My mother tends to show the whites of her eyes a lot, but that is because of arthritis in her neck.)

How much is "frequently"? It is rather subjective, but if you start out looking for the dog to flash the whites of his eyes and you see it once, you will probably continue to see it "frequently," because if the dog is flashing them a lot, you will be able to notice it more easily. On the other hand, if you look for it and see it once, and then realize that you have forgotten to keep looking, chances are the dog is not flashing them often enough to count as "frequent," and you have less to worry about.

I saw Bruce Willis being interviewed on a talk show once, and he was asked about what he learned in acting classes. He smiled, drew out an invisible gun, and held it at arm's length in front of him, using both hands overlapping on the trigger. He turned his head slightly to the side, showing clearly the whites of his eyes to his invisible opponent, and froze while he blared out a warning. He called this "stallion eye."

In Hawaii, while lecturing to a group of animal control officers, they demonstrated the local Hawaiian version by all turning their heads to the side and showing me the whites directly. "Stink eye," they called it.

The third and fourth items on the Bite-O-Meter are very closely related. They appear individually at first, but if the dog remains uncomfortable they will appear simultaneously, and then it is an obvious clue that the dog may be aggressive and often thinks of biting.

Number Four on the Bite-O-Meter

The dog will freeze for a tiny moment and then resume what he was doing. Often this dog will lower his head at this same time.

These pauses are tiny warnings the dog is giving that, if pushed, he may resort to some type of aggression. These freezes are hard to train your eye to see, because they're so brief. They will almost always happen because the dog does not like the proximity of the human, or does not like what the human is doing to him (this could be petting or restraint or hugging or almost anything). The dog almost always freezes when he would like to stop you from doing something he doesn't want.

Of course, good dogs often freeze when you touch them, because they are enjoying it and are calmed by your touch. If you're not sure what kind of

This dog has stiffened, frozen. His pupils are dilated and he is showing the whites of his eyes. He is snarling. This is his final warning to keep you away. If you don't retreat, he will bite.

freezing the dog is actually doing, stop whatever you're doing and see if the dog approaches you for more (the dog is friendly and less likely to be aggressive), or moves further away, stays where you left him or shakes you off (the dog is intolerant and more likely to be aggressive).

Unfortunately, by the time the dog is freezing *and* showing the whites of his eyes, he is very close to biting.

I had a client once who consulted me because her young German Shepherd Dog was occasionally aggressively going after and snapping at guests. The dog would let the guests *into* the home, but after they had been there awhile and they tried to get up and move about, she would lunge after them, growling and nipping at their behinds. My client said a very observant thing: She always knew when the dog was going to do it, because the dog would give a "whale eye." I asked her what she meant by "whale eye." "You know," she said, "whales have these huge bodies, no neck and small eyes on either side of their head, so in order to look anywhere, they can't turn their head. So they are always showing the whites of their eyes: a whale eye." How observant! And useful, since, if you can predict *when* a dog is going to bite, you can cut off the sequence and sometimes interrupt the dog before she bites.

The Rest of the Bite-o-Meter

The rest of the behaviors on the Bite-o-Meter are gross (not disgusting gross, but overt gross) and fairly obvious warnings that the dog may bite. In loose succession, they include growling, lunging, snarling, snapping, nipping (front teeth pinches, not breaking skin), biting, mauling, killing.

THE IMPORTANCE OF SELECTING CAREFULLY

In the absence of a shelter that does the preliminaries and does them well, carefully selecting a dog to adopt is important so you can be as sure as possible that you are bringing home a dog who will not physically hurt someone. This is especially important if you have young children in your household, or are planning on having children within the next five to 10 years. This is also important because even if you don't have any children, and don't plan to, there are still children on the planet and in your environment. The majority of dog bites to young children are delivered not by roving packs of stray dogs, not by the family pet, but by dogs who belong to friends, relatives and neighbors.

Not that it is any pleasure for an adult to get bitten, either. But adults can read a dog better and respond more quickly when warned, and adults can control their own actions to avoid bites. Children under the age of seven cannot do these things, and are at higher risk for being bitten. Children, if bitten, also tend to have the bites directed at their faces, since they are usually eye level with the dog, or in close contact, or on the floor when they are bitten.

Do You Have Young Children or Plan to within the Lifetime of your Dog?

If you answered "yes," I recommend sticking to the following rule: Do not adopt an unknown dog (stray or owner-surrendered without a really thorough behavioral history) older than two years of age. Unless the shelter you are adopting from has an excellent behavior department and behavioral staff (and sometimes even then), the risk of harm to your children is too great.

The older a dog is, the more force and damage he is likely to do when aggressive. Younger dogs tend to do a lot more snapping or inhibited biting, while an adult dog, experienced in aggression, efficiently and quickly bites to get what he wants. If you are going to inadvertently bring into your home a dog who ultimately will be incompatible with your children, at least minimize the amount of damage he is likely to do. Stick with younger dogs, or dogs who are very well known to the behavior experts at the shelter.

BEHAVIORAL REHABILITATION PROGRAMS IN SHELTERS

Recently more shelters around the country have been hiring trainers and behaviorists. And an increasing number of shelters that have these profession-als (particularly in urban areas, where there are more problem dogs) are imple-menting serious rehabilitation programs for problem dogs. This seems like it could be a good idea, because urban shelters do have an abundance of problem dogs. The rehabilitation programs involve an initial temperament evaluation (often each shelter has its own temperament assessment procedure) to deter-mine the type and severity of the dog's behavior problem. Then the shelter sets up a behavior modification program with, hopefully, a reasonable time limit.

These rehabilitation programs are not for simple dog-training issues (teaching the untrained dog to sit, stay, not to jump up on people, walk better on a leash and so on)— which can benefit the many, many young, untrained, enthusiastic dogs in shelters everywhere. Those kinds of training programs help put these dogs on the road to success—but I'm talking about dogs with no seri-ous behavior or temperament problems, just a lack of basic education. These training programs not only benefit a dog's behavior, but also, the mental stim-ulation helps him last longer in the kennels before deteriorating.

Behavioral rehabilitation programs for problem dogs, most notably aggres-sion problems, are a little more controversial. One of the most common aggres-sion issues to reveal itself in a dog during a temperament test is guarding resources. This means the dog will covet, growl, snap, snarl and in most cases bite and do harm if a human or (or another dog) approaches the dog while he has a resource: food, a toy, etc.

If you are looking for a good companion dog or have kids in your home (of almost any age), no matter how successful things might appear, my advice is to not adopt a dog who has been in any sort of rehabilitation. The dog may have been successfully rehabilitated to the point where the adopter can follow a few guidelines in the home for the rest of the dog's life, and effectively manage the dog. But unless you are an aspiring dog trainer or a single adult person looking to enter the field of dog behavior, choose a dog with no known aggression issues. Leave those dogs for the experts in the field—most of whom avoid these dogs like the plague because the experts all know how difficult it can be to live with a problem dog.

There is nothing simple or easy about continuing a behavioral manage-ment program for the rest of a dog's life. And, especially for aggression, things can go along great for many years, and then the dog bites and leaves you with a lawsuit. Management is never without slip-ups. Don't start out with a dog with known issues.

It is unfortunate, perhaps almost criminal, when a shelter adopts out its dogs without putting them through a reliable and thorough temperament test. Portions of this book will sound grim. But in so many ways there should be no need for a book like this at all. In the ideal world, shelters would provide all of these services and information for you, as the most important part of what they do. Until then, there are good dogs out there looking for good homes, and good people out there looking for good dogs. Don't be discouraged!

Chapter 5

How Do I Meet the Dogs?

Even if you think you've chosen your dog after you've seen just a few, force yourself to scour every last kennel and cage. My soul mate dog, Carmen, was the last of about 65 dogs at New York City Animal Care and Control. I went through every dog cage in every ward, and there, at the very end of the last ward, in a dark kennel partially hidden behind a mobile bank of puppy cages (I was not interested in adopting a young puppy), was Carmen—big, active, covered in dirt and motor oil stains, the future *love of my life*.

In this chapter, I'll explain what to do and what to look for as you are meeting all these dogs.

WHAT TO BRING WITH YOU TO THE SHELTER

- Post-Its

- A pen or pencil

- A bath mat

- A pig's ear or rawhide chew

- Two or three cans of dog food and a can opener (if they're not easy-open cans)

- An Assess-a-Hand (a fake rubber hand secured to a stick, used to safely temperament test dogs to find out if they will guard their resources)

- A toddler-size doll (for adopters who have children or are thinking of having children)

- A lifelike stuffed animal cat with black beaded eyes (if you have a cat at home)

WHAT YOU CAN EXPECT FROM THE DOGS

For the most part, you will encounter a room full of barking, jumping dogs. Often, people choose a dog who appears different from the rest, and in most cases, they'll select the "quiet" or "calm" dog. Unfortunately, sometimes the quiet or calm dog is merely frightened. "Frightened" can mean the dog just arrived recently at the shelter and is still freaked out, and in another day or two he will act like all the other dogs. Or it could mean the dog is by nature a fearful and suspicious dog—one who takes a long time to warm up to people—and that can sometimes translate into a dog who later becomes aggressive toward strangers, guests and visitors to your home. Or not. Later on, I will explain further how to gauge the severity of a dog's behaviors.

There are three basic possibilities for how shelter dogs may behave as you first walk through:

1. A dog might be sitting, or start standing up and end in a sitting position. He might scoot his butt toward you as you approach, or he might turn his body so that he is oriented sideways and smoosh himself against the front of the cage as you approach or reach out your hand, thereby placing as much of his body within your reach as possible.

2. A dog might be quite still, possibly sitting or lying down, usually in the rear of his kennel, sometimes in the middle, sometimes even just sitting or lying down in the front. He will not be barking or wagging his tail or moving around much. He will seem quiet or perhaps calm, or he might just be nervous and frozen.

3. A dog might be up at the front of his kennel barking, or barking and lunging, or barking and jumping up, or even growling, snarling and lunging.

A dog may react differently depending on whether you're a man or a woman, Caucasian, African American, Asian, big or small, hairy or bald,

This dog has turned her body so that she is oriented sideways, and has smooshed herself against the front of the kennel to offer you as much surface area as possible to pet. This, plus her soft-eyed expression, shows lots of friendliness.

bearded or shaved, a young child or an adult, facing him and leaning over or squatting sideways. Many years ago at our shelter, we had a nice medium-size black and tan shepherd mix for adoption. He was friendly and sweet with everyone at the shelter. He was adopted quickly, and within a few days the new owner called to report that Joey, as he was named, was very afraid of men and would bark whenever a man approached him. We hadn't seen this behavior at the shelter. Then we realized there were *no men working or volunteering at the shelter* at that time, and none had come through to adopt in the few days Joey was with us. The moral? Since men make up 49 percent of the general population, it is certainly worth finding out how a dog responds to men before sending that dog out into the world.

YOUR GENDER MATTERS

Why might a man get a different response from a dog than a woman? Men are generally bigger, have deeper voices, can have hairy faces in various designs (moustaches, goatees, Amish-type beards, huge sideburns and so on), can have hair or be totally bald. And so, dogs who are fearful are usually more fearful with men than women because men come in more varieties. Men are scarier than women. Women are generally smaller than men (or at least shorter); women have hair on their heads (at least in public) but not on their faces; women have higher pitched voices and tend to vary their inflection; women gesticulate more and move around and avert and change their gaze while greeting, while men tend to greet by facing you and staring directly at you. Dogs catch every nuance.

Fearful dogs are generally more fearful of men than of women because men are interpreted as more of a threat. Dominant aggressive dogs feel more challenged by men than by women. Dominant aggressive dogs see the head-on greeting and direct eye contact from men and respond to it as if it is a challenge. Dominant aggressive dogs don't generally feel challenged when meeting women. Fearful dogs are generally less afraid of meeting women.

If you're touring the kennels with a spouse or partner (same sex or opposite sex, same color or different color skin, same size or different size), you need to realize that the same dog may have a vastly different response to each person.

HOW WILL THE DOG BEHAVE WHEN MEETING GUESTS AND STRANGERS?

You are only a stranger to the dog once, when you first meet him. Thus, this may be your only opportunity to see what the dog is like when meeting strangers. How the dog responds when meeting new people in his kennel is consistent with how he will respond when meeting or being approached by people on the street, in the elevator, at the park, in the car at the drive-thru, etc. The responses you see in the shelter dogs in their cages are equivalent to the responses you might get at your front door when the doorbell rings and it's the pizza delivery guy.

You can test the dog's responses to meeting strangers by acting in ways strangers can and will act when meeting a dog, and flush out potential problems before you fall in love. If you just lean over and greet all the dogs and say hi, you make your body more neutral and less threatening and you upset the dogs less, but you also miss the opportunity to see each dog respond to realistic but difficult encounters with strangers. On the other hand, if you act like a stranger when first meeting the dogs, you miss out on going through the kennels and meeting and greeting all the dogs to see if you like them. If there are a lot of other visitors to the shelter on the day you're there, and you have a chance to observe the dogs when these strangers approach, do so. Use your observations of how the dogs react to other people as your test (especially watch the dogs' reactions to men, and even more especially, with different looking men—big, with sunglasses, different skin colors, beards, baldness, etc.)

Otherwise, do the test that begins on page 98 with each dog at the shelter, visiting every kennel, and then start fresh with the first dog again when you continue on with the test. Your new dog will meet hundreds upon thousands of strangers and guests and relatives and visitors in his lifetime, and if he growls at, lunges at, nips, bites or attacks these people, you will have a huge liability, not to mention a huge nightmare of a situation.

Also, the great beauty of meeting these dogs at the shelter is that while you elicit and observe the different responses, you are separated from the dog by a fence, and you are completely safe while you test.

As you walk past each kennel, if you turn your body to orient yourself directly to each dog, frontally facing them, you will elicit a different set of possible behaviors (depending on the dog's temperament) than if you turn your body to face off to the side, with more of an oblique orientation. If you make direct eye contact and sustain it, you will get a different response than if you avert your eyes or look downward as you interact with the dog.

Facing the dog directly can be interpreted by some dogs as a direct threat or challenge. Fearful dogs may become more fearful, thinking you are a threat, while dominant or aggressive dogs may become more aggressive, thinking you are challenging them. Submissive dogs may respond with more submissive body postures (lying down, lifting up one rear leg, curling their body into a C shape, lowering their bodies and squirting a little pee) to appease you in response to your perceived dominance.

Angling your body a bit more sideways to the dog is less of a threat and less of a challenge, and a lot more inviting for dogs. On the one hand, you may not want to inadvertently appear threatening or confrontational when meeting the dogs, because you may get unwanted responses. On the other hand, it can be very useful to determine the temperament and potential behavior problems in the dog by how he responds to your body. I'd rather get the unwanted responses up front and avoid the problem dogs, than fall in love, take the dog home and find out the dog snaps at strangers when the neighbors drop by.

That said, here's the test to gauge the dog's reaction to strangers. A **Pass Response** allows the tester to proceed with the dog to the next part of the test. If the dog passes all parts, he may be a good choice for adoption. A dog who gives a **Gray Area Response** is one whose behavior is questionable in some way. A Gray Area dog may display conflicted behaviors or offer responses that are not detailed in the test. This dog should neither be ruled out nor carelessly selected as a potential pet without the guidance of a professional dog behavior expert and trainer. The Gray Area dog is one who requires the expertise of a professional. A **Fail Response** immediately stops the test. It is an unsafe response and makes the dog potentially dangerous to continue with testing, and certainly unsafe to adopt.

1. **Approach the dog's kennel without saying anything, then turn and face the dog. Look neutral—neither threaten nor smile. Stand upright, make benign but direct eye contact with the dog, and hold your stare for a full five seconds (count "one Mississippi, two Mississippi . . .").**

Pass Responses

- The dog just wiggles and wags, avoids sustained, direct eye contact or glances into your eyes and glances away a few times, and squints. He has his ears back, and greets and greets and greets and solicits affection, not even noticing that you are standing like a zombie.

- The dog looks away within two seconds and offers gestures of apology (sitting or lying down, lifting one rear leg, curling his body with a low wagging tail or smearing his body lengthwise against the front of the kennel).

Gray Area Responses

- The dog stares for a few seconds, then gives one small brief bark and recovers immediately. (Make sure, if you take this dog out later to temperament test him, that you look for very, very sociable and affectionate responses, and he shows no further eruptions or suspiciousness of new people.)

Fail Responses

- The dog stares back, locks eyes with you, barks, growls, lunges forward or shoots backward while growling/barking. (This is not a good candidate for adoption—he will very likely be the kind of dog who bonds with one or two people and considers everyone else a threat, and may bite or menace guests, visitors, friends, delivery or service people. This dog can be a huge liability.)

- The dog does not stop barking long enough to notice that you are staring. This dog may already have been barking and leaping at the front of his kennel before you even took up a stance.

2. After staring at the dog for a count of five, turn your body sideways to the kennel, crouch down, smile and talk a little baby talk, and cajole the dog forward to make friends.

Pass Responses

- The dog immediately recovers and offers all sorts of apologies (sitting or lying down offset and not directly frontal to you, lifting one rear leg, curling his body with a low wagging tail, smearing his body lengthwise against the front of the kennel).

Gray Area Responses

- The dog barks or woofs one or two more times, stutters forward to greet you, changes his mind and scoots backward, comes forward and recovers, then offers all sorts of apologies (sitting or lying down, lifting one rear leg, curling his body with a low wagging tail, smearing his body lengthwise against the front of the kennel).

Fail Responses

- The dog remains in the back of his kennel, unable to approach you.

- The dog remains neutral, sitting or standing but not approaching, sniffing at the air in your direction.

- The dog remains suspicious, continuing to growl, lunge or bark.

TEMPERAMENT TESTING SHELTER DOGS

Many shelters claim to or actually do temperament test their dogs before placing them up for adoption. Temperament testing has become a generic term, like Kleenex, Clorox and Jell-O, but there are now many different formal and informal ways shelters perform temperament tests.

Many shelters perform useless temperament tests, just using the dog's aggression level (or lack thereof) during the incoming medical exam to determine the extent of his aggressive tendencies. This is particularly useless, since the most dominant aggressive dogs are often great patients during an exam (they're off-territory, they know they are in the presence of a dog professional and therefore they won't challenge anyone) and will not show the behaviors they would in a home, with the average owner.

Some dogs are temperament tested, and then made available for adoption no matter what shows up on the test. In other words, the dog has been temperament tested, but nothing was done with the information other than to record it somewhere. Or, if aggression was found, it was merely recommended that the dog not be placed with young children. Many shelters temperament test and either euthanize or permanently house the aggressive dogs, or send them away to a sanctuary.

Basically, every shelter is on its own. Some shelters temperament test in such a way that the dog responds to the tester, who is handling the dog as a dog professional. The dog knows the tester is a dog professional, and no behavioral information is gained about how the dog would act with the average person or a first-time dog owner or children. It is of no help to see a dog professional handle a dog, roll him over on his back, touch his ears, feet and mouth to see if the dog is aggressive, when the dog is responding to an authority figure. The dog is not likely to be adopted by this authority figure, or by a dog training professional. This dog is up for adoption as a pet—looking to be welcomed into a home with someone like you who is reading this book. So that shelter might claim to temperament test, but it offers no safer or more promising adoption than doing what this book says to do on your own.

Since there are no standards or formal guidelines for temperament testing and placement, I hope this book gives you a boost so that you can both choose the adoption option and come away with a safe, appropriate and wonderful family pet.

The temperament test I recommend is one called Assess-A-Pet, which I created and refined. I stand by it, having been in the shelter field studying temperament testing longer than anybody else. My test is also the most revealing, and its guidelines are the strictest. You will want strictness—remember, many people working or volunteering in the shelter are there because they love animals so much that sometimes their logic and knowledge of dog behavior is eclipsed by their emotion and hope for the dog's future. Sometimes a shelter worker will side with the problematic dog, hoping someone will adopt him and somehow make it all work out, and will not be adopting out the dog with *your* best interest in mind. Assess-a-Pet has your best interest *and* the dog's best interest in mind. The test is not just looking for a way out for the dog, but a way into the right person's home.

The following temperament test has been designed and created with the shelter dog in mind. It is a modified version of Assess-a-Pet, which is a formal temperament test for shelter professionals to use on their dogs. The responses you are looking for are not necessarily what you can expect from other owned and friendly dogs you know. It is not particularly useful to imagine how a dog you once owned, or a friend's dog whom you know well, might respond—owned dogs will not respond in the same ways as shelter dogs. The meaning behind the shelter dogs' responses may or may not seem logical to you. The responses from some of the shelter dogs may or may not be what you would expect from other dogs you already know.

You are not necessarily looking for logical, predictable responses. You are not looking for an obvious aggressive display. Assess-A-Pet neither looks for, nor reveals in obvious ways, anything familiar or overt in the dog. The temperament test has been created specifically for a dog who is in the shelter, and has been in the shelter, given up on, given away, lost, strayed or abandoned. The test takes into account that the shelter dog is unattached, unbonded, ready to re-bond and attach to someone new.

This temperament test is based on the fact that the dog you are testing has been in a kennel, a cage, for at least a couple of days. All dogs in this situation have experienced certain things. No matter how good the shelter is, how caring the staff and volunteers, dogs in shelters are deprived of the familiarities of home; they have been deprived of normal amounts of human touch, human contact, human attention, human comfort. Thus, knowing what the dog has been missing, you can expect certain responses from him. A dog who is neutral with, or doesn't care about people—the asocial dog—will not seek out human touch or attention when he comes out of his kennel, while the sociable and friendly pet dog will come out almost desperate for human touch.

Below are the steps you can take to evaluate more objectively the safety and temperament of each dog. Do not underestimate the importance or the seriousness of these tests. The steps unfold in a very specific order, each one building on the one before it for your safety's sake, and if the dog you are evaluating—even one you really like—doesn't show a positive/pass response at one step, *do not proceed any further*. If you cannot get this particular dog out of your mind, or believe he is really a good dog, or you still really want to meet him—put him back in the kennel and hire a professional dog trainer to come in with you and evaluate the dog. But bear in mind that it would not be safe for you to proceed with your own evaluation.

1. Preliminary Observations

Take note of the dog's tail. Tails can tell you so much about a dog. Don't concern yourself with whether or not the dog's tail is wagging, or how hard it is wagging. Wagging doesn't actually tell a lot about a dog's mood. In studying hours of video footage of dogs in different situations, looking at just the dogs' rear ends, I can tell you that many aggressive wags are virtually indistinguishable from friendly wags.

This Boxer–Pit Bull mix shows a relaxed and low tail carriage.

This mixed breed's tail carriage is high, and the tail is raised up over her back. Her tail came up as she snarled. She was guarding a stick on the ground in front of her.

What is very useful, however, is to take note of the dog's tail *carriage*. Tail carriage refers to how high or how low the dog holds his tail. Look to see how high the dog carries his tail, when it goes up and when it goes down. In general, look for a dog who carries his tail mostly level or low. If you are interested in a dog who seems to carry his tail mostly level and high, then at least look for the dog to lower his tail when you approach or interact with him, and raise it higher only when puttering about the environment or when he sees another dog or you take him outside for a walk. Tails, no matter what level the dog starts out carrying them, should be lowered during greetings and lowered when you are making him do anything he doesn't want to do.

There are three main tail levels:

1. **High tail carriage**—the base of the tail and the tail itself is higher than the plane of the dog's back

2. **Level tail carriage**—the dog's tail is on a level plane with the dog's back

3. **Low tail carriage**—the dog's tail is lower than the plane of the dog's back

You will frequently be interrupting your temperament test to observe and to note down what is happening with the dog's tail. In general, especially if you have young children, select a dog who carries his tail level or low and rarely, if ever, raises it much above his back. Look for a dog whose tail is higher when he is investigating the environment or when he hears or sees something novel, but lower whenever you are petting him or leaning over him or making him do something he might not be pleased to do. Even dogs with bobbed tails, docked tails or almost no visible tails can be evaluated the same way. Concentrate on the base of the dog's stub and you will see if it is high, level, low or tucked, and you can even see a circular wag. Since it is the *base* of the dog's tail that is most significant, the same observations can be made with stub tails.

While in his cage or kennel, is the dog's tail carriage:
High ❑   Level ❑   Low ❑
(If it was high, it should lower; if tucked, it should relax to low or level.)

When you call him forward to the front of his cage or kennel to say hi, is the dog's tail carriage:
High ❑   Level ❑   Low ❑
(If it was high, it should lower; if tucked, it should relax to low or level.)

2. Extend Your Hand

Bend down slightly and extend your hand, fingers facing the dog, palm down, knuckles up, until it is resting on the chain-link or bars (make sure no flesh is sticking through!). Your hand should be at the kennel at the same height or level as the height of the dog (in other words, don't offer your hand so high that the dog has to jump up to seek it out, nor so low that he has to go to the floor to reach you). No matter what, you are looking for a dog who will approach you or your offered hand and make a sustained connection.

Many dogs will look friendly and seem to be at the front of the kennel, jumping at you and trying to get your attention, but some are, in fact, only trying to get your attention so that you will open their kennel door and let them out. I know that may sound devious, but it's true. While inside his kennel, he will seem to look adoringly up at you or jump up and at the front of the kennel as if he cannot get close enough to you. But when you open the kennel or a staff member lets him out (on a leash, of course), the dog becomes his own independent spirit, having no further interest in or use for humans. Freedom is what he really wanted.

This truly sociable dog has changed the position of his body so that he is sideways to the front of the kennel, offering as much surface area as possible for this visitor to touch.

When you bend down and extend your hand, is the dog's tail carriage:
High ❏   Level ❏   Low ❏
(Level or low is ideal. High is acceptable, as long as the tail lowers once the dog is out of the kennel.)

Pass Responses

- The truly sociable and sincerely friendly dog will immediately approach your offered hand.

- The truly sociable dog may nose, nuzzle or lick your hand.

- The truly sociable dog may change the position of his body so he is sideways to the front of the kennel, offering as much of himself as possible for your touch.

- Sometimes you will come across a dog who rolls over on his back and remains prone, with his rear leg raised in submission.

- The truly sociable dog will sustain contact with your hand for two seconds or longer.

Gray Area Responses

- Same as the Pass Responses, except interactions last less than two seconds.

- The dog starts out with one or more of the Pass Responses, but loses interest or discontinues for whatever reason after a few seconds.

Fail Responses

- The dog barks at you and ignores your hand.

- The dog looks friendly but ignores your hand completely.

- The dog growls at you.

- The dog sniffs at your hand, but offers no sociable behaviors as listed in the Pass Responses.

If the dog shows any of the Fail Responses, don't take this dog out unless it's under professional supervision!

3. Move Your Hand Four Inches in All Directions

The next step is to see if the dog is truly interested in interacting with you (via your hand) or is only interested in capturing your attention so you will let him out. You can do this while he is safely behind bars, before you need to risk having him out and about. Move your hand four inches in each direction—that is, move it sideways four inches to the right and then pause there for a second. Then move your hand straight down toward the floor another four inches, pause for a second, and then, tracing a square, move it sideways to the left four inches. Pause for another second, then move your hand up four inches.

Pass Responses

- The truly sociable dog will follow your hand wherever it moves.

- The truly sociable dog may smoosh his body broadside along the front of the cage to get you to touch him anywhere.

Gray Area Responses

- The questionable dog follows your hand on the first two moves, but then loses interest.

- The questionable dog follows your hand for only the first move, but then loses interest.

Fail Responses

- Watch out for the dog who jumps up on the front of the kennel and ignores your hand.

- Watch out for the dog who jumps up to get clear from your hand, as if it is in the way.

If the dog shows any of the Fail Responses, don't take this dog out unless it's under professional supervision!

4. If You Make It Far Enough into the Evaluation to Meet the Dog Outside the Kennel or Cage

Find a relatively quiet, indoor area away from the kennels—a small room, even the lobby if it is not too busy, or someone's office (with permission, of course!) or even the bathroom, if that is the only private, quiet, indoor area. If the staff member brings the dog to you, have them hand you the leash and walk away from the dog, not looking back, and remain out of reach of the dog.

You will remain completely neutral, almost like a zombie at first, for a very specific amount of time. Take the leash and stand upright, feet planted firmly on the floor. Hold the leash so you offer the dog between three and four feet of slack, and stand in the middle of the room so that the dog cannot reach objects and/or people in the room that would be more distracting.

Once you are holding the leash, are in the room with the door closed and are in position, look at your watch or a clock and begin timing 60 seconds. Stand up, hold the leash firmly, watch the dog carefully, but resist any temptation to initiate a response from the dog. What can happen in 60 seconds?

This is where observing signs of sociability and seeing true friendliness in the dog becomes most critical. In fact, this is, perhaps, the most critical part of the test. If the dog does not initiate and strive to get your attention for affection—if the dog isn't trying to wake you up to get you to pet him and hold him and touch him and say loving things to him—then he is not likely to allow anything from you that he finds remotely undesirable. If a dog who comes out of a kennel does not come out requesting all the good things a human has to offer (petting, praise, touch, loving, holding), then he is not likely to tolerate the things a human sometimes has to do that are humane, fair, routine, but unwanted by the dog at the time. This is the most common source of what is called dominance aggression, which is the dog's tendency to inflict harm on you when you make him do something he doesn't want to do or prevent him from doing something he really wants to do.

I was fostering a 12-week-old puppy who turned around and attacked me, biting at my arm and hand and trying to get at my body, because I casually held him by the collar so I could let all my other dogs out the door, only wanting to keep the puppy inside to play with him. The puppy wanted to go out with the other dogs. And he told me so by throwing a violent temper tantrum. It's not wrong for the puppy to disagree with my intentions or not want to do what I need him to do. It's wrong for him to choose aggression as a means to get his way.

What if I was trying to rent out a room in my house? I place an ad, I interview a few applicants, and I finally interview a woman I like immediately who has a lot in common with me. She shares similar likes and dislikes, hobbies and evening pastimes. She is by far my favorite applicant, her references check out and she is financially capable of paying the rent. The first two weeks are bliss; she moves in quickly and we get along famously. We enjoy each other's company, eat dinner together after returning home from work each evening, enjoy lots of good conversations. On the second weekend after moving in, we wake up on a Saturday and I suggest we clean the house that day—a really good spring cleaning. She nods. I then suggest, "You vacuum, I'll dust." She walks into the kitchen, pulls out a cleaver, walks toward me and holds the blade against my throat saying, "I don't vacuum." Then she starts hacking away at me while informing me she hates vacuuming.

What other choices did my new roommate have to let me know that she doesn't like vacuuming? She could have simply said, "Oh, I don't like to vacuum. Could you vacuum and I'll dust?" Or, "I hate vacuuming; I'd rather pay to have someone clean the house!" The problem is not that she doesn't like to vacuum, it's how she chooses to handle being asked to do something she doesn't want to do. I would have liked to know about her violent tendencies before she moved in.

Equally important, and sometimes very, very hard to detect, is how a dog will respond when he is first made to do something he doesn't want to do. Just as your dog hopes you will not use violence against him when he makes you do something you don't want to do (such as taking him out in the middle of the night because he has diarrhea, not letting him off the leash when walking, brushing his hair every day), you hope he will not use violence against you when you make him do something he doesn't want to do (such as moving him off the couch so that you can sit down, pulling him out of the kitchen trash can or drying off his feet when he comes in from the rain). Living with a dog (let alone another human being) is a constant give and take, and there's nothing wrong with being reluctant to comply with the things you don't enjoy. But there is something wrong with harming another living being so you can have your way.

While you are standing in the middle of the room with the dog on a leash, being unresponsive, is the dog's tail carriage:
High ❏   Level ❏   Low ❏
(Look for a level or low tail carriage. If high, the tail should lower to level or below when/if the dog initiates contact. If the tail is tucked, it should relax during the interaction.)

Pass Responses

- The dog initiates social, affectionate interactions with you within 60 seconds, and sustains each interaction for two seconds or longer.

- The dog nuzzles, or licks or nudges your hand for two seconds or longer at a time.

- The dog may jump up on you, but is gentle when he does and he lingers for two seconds or longer at a time.

- The dog makes at least three attempts to engage you socially.

Gray Area Responses

- The dog initiates social, affectionate interactions within 60 seconds, but interactions do not last for two seconds.

- The dog uses his mouth on your skin/hands/body (gets mouthy) while maintaining interaction for two seconds or longer.

- The dog initiates social interaction but spends less than 50 percent of the time interacting with you.

- The dog leans against you for more than 50 percent of the time, but offers little or nothing else.

Fail Responses

- The dog does not interact with you in 60 seconds.

- The dog jumps up on you, not stopping at all or stopping for less than two seconds; the jumping is brutal.

- The dog initiates an interaction, but the contact involves his mouth (mouthing as opposed to licking) or jumping on you or at you.

- The dog sniffs you but offers no other signs of affection, such as licking, nudging or nuzzling.

If the dog shows any of the Fail Responses, do not continue further with the test. Have a shelter staff member put the dog back into his kennel.

5. Three Back Strokes

Stroke the dog starting on the back of his neck and traveling down to the base of his tail. Stand up and count to one before repeating twice more for a total of three strokes, with a one-second pause between each stroke. Stand up between strokes. Notice only the dog's position relative to you.

This is a very informative test. The dog who comes out of a kennel, gets stroked in a pleasing way and *doesn't* turn back toward you to request more, who *doesn't* seek out more affection, is *not* a social, friendly pet dog. Although you're not looking for an aggressive response, the lack of a sociable, come-closer-to-seek-out-more-affection response is indicative of future aggression in the home. It's hard to trust this. It's hard to predict aggression without an overt sign of aggression. But the whole point of this test is to predict and help you or a member of your family avoid getting bitten by a dog—*before* the dog feels he has to bite.

It's hard to be in a room with a dog whom you have taken out of his kennel because you felt an emotional connection, and then to dispense with your emotional connection because you believe a seemingly neutral response is so indicative of future problems.

But believe it. It *is* indicative of future problems.

While you are stroking the dog, is his tail carriage:
High ❑   Level ❑   Low ❑

Pass Responses

- The dog moves closer to you in between strokes at least two out of three times.

- The dog snuggles closer, and leans against you and remains touching for two seconds or longer, at least two out of the three strokes.

- The dog turns around between at least two of the three strokes with his ears back, tail level or low, and nuzzles or licks your hands.

- The dog remains gentle, eyes soft and squinty, ears back. His tail starts wagging or wags harder, with the tail level or lower during and in between stroking.

Gray Area Responses

- The dog moves closer but then passes by you and ends up further away.

- The dog remains where he is, neither moving away nor coming closer.

This pretty merle-colored herding dog mix has snuggled closer and leaned against me, and he remains in physical contact for more than two seconds. This indicates a highly social and friendly dog.

- The dog turns around in between only one stroke, but does snuggle closer and remain with a soft-eyed expression during this one interaction.

Fail Responses

- The dog moves closer only once out of three times, or not at all.

- The dog shakes you off as if he was shaking off rainwater.

- The dog gets more excitable and stimulated, but remains in place or moves farther away.

- Watch out for the dog who stiffens and freezes, and especially one who stiffens and freezes and slowly turns his head to stare at you.

If the dog shows any of the Fail Responses, do not continue further with the test. Have a shelter staff member put the dog back into his kennel.

6. Sit in a Chair

Without saying anything, sit in a chair. A truly sociable dog, even one who has lived outside his whole life, recognizes a human in a chair as an excellent opportunity to come over for some affection and attention.

While you are sitting in the chair, is the dog's tail carriage:
High ❑   Level ❑   Low ❑
(Look for a dog who carries his tail level or lower, or, if he starts out with a high carriage, lowers it to level or low during the Pass Responses; or, if tucked, the tail relaxes and comes up to maximum of level during interaction.)

Pass Responses

- The dog comes to you immediately (within five seconds), sits between your legs and nuzzles up against you or rests his head on your lap.

Gray Area Responses

- The dog comes over within five seconds, jumps up on your lap, fusses around your face and makes you lean backward to get out of his way.

- The dog has passed every previous test with no Gray Area Responses, but does not come over within five seconds.

Fail Responses

- The dog ignores you completely, and has had mostly or many Gray Area Responses in the previous tests.

- The dog ignores you completely, and does not come over within 20 seconds.

If the dog shows any of the Fail Responses, do not continue further with the test. Have a shelter staff member put the dog back into his kennel.

7. 20 Seconds of Petting, Praise and Affection

Remain sitting, and check your watch, time 20 seconds, and during that time pet, pat, praise, stroke, thump, ruffle up the hair and talk in baby talk to the dog. Do not hold him next to you; do not restrain him near you. Give him as much leash as he wants.

As you interact with the dog, is his tail carriage:
High ❑   Level ❑   Low ❑

Pass Responses

- The dog comes right over, snuggles close and remains with you for the full 20 seconds.

- The dog may lick, nuzzle, nudge or crawl gently into your lap.

Gray Area Responses

- The dog comes right over, remains for the full 20 seconds, but gets more and more excited.

- The dog may start mouthing (putting his mouth on your hands and clothes) or get "playful."

- The dog starts out sociable, but doesn't remain for the full 20 seconds.

- The dog takes five seconds or more to come over to socialize.

- The dog was more sociable when *he* initiated the contact, as opposed to when *you* initiated sociability.

Fail Responses

- The dog ignores you or doesn't come over at all.

- The dog begins playing tug of war with the leash.

If the dog shows any of the Fail Responses, have a shelter staff member put the dog back into his kennel.

8. Test for How Well the Dog Listens to You

Free up both your hands by looping the end of the leash around one wrist. Give the dog as much leash as he wants. Allow the dog to investigate the area and sniff if he wants. Wait until the dog becomes involved in investigating or sniffing an object (not a person), and then, standing *behind* him, clap your hands twice, loudly and sharply, while yelling "Hey!"

Pass Responses

- The dog immediately stops what he was doing, turns around, comes to you and offers some apologies (low tail, nuzzling or licking your hand, lowered body, lip licking, lifting up one hind leg, maybe even a tiny squirt of pee).

- The dog immediately stops what he was doing, turns around, comes to you and snuggles next to you, making sustained physical contact with your body; he may face away, but he remains cuddled up next to you.

Gray Area Responses

- The dog stops what he was doing, turns around to face you, softens his expression (puts his ears back, wags a low or lowered tail, squints his eyes a little), but then either moves to investigate something else in the room or goes back to investigating what he was originally interested in.

- The dog stops what he was doing, turns to face you, offers a play bow (faces you, butt up in the air, front end on the floor) comes back to you, but offers no apologetic behaviors as above.

Fail Responses

- The dog totally blows you off, barely, if at all, glances back, but continues right on doing what he was doing.

- The dog stiffens and doesn't turn around.

- The dog growls or raises the hair on his back.

TESTS TO LEAVE FOR THE PROS

For these next important tests, you will need to find a shelter employee or qualified volunteer willing and able to assist you. You will provide them with some equipment (the Assess-A-Hand, a pig's ear, a bath mat, etc.), and then ask them to perform the following tests.

These next tests are to determine the likelihood that the dog will harm someone when he has something that he considers valuable. We first use a pig's ear, which is an easy and handy chew toy that most dogs will chew on during the test. We are not actually evaluating whether the dog will bite someone over a pig's ear (although we can tell using this test); we are evaluating what the dog's basic response will be, in your home or out on a walk, when he puts something in his mouth that he considers valuable, or even just stands over something he considers valuable.

Different dogs find different things valuable. I knew of a chocolate Labrador Retriever who belonged to a family. The family sought the advice of a trainer because, at the age of eight months, the dog was seriously going after anyone in the family who tried to go near her or take something away. The trainer downplayed the problem, and instructed the family to not keep bones and rawhide chews and pig's ears around (since the dog guarded those routinely). But then one day the 10-year-old daughter's beaded necklace broke and all the tiny, colorful beads scattered across the living room floor. The daughter immediately went down on her hands and knees to salvage as many beads as possible. The mother watched in horror when the Labrador dove to the floor to scarf up the beads, too (this dog wanted to eat them). Without thinking, the daughter went to push the dog away from her beads. The mother screamed and pulled the dog away from the daughter just before a tragedy. They decided then and there that this resource-guarding behavior was too dangerous to live with.

Another dog guarded his own vomit when the owner leaned down to clean it up.

Another dog bit the visiting uncle on the face during a Sunday dinner. While the roast was cooling on the kitchen counter, the family stood around chatting and waiting for it to cool so they could carve it. The uncle, who was petting the dog (who was just sitting among the people in the kitchen), bent down to put his arm around the dog in a chummy way, and was bitten hard enough to puncture skin. No one expected the dog to guard the food that was safely up on the counter.

Another family adopted an adult Akita from a rescue group that routinely placed dogs who growled around their food bowl, or growled when disturbed

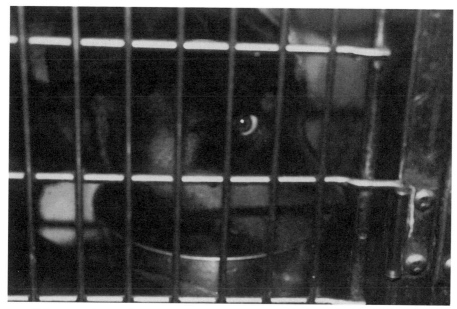

This young Rottweiler is guarding his water bowl. Many people believe a dog will just guard one item, and if that one item can simply be eliminated from the dog's life, he will not be aggressive. Dogs who guard resources will never just guard one thing. A resource-guarding dog will find many everyday things in his life to guard. These dogs can be extremely dangerous.

while eating. The rescue group never placed their dogs with families with children under the age of 11, and warned every adopter about the problem. They counseled every adopter about the breed's tendency to guard food and instructed them to always feed the dog in his crate, and not to disturb him or let him out of his crate until the bowl was empty and the dog was clearly finished eating. All went well for the first few months, until the evening the mother was in the kitchen preparing a chicken dinner for the family. She was marinating raw chicken thighs on a glass platter on the counter. Her Akita (whom she adored) sat at the edge of the kitchen, just keeping his owner company. While transferring the platter from the counter to the oven, the woman accidentally dropped the platter, and it shattered all over the kitchen floor, shards and splinters of glass mixed in with marinade and raw chicken. The dog, naturally, stepped forward to investigate, and, without thinking, the woman—terrified her dog would lap up or step on the glass—put out her arm to block the dog's path forward. The dog bit her in the forearm hard, twice, puncturing the skin both times. They returned the dog to the rescue group.

These are examples of how a food guarding problem manifests itself in real life. Certainly, not all dogs that growl over a bone or food end up biting. But at the shelter there is no way to tell which dogs will growl but not bite. My advice is, whether or not you have young children in the home, stay away from any dog with any hint of a resource guarding problem. It is most often the tip of a behavioral iceberg.

9. Test for Guarding the Pig's Ear

1. **Find an indoor room that's as quiet as possible, and have the shelter staff member hold the leash of the dog.**

2. **You place the bath mat on the floor somewhere near the dog. You don't need to say anything.**

3. **Hand the pig's ear to the shelter staff member, and have them offer the pig's ear to the dog.**

4. **Wait for the dog to (hopefully) take an interest in the pig's ear, and settle down to chew it on the bath mat you provided.**

Pass Responses

- The dog settles down next to the helper, not adjusting his position at all, just lying down wherever he ends up after taking the pig's ear.

- The dog may toss the pig's ear to the helper as if to engage the helper in play, or try to get the helper to toss it back.

- The dog settles down to chew it, occasionally (and unprompted) interrupting himself to look up at the helper, put his ears back, squint his eyes and wag his tail.

Gray Area Responses

- The dog snatches the pig's ear from the shelter staff member's hand and has trouble settling down to chew it. He may try a few different directions before finding a comfortable position in which to settle and chew.

- The dog snatches the pig's ear from the shelter staff member, and abruptly lies down and begins to chew frantically and voraciously.

Fail Responses

- The dog snatches the pig's ear and immediately becomes agitated and tries to find a private place to chew, but he cannot find the right place. He may pace from one corner of the room to the other.

- The dog gives furtive glances as soon as the pig's ear is in his possession, glancing from the helper, to the pig's ear, to a hiding spot, and back to the helper.

- The dog lies down facing the helper, or deliberately with his back facing the helper, and freezes or growls or glares at the helper with the whites of his eyes.

5. **After the dog is chewing on the pig's ear, holding it solidly between his paws, ask your helper to take one step (roughly 12 inches) closer to the dog.**

Pass Responses

- The dog pauses in his chewing to put the pig's ear down and look up at the helper, squint his eyes, start wagging his tail or wag it harder if it was already wagging, or put his ears back.

- The dog picks up the pig's ear, gets up and brings it to the helper.

Gray Area Responses

- The dog repositions himself so that the pig's ear is further away from the helper or you.

- The dog begins chewing faster or frantically.

Fail Responses

- The dog snatches up the pig's ear and repositions himself, and freezes as he stares back at the helper, showing the whites of his eyes.

- The dog repositions his shoulder further around the pig's ear, at the same time shouldering the helper farther away from it.

- The dog freezes, showing the whites of his eyes.

- The dog growls, snarls or bites.

6. Discreetly hand your helper the Assess-A-Hand, trying to make sure the dog does not see it, get distracted by it and lose interest in his pig's ear. Sometimes it works better to exchange the Assess-A-Hand behind your backs.

7. Have your helper begin stroking the dog on his back with the Assess-A-Hand and telling the dog he is a good dog in a soothing voice.

Pass Responses

- The dog pauses in his chewing to put the pig's ear down and look up at the helper, squint his eyes, start wagging his tail or wag it harder if it was already wagging, or put his ears back.

- The dog picks up the pig's ear, gets up and brings it to you or your helper.

Gray Area Responses

- The dog repositions himself so that the pig's ear is further away from you or the helper.

- The dog begins chewing faster or frantically.

Fail Responses

- The dog snatches up the pig's ear and repositions himself, and freezes as he stares back at the helper, showing the whites of his eyes.

- The dog repositions his shoulder further around the pig's ear, at the same time shouldering the helper farther away from it.

- The dog freezes and shows the whites of his eyes.

- The dog growls or bites.

8. Have your helper pat the dog gently on the top of his head with the Assess-A-Hand and continue praising the dog.

Pass Responses

- The dog pauses in his chewing to put the pig's ear down and look up at the helper, squint his eyes, start wagging his tail or wag it harder if it was already wagging, or put his ears back.

- The dog picks up the pig's ear, gets up and brings it to you or your helper.

Gray Area Responses

- The dog repositions himself so that the pig's ear is further away from you or the helper.

- The dog begins chewing faster or frantically.

Fail Responses

- The dog snatches up the pig's ear and repositions himself, and freezes as he stares back at the helper, showing the whites of his eyes.

- The dog repositions his shoulder further around the pig's ear, at the same time shouldering the helper farther away from it.

- The dog freezes and shows the whites of his eyes.

- The dog growls or bites.

9. **Instruct your helper to move the fake hand slowly and hesitantly toward the dog's mouth and the pig's ear. Remind your helper to treat the Assess-A-Hand as a real hand, and to whisk it away if he thinks the dog might snap.**

10. **Three times in a row, instruct your helper to slowly approach the pig's ear with the fake hand. Just when the Assess-A-Hand touches the pig's ear, the helper will withdraw suddenly, as if the helper is scared the dog will guard it and worried that the dog will strike out.**

Pass Responses

- The dog pauses in his chewing to put the pig's ear down and look up at the helper, squint his eyes, start wagging his tail or wag it harder if it was already wagging, or put his ears back.

- The dog picks up the pig's ear, gets up and brings it to you or your helper.

Gray Area Responses

- The dog repositions himself so that the pig's ear is further away from you or the helper.

- The dog begins chewing faster or frantically.

Fail Responses

- The dog snatches up the pig's ear and repositions himself, and freezes as he stares back at the helper, showing the whites of his eyes.

- The dog repositions his shoulder further around the pig's ear, at the same time shouldering the helper farther away from it.

- The dog freezes and shows the whites of his eyes.

- The dog growls, snarls or bites.

11. **After the third approach, instruct your helper to slowly and gently try to push the dog's muzzle away from the pig's ear. The goal is only to try, ever so slowly, to push the dog's muzzle about five inches away from the pig's ear.**

Pass Responses

- The dog pauses in his chewing to put the pig's ear down and look up at the helper, squint his eyes, start wagging his tail or wag it harder if it was already wagging, or put his ears back.

- The dog picks up the pig's ear, gets up and brings it to you or your helper.

Gray Area Responses

- The dog repositions himself so that the pig's ear is further away from you or the helper.

- The dog begins chewing faster or frantically.

Fail Responses

- The dog snatches up the pig's ear and repositions himself, and freezes as he stares back at the helper, showing the whites of his eyes.

- The dog repositions his shoulder further around the pig's ear, at the same time shouldering the helper farther away from it.

- The dog freezes and shows the whites of his eyes.

- The dog growls or bites.

10. Test for Guarding the Food Bowl

For this test you will need a large dog bowl filled to the brim (don't worry, the dog isn't going to eat it all) with a mixture of canned and dry food. It does not matter whether the dog has already eaten that day, or at what time. The dog need only be hungry enough to have the desire to eat.

1. **Hand the filled food bowl to your helper, and instruct your helper to place the bowl on the floor, between you and him.**

2. **Wait for the dog to take an interest in the food.**

As the dog shows interest in the food, is his tail carriage:
High ❑   Level ❑   Low ❑

3. **Instruct your helper to take one step toward the food bowl.**

Pass Responses

- The dog pauses in his eating and looks up at the helper, squints his eyes, starts wagging his tail or wags it harder if it was already wagging, and may put his ears back.

- The dog continues eating at the same speed, may look up at the helper while continuing to eat and may begin wagging his tail or wag harder while eating at the same speed.

Gray Area Responses

- The dog repositions himself so that he is between the helper and the food bowl.

- The dog begins eating faster or frantically gulping.

- The whites of his eyes show as he eats quickly and tensely.

Fail Responses

- The dog changes where he places his muzzle to eat and begins eating out of the side of the bowl closest to the helper, thereby blocking the helper from the food bowl.

- The dog repositions himself by thrusting his shoulder out, and further blocks the helper from the food bowl.

- The dog freezes as he stares back at the helper, showing the whites of his eyes.

- The dog growls or bites.

4. **Instruct your helper to begin stroking the dog on his back, slowly and gently, keeping the Assess-a-Hand between himself and the dog, while telling the dog in a soothing voice that he is a good dog.**

While he is being stroked, is the dog's tail carriage:
High ❑   Level ❑   Low ❑

Pass Responses

- The dog pauses in his eating and looks up at the helper, squints his eyes, starts wagging his tail or wags it harder if it was already wagging, and may put his ears back.

- The dog continues eating at the same speed; he may look up at the helper while continuing to eat, and may begin wagging his tail or wag harder while eating at the same speed.

Gray Area Responses

- The dog repositions himself so that he is between the helper and the food bowl.

- The dog begins eating faster or frantically gulping.

- The whites of his eyes show as he eats quickly and tensely.

Fail Responses

- The dog changes where he places his muzzle to eat, and begins eating out of the side of the bowl closest to the helper, thereby blocking the helper from the food bowl.

- The dog repositions himself by thrusting his shoulder out, and further blocks the helper from the food bowl.

- The dog freezes as he stares back at the helper, showing the whites of his eyes.

- The dog growls or bites.

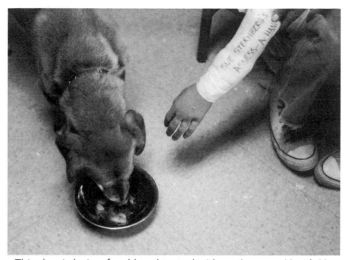

This dog is being food-bowl tested with an Assess-a-Hand. He is showing a pass response; he is eating out of the center of the bowl and his body posture is relaxed, neither thrusting his shoulders to shove the tester away from the bowl, nor looking up at the tester with a furtive, whites-of-the-eyes glance.

5. Instruct your helper to pat the dog very gently on the top of his head, using the Assess-a-Hand, while continuing to praise the dog soothingly.

Pass Responses

- The dog pauses in his eating and looks up at the helper, squints his eyes, starts wagging his tail or wags it harder if it was already wagging, and may put his ears back.

- The dog continues eating at the same speed; he may look up at the helper while continuing to eat, and may begin wagging his tail or wag harder while eating at the same speed.

Gray Area Responses

- The dog repositions himself so that he is between the helper and the food bowl.

- The dog begins eating faster or frantically gulping.

- The whites of his eyes show as he eats quickly and tensely.

Fail Responses

- The dog changes where he places his muzzle to eat, and begins eating out of the side of the bowl closest to the helper, thereby blocking the helper from the food bowl.

- The dog repositions himself by thrusting his shoulder out, and further blocks the helper from the food bowl.

- The dog freezes as he stares back at the helper, showing the whites of his eyes.

- The dog growls or bites.

6. **Instruct your helper to move the fake hand slowly and hesitantly toward the dog bowl. Remind your helper to treat the Assess-A-Hand as a real hand, and to whisk it away if he thinks the dog might snap. Repeat for a total of three advances and retreats.**

Pass Responses

- The dog pauses in his eating and looks up at the helper, squints his eyes, starts wagging his tail or wags it harder if it was already wagging, and may put his ears back.

- The dog continues eating at the same speed; he may look up at the helper while continuing to eat, and may begin wagging his tail or wag harder while eating at the same speed.

Gray Area Responses

- The dog repositions himself so that he is between the helper and the food bowl.

- The dog begins eating faster or frantically gulping.

- The whites of his eyes show as he eats quickly and tensely.

Fail Responses

- The dog changes where he places his muzzle to eat, and begins eating out of the side of the bowl closest to the helper, thereby blocking the helper from the food bowl.

- The dog repositions himself by thrusting his shoulder out, and further blocks the helper from the food bowl.

- The dog freezes as he stares back at the helper, showing the whites of his eyes.

- The dog growls or bites.

7. **Three times in a row, instruct your helper to slowly approach the dog bowl with the fake hand, and just when the Assess-a-Hand touches the dog bowl, the helper should withdraw suddenly, as if the helper is scared the dog will guard the food and worried that the dog will strike out.**

8. **After the third approach, instruct your helper to slowly and gently try to push the dog's muzzle away from the dog bowl. The goal is only to try, ever so slowly, to push the dog's muzzle about five inches away from the dog bowl.**

While the helper is gently pushing the dog's muzzle, is the dog's tail carriage:
High ❑   Level ❑   Low ❑

Pass Responses

- The dog pauses in his eating and looks up at the helper, squints his eyes, starts wagging his tail or wags it harder if it was already wagging, and may put his ears back.

- The dog continues eating at the same speed; he may look up at the helper while continuing to eat, and may begin wagging his tail or wag harder while eating at the same speed.

Gray Area Responses

- The dog repositions himself so that he is between the helper and the food bowl.

- The dog begins eating faster or frantically gulping.

- The whites of his eyes show as he eats quickly and tensely.

Fail Responses

- The dog changes where he places his muzzle to eat, and begins eating out of the side of the bowl closest to the helper, thereby blocking the helper from the food bowl.

- The dog repositions himself by thrusting his shoulder out, and further blocks the helper from the food bowl.

- The dog freezes as he stares back at the helper, showing the whites of his eyes.

- The dog growls, snarls or bites.

11. Take the Dog for a Walk

Don't worry so much about the dog pulling on the leash. This is likely a training issue that can be remedied with the proper equipment, and is almost always a part of a good training class. So even if the dog you are interested in seems to be a blithering idiot on leash, don't worry. Signing him up for training classes will help.

On the other hand, *usually* the more force and strength a dog puts into hauling you on leash, the more dominant the dog. It's the degree to which he uses his strength to pull, and also how high or low he carries his tail, along with his ability to be sociable outdoors, that together combine to produce a dominant/dominant aggressive dog, or a safe dog who will just require some time, effort and training.

It is unrealistic to expect most young children to be able to walk most dogs, even smallish dogs. The sudden lunge of a dog who sees a squirrel, an accidentally dropped leash—there are too many unpredictable events that could make it unsafe for both child and dog. So don't try to visualize this shelter dog being walked by your seven-year-old child, or think there is something wrong with the dog if that's not working out. There is nothing inherently or temperamentally wrong with a dog who pulls. A dog can pull on leash and still be respectful of and acknowledge people.

On the other hand, if you take out a dog and he is completely body insensitive, slams into your knees a few times, leaps up and bounces off you, starts yanking and playing tug with the leash, jumps up and down and starts mouthing your hands or clothes, or you can envision the dog mowing down your children, this is probably a temperament issue and the dog may not be an appropriate choice for an inexperienced person or for a family with children.

1. **Take the dog for a walk. Have the shelter staff member come along, but you hold the leash.**

Pass Responses

- The dog may or may not pull moderately on the leash.

- The dog is interested in the environment but checks back often with you, looking at you, putting his ears back and softening his expression when he does.

Gray Area Responses

- The dog pulls hard.

- The dog strains against the leash a lot and is hard to move away from an area he is sniffing.

- The dog rarely, if ever, checks back with you.

- The dog is very nervous outdoors, tail tucked, ears plastered back, eyes wide. He makes sudden dashes and then stops, darts out to the end of the leash and gets snagged there, wild-eyed or frozen.

- The dog shies from or panics around moving vehicles or loud but common outdoor noises (trucks passing, horns honking, etc.).

Fail Responses

- The dog gets much more stimulated, and bruises you or causes you pain.

- The dog starts to yank or tug on the leash with his mouth.

- The dog puts his mouth on your hands, or clothes or feet.

- The dog uses you as a springboard, and leaps up at your face and rebounds off your body.

- The dog basically never stops pulling and never looks back at you.

2. **Stop walking for a minute at a fairly nondistracting place, and, without pulling or reeling him in by the leash, call the dog and cajole him to come over to you. Try to get his attention just with your voice, and encourage him in any way other than with treats or the leash to come to you.**

Pass Responses

- The dog stops when you stop, turns immediately and readily comes to you.

- The dog comes to you readily and leans against you or nestles in close for attention.

- The dog comes over and lingers near you, wanting attention or affection.

Gray Area Responses

- The dog comes over to you but requires more than two seconds of cajoling before he turns toward you.

- The dog comes within two seconds, but leaves again instantly.

- The dog turns around and stops his forward motion, acknowledges you, but doesn't come over to you.

- The dog is very nervous outdoors, keeps his tail tucked, his ears plastered back, his eyes wide, and gets stuck in position and doesn't come readily because he is nervous.

12. Test with the Toddler Doll

This test is much more important if you actually have children in your family, or are planning to, but the first part of the test should be done by everyone and anyone. To live safely with young children, a dog cannot merely tolerate them. To live with young children, a dog must adore them, actually prefer them to adults. Nothing is more important than finding a safe and appropriate dog for a family with young children. But practically, you can't risk or sacrifice children in the name of testing dogs. So dolls can help.

Testing a dog with a doll is not helpful in determining any useful information about how most dogs might be with real children. But using the doll can help flush out dogs who hate children on sight, and will lunge and bark when they see them. Not only do you not want a dog like this whether you have kids or not—but you don't really want this dog on the planet, because this planet is filled with children. The doll will also help you pinpoint the other extreme: Dogs who adore young children.

1. **This test should be done with all the dogs back in their kennels. If you still have the dog you are interested in out with you, have a staff person put the dog back in his kennel. Take your toddler doll and, holding onto one of her hands, walk her, posing her and treating her just like a real child. You may feel foolish, but remember, aggression toward children is the most feared and critical reason to temperament test, and the hardest problem to root out.**

As you walk down the aisles with your doll, pretend to be introducing your doll to the dogs. Stop in front of the kennels of some of the dogs you are interested in, have the doll face the dog, and extend the doll's hand to the dog, as if the doll were going to pet the dog. Talk to the dog and the doll as if really introducing them, "Hi, dog, do you want to say hi to my son, Timmy?"

For the majority of dogs this test doesn't glean much information out of the dog, since many dogs don't consider the doll to be a real child. Many dogs will either ignore or be somewhat afraid of the doll, in which case the test doesn't necessarily tell you much at all.

When you stop with the doll in front of the kennel, is the dog's tail carriage:
High ❏   Level ❏   Low ❏

Pass Responses

- The dog comes to the front of the kennel, orienting toward the child, with his tail low and with a sweeping or circular wag. The dog's ears should be back, his eyes squinty and soft, and he should be licking or nuzzling, but not mouthing.

- The dog will usually greet the child's face with all of the above expressions, and then sniff and orient toward the doll's hand.

- Even after sniffing and discovering the child is fake, the dog will almost try to convince himself that the doll is real, and try regreeting, or nuzzling or licking again.

Pass Responses on this test aren't like other Pass Responses. A Pass Response to the doll means the dog is allowed, assuming he has passed every other single test, to actually meet your real live human children.

Gray Area Responses

- Any other response not described in the Pass or Fail categories.

Fail Responses

- The dog lunges and barks and growls at the doll as he sees it approach.

- The dog goes up to the doll tentatively at first, and then growls and may put up his hackles (the hair on the back of his neck), then barks or growls and shoots backward, or lunges forward.

- The dog strains at the front of the kennel, whining in a high-pitched tone. You may *think* the dog wants to play, but he does not. He wants to get to the child out of a predatory response, which is often mistaken for keen interest in playing with something.

If you see any of these Fail Responses, notify a shelter staff member immediately, as this dog is a serious threat and a potential danger to the public. He needs further professional evaluation before leaving the shelter.

If the dog passes this initial doll test, proceed to the next child test.

2. **Have your entire family in the get-acquainted area room. No treats, just people.**

3. **Have the helper bring the dog in on a loose leash.**

4. **Everyone can say hi and try to call the dog over to them, or they can be quiet; it doesn't really matter.**

5. **Instruct the helper to merely follow the dog, but not guide him or pull him *except to pull him off or away from your child if he is too rough or anyone senses any problems*.**

6. **Have the helper allow the dog to go to whomever he wants.**

Pass Responses

- The dog goes to the children first and greets them.

- The dog may roll over on his side and lift up one rear leg when the children pet him.

- The dog goes to the children first, but then makes the rounds and ends up visiting everyone in the room.

Gray Area Responses

- The dog orients toward adults first, but within two seconds goes over to greet the children on his own.

- The dog does any or all Pass responses, but is a little rough—does some gentle jumping up, but never scratches or plows into the children.

Fail Responses

- The dog ignores the children or huddles around the adults.

- The dog becomes aroused or overstimulated.

- The dog gets excited and begins whining or poking at or nudging the children in any way.

This dog shows a soft eye, sweet expression, relaxed body posture, and level to low tail carriage with this young boy. The boy is slightly restraining the dog, but the dog does not struggle to get away. This indicates a social, friendly response with the child.

- The dog is rough and physical with the children, knocking them over easily, jumping on them and taking over their space.

- The dog is mouthy (puts his mouth on any part of a child or his clothing for any reason, even in play).

- The dog exhibits any growling, lip curling or snarling, or makes any sound that someone hears that makes them wonder, "Hey, was that a growl?"

- The dog shows no interest in children and never approaches them to be petted.

- The dog never stays with any child for more than two seconds.

If the dog passes that part of the test, then proceed to the next part.

7. **Have whichever adult the dog has lingered around the most call the dog over and begin hugging and stroking him, engaging the dog. Kind of overdo it with love and attention.**

8. Ask one child to approach.

9. Watch the dog's responses carefully.

Pass Responses

- The dog readily moves or shifts himself to meet and greet the approaching child.

- The dog doesn't greet the child, but stays where he is without shifting his position.

Gray Area Responses

- The dog readily moves or shifts to the other side of the adult, or moves away to either investigate other things in the room or visit with other people.

Fail Responses

- The dog wriggles and moves in such a way as to cut off the child's access to the adult.

- The dog may remain where he is and look back and forth from the adult's face to the child's face.

- The dog cuts in between adult and child, and moves around in such a way as to try to separate the adult from the child.

- The dog shows no interest in children and never approaches them to be petted.

- The dog never stays with any child for more than two seconds.

If the dog passes that part of the test, proceed to the next part.

10. Have someone hold the dog in one corner of the room, away from your family.

11. Have one of the children get onto a parent's lap, and have the parent audibly coo, talk to the child, and shower the child with praise while hugging or stroking the child.

12. Let the dog go free.

13. Carefully watch the dog's responses.

Pass Responses

- The dog comes over with a low tail wag, ears back, eyes squinty, and visits with or greets any person in the room, adult or child.

- The dog doesn't necessarily come over to the parent and child, but is engaging other family members for attention.

- The dog comes over to the parent and child combination and visits with, engages, and greets or licks or nuzzles close to both parent and child.

- The dog engages, sits or snuggles next to, licks or rolls over for any child in the room.

Gray Area Responses

- The dog may sniff the room, but check in frequently with humans, using eye contact, making sure you're all still in the room with him. He actually comes over for affection at least one time—that is, the dog shouldn't just be solely interested in the environment—but he doesn't have to approach humans immediately to pass.

Fail Responses

- The dog cuts in between the parent and child, and moves around in such a way as to try to separate the parent from the child.

- The dog shows no interest in children, and never approaches them to be petted.

- The dog never stays with any child for more than two seconds.

Please be very critical and objective here. This will be difficult, because any time you actually introduce a dog to your children, they will want him and it will be emotional to tell them the family can't have that dog. But never lose sight of the fact that you are basically using this book to prevent bringing a dangerous predator into your home. If the dog shows any Gray Area Responses during these tests with children, or offers responses not listed here that confuse you, hold off on adopting the dog and hire a professional to help observe the dog and offer advice.

The bigger the dog, the pickier and more suspicious you should be. Never err on the side of assuming the dog "is OK" or will "be fine." You are making a lifelong commitment. I want this dog to be the dog of your dreams, the dog of a lifetime.

13. Test to See What the Dog Is Like with Cats

You only need to conduct this test if you have cats at home, or if you think you might want to adopt a cat in the future. There is nothing quite like seeing a close friendship between a cat and a dog. When a cat and a dog get along, they will often sleep together and play together. We adopted out a wonderful adult female Pit Bull a few years ago to a man who later adopted a kitten. This Pit Bull was in a shelter in North Carolina that has a policy to euthanize all Pit Bulls, regardless of temperament. A dog trainer friend of mine was volunteering at this shelter and was temperament testing their dogs, and came upon this lovely Pit Bull. We transferred the dog to our shelter, since we consider all dogs as individuals and will place any dog, regardless of breed or reputation, if it passes the Assess-a-Pet test.

We received photos from the Pit Bull's new owner with a thank you letter in appreciation of the dog he adopted. One photo showed a tiny kitten sharing a bowl of food with the gigantic Pit Bull. In the photo, the Pit Bull is obviously deferring to the little kitten, who has complete control of the bowl. The other photos showed the two species sleeping snuggled up against one another on a large dog bed. The lives of both the kitten and the Pit Bull (not to mention the owner's life) are enriched by living together and enjoying each other's company.

This test is the least predictable of all the tests. It has been my experience that there are two kinds of dogs: The first kind are OK living with a cat as long as the cat stands his ground with the dog, maybe even hissing and clawing to control the dog, but he doesn't flee when the dog approaches, thereby causing the dog to chase. The second kind are dogs who are OK living with a cat as long as the cat doesn't stand his ground and hiss and claw at the dog. This test is not good at predicting if the dog would do well if he had one type of cat but not the other. But at least it can give good, solid warning clues that the dog may be a cat killer.

Because of safety considerations for the cat, it is necessary to keep him protected in a wire enclosure—so you cannot see what the dog would be like if the cat is the type who flees. But we do the best we can do, and the test can at least usually weed out the potential cat killers.

Unfortunately, you will need a cat, and a cat who won't be permanently traumatized by helping you assess your dog. Please don't think you need to bring your own cat, or borrow one! You will, however, need to inquire whether the shelter has a cat they could use to help you assess the dog you are interested in. Ideally, the shelter will have an office or resident cat who is savvy with dogs, and they can find a portable wire cage or wire dog crate. Really, you don't want to stress out a cat in the name of testing a dog.

1. The safest way to test a dog for compatibility with cats is to secure the cat in a wire crate, and place the crate on the floor in a quiet room.

2. Have someone from the shelter bring the dog into the room on a leash.

3. Allow the dog the length of the leash, and let him go where he wants to go.

4. Watch his reactions as he locates and approaches the cat. After the dog has been with or next to the cat for at least 30 seconds, try to interrupt the dog's interest in the cat by calling him and cajoling him to come over. Don't use the leash to get him to you; see if you can get him to disconnect from the cat with just verbal encouragement and hand gestures.

Pass Responses

- The dog approaches the cat casually, without straining on the leash, and may sniff at the cat.

- The dog may begin wagging his tail while greeting the cat, but the tail will be level or low when wagging.

- The dog shows mild interest in the cat and looks away, turns away or leaves the cat alone at least once.

Gray Area Responses

- The dog approaches the cat readily, with ears up and tail level or high.

- The dog may approach the cat with some pulling on the leash, but does not make an intense beeline for the cat.

- The dog may bark a few times, play bow (front paws on the ground, butt up in the air) and poke at the cage once or twice with his nose.

- The dog disengages on his own from the cat and looks away, turns away or leaves the cat at least once of his own volition.

These dogs tend to do best with cats who won't flee, but will stand their ground or confidently ignore anything the dog does, go up to the dog and rub up against him, or sit right in front of the dog and groom.

Fail Responses

- The dog focuses in on the cat and strains and pulls his way to the cat.

- The dog stares at the cat with intense focus.

- The dog stares at the cat and trembles.

- The dog stares at the cat and cannot be verbally called away or cajoled away; his gaze cannot be interrupted.

- The dog stares at the cat and puts a razor-thin line of hair (hackles) up the back of his neck or between his shoulder blades.

- The dog begins whining, or whining and growling.

- The dog circles the cage, trying intensely to break into it and get at the cat.

- As your helper tries to pull the dog away, the dog begins growling and lunging, or puts the hair up on his back.

These responses indicate a high predatory instinct. Although sometimes these dogs may look like they want to play, they don't. They usually want to kill.

5. **In the absence of a real live cat, the next best thing is to bring a soft, white (white objects show up better and seem to entice dogs more to chase), fluffy stuffed cat toy. Tie a dog leash to the toy cat, so you can drag it along the floor by holding one end of the leash. Have your helper restrain the dog on a leash, in an indoor or out-door area. You have the toy cat; stand about 10 to 20 feet away from the dog. Flick the toy and tease the dog, from that distance, to get the dog's attention. Once the dog is focused on the toy cat, begin hissing and flick the toy behind you as you run. Run back and forth in front of the dog three times.**

Pass Responses

- The dog looks with mild interest as you make a fool of yourself, hissing and running back and forth with this toy.

- The dog does not strain on the leash or pull forward at all, but remains in place watching the toy.

- The dog may disengage at least once.

Gray Area Responses

- The dog perks up immediately, puts some pressure on the leash, but remains standing on all four legs.

- The dog may play bow or bark once or twice, or may turn around to the helper and bark and turn back to the toy.

Fail Responses

- The dog focuses in on the toy immediately, strains forward on the leash and spends most of the time pulling or jumping up and down, trying to get to the toy.

- The dog whines or growls while straining forward (a dog who growls but is backing off is just scared).

- The dog continues to strain and/or whine and/or bark even after you have stopped running and the toy is still.

Using the toy as a test for cat compatibility is even less predictive than using a caged cat, so if the dog you are very interested in passed in all the other tests but failed the cat test, it is worth getting a second opinion from a dog trainer or dog behavior expert.

THE WRAP-UP

This may seem like an awful lot to go through to select a dog whom you have such a good feeling about. You probably feel that you have a "good gut sense" about dogs. That you can "read them well." I think that about myself, especially after 23 years in the field. I think I have a really good gut feeling about dogs. And yet I use the temperament test to know a dog. I will not place a dog out of my shelter, no matter how good I feel about him, without performing a thorough Assess-a-Pet evaluation.

I have to trust the temperament test over my own gut feeling about a dog. I have learned this the hard way: by placing dogs based on what I thought were good gut feelings, and having them returned after horrifying the families with serious, surprise behavior problems.

The shelter world is an emotional one. It helps to have something solid to depend on to either back up or see through your highly charged and emotional feelings about a dog.

Chapter 6

What Have I Done?

Sometime during your first week with your new dog, probably on your way home from work, when you are tired and the novelty, fun and excitement of having a dog has worn off just a bit, you will suddenly wonder, "Oh, my God, what have I done?" The enormity of the responsibility and commitment, the "forever-ness" of your decision, the permanency of this dog at home needing so much attention, finally sinks in and fear engulfs you.

Or you may be at home with your new dog, and he may do something bad—it could be anything from pooping on the rug *again* to lifting his leg on your couch to panting, drooling or licking—and you think, "Have I made a huge mistake?"

You **will** feel this way. If you have adopted a cute young puppy, you won't feel this way for another few months, since you will be caught up in the cuteness of the puppy. If you have adopted an adult dog, you may not ever feel this way (although many people will), since many adult dogs fit your lifestyle so perfectly that they seem custom made for you. But those of you who have adopted adolescent dogs or puppies heading quickly into adolescence will feel this fear.

Behaviors can start appearing, or flash by, especially in the first week, that will make you think it is just the tip of a horrible behavioral iceberg, and you will feel you have made some huge mistake. Every housebreaking setback seems to be a marker of this dog's inability to be house-trained. Every chewing episode seems to be proof that this dog will chew destructively forever, and that chewing must be the real reason someone gave him up. When he barks at something and you can't shut him up, you believe (especially now that this is the third time in one week he has repeated this behavior) he is a terrible, permanent barker, and that barking must have been the real reason the previous owner gave him up.

During this first week, no behavior feels meaningless, none is a fleeting problem. All your dog's behaviors will seem like proof of his future, permanent and problematic temperament. It is during this first week that many people worry that they have chosen the wrong dog.

These worries about your new dog are universal. It seems everyone who has adopted a new dog, particularly an adolescent, shares these worries. That includes professional dog trainers. I myself have had these feelings each and every time I have adopted a dog. My last five dogs were all adopted at the peak of adolescence (from six months to 10 months). In each case, I was initially excited (after all, I chose each dog because I fell in love, not because I *needed* another dog). But then, at the first sign of less-than-perfect behavior (which no adolescent dog is without), I would worry about the terrible mistake I must have made.

This is why training is so important right from the very start. Each day with your new dog is a struggle to rack up more points on the "good dog" team than the "bad dog" team. Every day you must score points for the good dog inside your dog, so that ultimately, when your dog is all grown up and settled into a routine, his good dog points far outnumber his bad dog points, and, as in any relationship, you don't notice his bad dog qualities anymore because you have compromised and incorporated them into the total relationship; they have become part of the package of overall love and acceptance—as your dog does with your bad qualities. What he found so irritating about you in the beginning (how whiny your voice is or how inconsistent you are—allowing him to jump up on you one moment and then getting angry about the same thing a moment later), he learns is just part of you, and he adores you anyway.

During this first week and beyond, you need to instill in your dog all the ways you want him to behave, train him in all the behaviors you want to become habits, and hope that the unwanted behaviors will be covered, over time, by the good ones you keep encouraging. But one week is not enough time to see an overall future, or the big picture. During this first week you can only see the moments of bad and good behavior—and the bad ones will seem permanent and the good ones fleeting. Keep plugging away! You have chosen this dog for some reason. Some quality in him touched you and helped you select him. It was no accident. And it will all come together.

It just won't seem so in the first week.

In addition to training (which I will talk about in detail in the next chapter), you'll probably spend that first week trying to figure out as much as you can about your dog. Some dogs come from a shelter with lots of information about their past and present, and some are real unknowns. The more you can figure out about your new dog, the better you'll both be able to understand one another. Let's start with the basics.

WHAT GENDER IS YOUR DOG?

This may seem obvious, but it has been my experience that many a dog has been mistakenly labeled as the opposite sex. Many dogs are tagged by gender when they come in to the shelter, and will, for instance, be given a pink or red colored identification collar or tag if they are female and a blue one if they are male. But the tags are not always correct.

While I am urging you not to limit your selection by preferring one gender over another, knowing the true gender of your dog is useful for determining how you want to handle the dog, giving the dog a name (unless you want to go with a unisex name like Chris, Pat, Leslie, Robin, Dana or something similar), and making an appointment for the correct surgery for sterilization.

A male dog's penis is basically located on his underbelly. A female dog's underbelly is smooth, and she has a vulva way back as far as you can go underneath her toward her tail, but before you get to her anus. That's putting it bluntly.

GUESSING THE AGE OF A DOG

Being able to accurately determine the age of a stray or unknown dog is beneficial for everyone who will come in contact with the dog—starting with the shelter personnel. As much as possible, it is important for them to gauge the age of a dog before looking at his temperament, and certainly before he's handled in the shelter. Why? If you are going to approach and handle an unknown dog and the dog is going to be aggressive during this event, you are more at risk for damage from a mature adult dog (one to two years or older) than from an adolescent or puppy.

If you are a family with young children looking to adopt, or a young single person or couple entertaining the possibility of having children within the next five years, it is particularly helpful to have this inside knowledge about the dog's age. The older the dog is you're thinking of bringing into your home, the more carefully you will have to assess his temperament and behavior, because the more likely he is to cause harm and serious damage to you and your family. That is not to say that all mature, adult dogs will bite you or hurt you if you approach and handle them. It's just that your family is more at risk.

What follows is a list of development traits to look for that will help you determine the age of a dog. Some of the tips will be safe for your dog trainer or dog obedience instructor or veterinarian to look for on a dog you are thinking of adopting. Or, if you're at the shelter, it is appropriate to ask a shelter employee or volunteer to help you by doing some of the handling. It is *not* safe for an inexperienced person to look at the teeth, genitals, eyes or ears of unknown dogs of any size! If you have already adopted the dog, it should (hopefully) be safe for you to look for these things.

Birth to 48 Hours

The eyes and ears are sealed. Pigment on the lips and paw pads is a bright, cherry red color. Poop is often bright yellow.

Seven to 14 Days

The eyes and ears start to open, and will be open by 14 days. Before 14 days, the ears look like gerbil ears—small and rounded. The eyes will be a cloudy blue.

Four to Five Weeks

Play behaviors start to show up. Different personalities appear in the puppies within the same litter. Eye color is still a hazy, cloudy blue.

Six to Eight Weeks

Eye color begins to change to a clear, more adult, final color. The pups show fairly good coordination, and are ready to be adopted. Teeny tiny sexual organs (penises and testicles, nipples and vulvas) are visible.

Eight to 16 Weeks

The puppy will have all baby teeth (baby incisors and baby canines). Baby teeth are comparable in color to skim milk, while adult teeth are comparable to Half & Half. The closer in age the puppy is to eight weeks, the closer together the baby incisors are; the closer to 16 weeks, the more space there is between the incisors. (The incisors are the pointed teeth in the very front of the mouth. The canines are the long, fanglike teeth on either side of the incisors. The back teeth are the premolars and molars.)

Females will have prepubescent, teeny nipples and vulva. Males will have a tiny penis and teeny testicles, very tight and close to the body.

Four Months

The baby incisors will begin to be replaced by adult teeth. The front two incisors will be the first to loosen and be replaced. The puppy's two front teeth will look like beaver teeth, compared to his other incisors, which are smaller because they're still baby teeth.

Four and a Half to Five Months

The adult incisors are coming in. The closer the puppy is to four and a half months, the more spaced out the adult incisors will be. The closer he is to five months, the closer together the adult incisors will be. The pup will still have baby canine teeth.

Five Months

This is the "nub" age: The adult upper canines (thicker and less sharp-tipped than baby canines) will be crowning—just showing a nub. All adult incisors will be snug in a row.

Six Months

The adult canines are about halfway down. This is the age where the puppy's body type changes, and he begins to look more in proportion and less puppyish (that is, he begins to "lose" his knobby joints, big ears, and big feet). He may be mistaken for an older adolescent at this age, until you see him grow more and, upon looking back, you realize how puppyish he still was at six months.

Seven Months

The canines are about three-quarters down; they may look fully descended, but the base of the tooth near the gum line will still be small. Females are likely to go into season shortly.

10 Months

The canines have fully dropped, and the bases are thick. All premolars (the teeth directly behind the canines) have descended. These choppers can do the work of a predator! The toenail beds (at the base of the nails) are starting to thicken, and the nail ends are blunter and less pointy.

For sexually intact dogs, a male will have larger testicles, and they may hang slightly lower than on younger dogs. The penis size is enlarging as testosterone increases. A female may be in her first heat cycle. If the nipples and vulva are slightly larger than they were during prepubescence, she may have finished her first heat cycle. (A prepubescent or spayed female will have tiny nipples and vulva.) If the nipples and vulva of a sexually intact stray female suggest she has finished a heat cycle, she is likely in the early stages of pregnancy.

About One Year

The dog's overall appearance is less juvenile, less gawky and adolescent. The chest is dropping, but the ribs have not yet expanded the chest to its full circumference. There is no discernable wear on the incisors yet. Don't concern yourself with tartar on the teeth, which is never a reliable determiner of age.

One to Two Years

The dog's overall body type is still youthful, his chest is undeveloped, and his ribs are narrow. All the adult teeth are in, but there is no wear on the incisors and there should be relatively no chipping or wear on the premolars. The base of the toenails is thick, and the nails are thicker and blunter than on younger dogs.

A sexually intact male will have larger testicles, and they will start to hang more. The nipples will still be undeveloped. For a female, if the nipples and vulva are a small, prepubescent size, there's a good chance she has already been spayed, and was before her first heat cycle. If she hasn't been spayed, the nipples and vulva will be enlarged but not huge.

Three to Five Years

You will see some flattening of incisors, and some chipping on the teeth is possible. Certainly, they will look less pristine. The chest will be fully developed, and the dog will have a hefty, filled-out look.

Sexually intact males will have a large penis. The testicles are beginning to dangle. The nipples are usually small. There will be some bulging of the area directly below the anus. If the dog is neutered at this age or older, the scrotal sac will usually hang like a flattened pancake. Intact females will have enlarged nipples and vulva.

Five to Seven Years

You'll see considerable flattening of incisors, overall yellowing of all teeth and probably some chipping. The dog will have more nicks and scars overall, and some calluses are usually present on the elbows and hocks (the joint that points backward on the lower legs). You may see considerable "leaking" of brown eye color from the corners of the eyes and even into the whites of the dog's eyes.

On a sexually intact male, the testicles will be dangling considerably and penis size will be substantial. The nipples will be enlarged

The underbelly of this intact female shows enlarged nipples, indicating she is a sexually intact, mature dog.

and sometimes gnarly and gross looking! There will also be considerable bulging of the area directly below the anus. A sexually intact female will have enlarged nipples, usually black in color unless she is in season, and enlarged vulva. If she has been bred extensively, the nipples will hang low in two racks. Check for mammary tumors; the principal sign is a painless lump or mass.

Seniors (More Than Eight Years)

Older dogs will have less muscle tone and mass. Often the topline (the line along the top of the back, from the base of the neck to the base of the tail) will have a dip or appear knobby. The teeth will show considerable overall wear and yellowing, and gum disease and heavy tartar and plaque will often be present. Cataracts and clouding of the eyes are common. The muzzle may be graying. You'll see a much lower activity level than in younger dogs; older dogs may walk instead of trot.

GUESSING THE MIX OF YOUR DOG

Most people who own mixed breed dogs know their single most important quest in life is to try to figure out the origin of their dog. We all like to believe that every mixed breed is a cross of two distinct purebreds, but the truth is that most mixed breeds are the result of one mixed breed dog breeding with another. At best (and not very often), a mixed breed is the offspring of one purebred parent and one mixed breed. Still, it gives us great pleasure to try to come up with the exact combination of breeds that might make up our unique mixed breed.

The best (and most fun) way to really delve into the world of purebreds and help you see one or more possible purebreds in your own particular mixed breed is to attend an American Kennel Club or United Kennel Club dog show. Never will you see more examples of each breed in one place. Ask handlers if you can pet their dogs. Ask handlers all about their dogs. (Then, take whatever they say with a grain of salt, because each handler, each owner thinks their breed is the best, the smartest, the most loyal, the most devoted, the best with kids, etc.)

Watch the different breeds trot around the ring; watch them move. Movement and style are the very essence of a purebred that will sometimes remind you of something in your own dog. We had a large, hairy mixed breed

Best breed mix guess: half Pug and half Chow Chow.

at our shelter, and, because I know the breed well, I *knew* beyond a shadow of a doubt that this mixed breed was part Bernese Mountain Dog. I knew because of the dog's thighs, legs and bone structure. His rear end was the very essence of a Bernese Mountain Dog.

Sometimes you will think you see some very rare purebred in the mix of your own dog. Others will make fun of you or humor you, but not really believe you. But you may be right. The more uncommon or rare the purebred, the less likely it is to be spayed or neutered because so many rare breeds are considered show or breeding quality (since their gene pool is so limited). That means many of them are left intact. Sometimes the more rare the purebred, the less experienced the owner. Many novice pet owners will seek out and purchase the rarest, most exotic, trendy purebred dog, and then not be experienced enough or educated enough about breeding, spaying and neutering.

Another favorite activity of the mixed breed dog owner is to peruse the encyclopedias and atlases of purebreds, locate a photograph of an incredibly rare and foreign breed, decide it is the spitting image of their own mixed breed, and then believe their dog to be a Podengo, a Lesser Munsterlander or a Drever.

And who knows?

Shelter Shorthand

Animal shelters seem to boil down all breeds and mixes to four basic types:

1. If the dog is black, no matter how big or small, how short or long his hair, the dog is a "Labrador mix."
2. If the dog has wiry hair, it's a "terrier mix."
3. If the dog is a Pit Bull type, it's a "Lab-Boxer mix."
4. If the dog is black and tan, no matter how big or small, how short or long his hair, the dog is a "shepherd mix."

We make these gross breed type simplifications so that we can at least find some way to categorize some of the mixes we get. There is little information out there for shelters to access in terms of determining mixes and cross-breeds.

Dr. Leon F. Whitney, in his book *How to Breed Dogs*, did numerous breedings to study the inheritance of various physical characteristics of purebred dogs. He came up with some interesting genetic marking points, which, if I am interpreting them correctly, can help the owners of unknown mixed or cross-bred dogs. From my experience, and following what Dr. Whitney wrote, the following conclusions can be drawn:

- Leg length: Breed a short-legged breed to a long-legged breed (say, a Basset Hound to a German Shepherd Dog) and leg length of the first-generation puppies is somewhere in between.

- Ear length: Breed a long-eared breed to a short-eared breed (for example, a Coonhound to a Labrador Retriever) and ear length of the first-generation puppies is somewhere in between.

- Coat length: Breed a long-coated breed to a short-coated breed (say, a Collie to a Doberman Pinscher) and the coat length of the first-generation puppies is likely to be short.

- Ear carriage (erect, semi-erect, drop, pendulous): Breed a breed with long, pendulous ears to a breed with prick ears (for example, a Beagle to a Siberian Husky) and the ears of the first-generation puppies will neither be fully dropped (like the Beagle) nor fully erect (like the Siberian Husky).

What I have found useful in determining the heritage of a mixed breed dog is to observe the traits of each breed you think might be part of the mix, and rule out certain possibilities. For instance, a Labrador Retriever crossed with a Siberian Husky would produce a dog whose ears would not be fully dropped like a Labrador, nor be fully, naturally erect like a Siberian. A Labrador Retriever crossed with a Golden Retriever (or any of the setters, spaniels or pointers) could have fully dropped ears, since all those breeds have fully dropped ears. A Siberian Husky crossed with a German Shepherd Dog would likely have naturally fully erect ears, and, if the ears bent over at the tips (called "tulip" ears) or were folded back and somewhere in between an erect and drop ear, then the mix is unlikely to be of a purebred Siberian to a purebred German Shepherd.

An American Cocker Spaniel crossed with a Border Collie would be very unlikely to produce a dog with naturally erect ears, since the Cocker's ears are so long, pendulous and heavy.

The progeny of two purebreds could not be substantially larger or smaller than the extreme of either breed. So the puppy of an American Cocker Spaniel crossed with a Border Collie could be no smaller than a small Cocker Spaniel, and no larger than the largest Border Collie.

A Labrador Retriever mixed with any of the setters (English, Irish or Gordon) would be unlikely to have a long, feathered coat, since I believe Whitney showed in all of his test breedings that the first generation of long coats bred with short coats were short coated. Same for a Labrador Retriever mixed with a Golden Retriever.

Some breeds have short coats (Labradors, German Shepherds, Australian Cattle Dogs, Corgis and many more), but other breeds have very fine short coats (Doberman Pinschers, Pit Bull Terriers, Greyhounds, Pointers and others). Only two finely coated breeds could produce a dog with the same fine coat. A Labrador Retriever bred with a Collie would likely produce puppies with short coats, but not with the extra-fine coat like that of a Greyhound.

Sometimes a particular purebred will send up an obvious flare, declaring its role in a mixed breed dog. The baying of a Coonhound or any scenthound cannot belong to any other type of purebred. The exaggerated dipped head, hard stare and forward crawl of a Border Collie are unmistakable in a Border Collie mix.

Then again, as Freud said, "Sometimes a cigar is just a cigar." Sometimes a mixed breed is just a mixed breed, with no particular purebred represented for many generations.

Chapter 7

Basic Manners

PLEDGE FOR NEW DOG ADOPTERS

❏ I pledge to make a reasonable commitment of time and effort, and to affect scheduling and lifestyle changes to make this relationship work.

❏ I pledge to make sure my dog is not exposed to the elements of weather without proper shelter, shade cover, dry ground, access to fresh water and at least one hour of loving companionship and play each day. I understand this is a minimum and will strive to keep the dog with me as much as possible and treat him/her as an important member of my family.

❏ I pledge to provide appropriate and timely veterinary care for the life of my dog.

❏ I pledge to provide my dog with the proper nutrition for optimum health, and to keep my dog at the proper weight, neither obese nor emaciated.

❏ I pledge to keep my dog indoors at night, and to include him in the activities of the household while we are home, as much as possible.

❏ I pledge to keep my dog groomed and free of external parasites and matting (particularly behind his ears, under his elbows and on his tail and thighs).

❏ I pledge to spay or neuter my dog, if this has not already been done.

❑ I pledge to give my dog ample aerobic exercise daily, and make sure that at least three times a week he has the opportunity to run and play and get tired out.

❑ I pledge to provide my dog with mental stimulation in the form of either play, interactive toys, training or off-territory leash walks *every day*.

❑ I pledge to provide my dog with enough training and/or behavioral management to enable him to be a welcome part of my community or to be managed safely.

❑ I pledge to provide my dog with ample outlets for his instincts (such as off-territory leash walks, running, opportunities to sniff and explore the natural world, agility training, trick training, fun and rewarding obedience training, play with other dogs, etc.), so that he does not feel constantly frustrated or develop behavioral problems because he is neglected or understimulated.

❑ I pledge to provide a home in which my dog clearly knows there are certain rules I will insist on and he can count on.

❑ I pledge to provide my dog with enough toys to satisfy his urge to chew.

❑ I pledge to get professional help if my dog has or develops behavior or temperament problems, and, if safe, to manage my dog carefully so as not to endanger the people and other pets in my community.

❑ I pledge do everything I can to keep my dog from becoming a nuisance in my community.

❑ I pledge that I will not allow my dog to run free or out of my control, or to chase cars, bicycles, children, etc.

❑ I pledge that I will keep my dog quiet, or seek professional help to get him to be quiet, when I am home and away, so as not to disturb my neighbors.

❑ I pledge to scoop my dog's poop when we're off my property, so that my dog and other dogs will always be welcome in public.

❑ I pledge that if I have to move to another residence for any reason, I am aware that finding housing that accepts pets can take longer than average, but that I will commit to moving with my dog, as I would move with a member of my family.

❑ I pledge that if, for any reason, I can no longer keep my dog, I will not abandon him; I will return him to the shelter (if required) or leave ample time to find him a new, appropriate home; I will tell the new owners truthfully all the dog's behaviors, good and bad; and I will follow up occasionally to make sure the dog is safe and content.

WHEN SHOULD I START TRAINING?

You don't want to wait until you *need* to enroll in a dog training class; you should enroll in a dog training class as soon as there is an opening. Dog training today is quite different (or at least it should be!) than it was 10 years ago. Joining a dog training class is not just for people looking desperately for help or control of their dog. A good class can put you in a room full of other new dog owners just like yourself (so you won't feel too alone) and can answer all your day-to-day questions and address the minor issues that arise every day. A good dog training class can teach you how to teach your dog anything, and can teach your dog how to learn anything. A good dog training class can cement the bond between you and your new dog, and provide an introduction to a lifelong relationship of cooperation and learning.

Remember, a dog is always learning—whether you're trying to teach him anything or not. When he barks as the letter carrier delivers the mail, and the letter carrier then goes to the next house, your dog "learns" that barking gets the letter carrier off his territory. When your dog pokes your hand with his nose and you pet him, your dog learns that he can get you to do things for him by poking you. Your dog learns that if he looks at you cutely and wags his tail and barks, you will get up and let him out into the backyard to go to the bathroom.

With your dog learning all the time, it behooves you to start teaching your dog all the things *you* want him to learn. Besides, it's really fun.

WHAT KIND OF TRAINING CLASS?

When we think of dog obedience classes, we may think of the British dog trainer Barbara Woodhouse (now deceased) and the military-school style of dog obedience classes of that era. Dog obedience training has changed at lot since then. The word "obedience" implies a slavish, submissive response from the dogs. Obedience used to refer to six commands that were thought to be the key to gaining power in your relationship with a dog. These six commands are sit, lie down, stand, stay, come and heel. Lie down was considered to be a very subordinate position to command a dog into, yet play dead or roll over were thought to be "silly pet tricks" and not subordinate positions at all. In reality, if you believe that commanding your dog into different positions makes you more dominant, then play dead or roll over should be worth more than plain old lie down. I teach my dogs positions as if all of them were tricks: sit, sit pretty, lie down, play dead, roll over, stay, come, take a bow, stand, spin, and so on. I assert my leadership in ways and at times that do not have anything to do with teaching my dogs different positions.

It would not have been helpful if my third grade math teacher had picked me up by my ears, stared me in the face and commanded "72–69=3" over and over again to assert herself as the authority, nor would it have helped me understand subtraction. I learned to respect my teachers as authorities not because they asserted themselves in the middle of trying to teach us a lesson, but because of how they behaved and treated us elsewhere.

All the tricks of obedience should be taught to your dog in the most positive, rewarding and efficient way. Treats are, without a doubt, the fastest way to teach a dog to do anything. Life isn't all positive, and neither is every element that goes into training your dog, but all the teaching is most quickly and effectively done using food rewards. This does *not* mean the dog is only working for food, and it does not mean he is not "doing it for you." It simply means that while you are teaching a behavior, food treats are used to lure and/or reward the correct responses. Once a behavior is learned, using many *different* rewards (food, petting, praise, play, going outside for a walk, games) makes for a very strong and reliable response.

With my own dogs, I raise my voice or clap sharply while yelling "Hey!" or "No!" during normal, everyday interactions that require me to stop or interrupt an unwanted canine behavior. But they learned how to learn, and they initially learned all their commands, with food treats. They do not beg at the table (they don't get fed at the table). They do not think I am a pushover (I keep order and control through strong, calm leadership and setting limits). My dogs do not just work for food (they will respond just as well whether I have food or not, whether or not they can see if I have food).

In looking for dog training classes, ask if you can observe a class before signing up your own dog. Good dog training schools welcome observers. Just as you don't want someone abusing your dog physically or verbally in the name of training, neither should you accept an instructor who abuses the human students verbally. The only way for a dog trainer to train your dog is to *teach you* how to train your dog. You needn't be yelled at or demeaned during this process. You shouldn't care if your dog is well behaved for the dog trainer; you should care if your dog is well behaved for you.

If the class has more than 10 students for each instructor, or the room is so stuffed full of students and their dogs that you and your own dog can't get more than four feet away from another dog, the class is too crowded and this adds extra stress to your dog.

If most of the class time is spent heeling the dogs around the room in a circle, find another class. Heeling in a group can be useful at times for teaching the dogs to walk on a leash without pulling, but spending a lot of class time doing it, or starting out with group heeling, is an old-fashioned technique used to wear down your dog and make him more inhibited. That's not teaching any-thing—it's suppressing your dog's personality. Look for a class that spends most of its time on teaching good manners and behaviors you want from your dog, rather than inhibiting him or beating down unwanted behaviors.

Look for a class that teaches behaviors that are applicable and useful to your life, not just commands to be practiced in a classroom. The reason to teach the sit-stay is to keep a dog from jumping up, or to have him remain in one position so you can get his leash on or off when going for a walk, or to keep him from lunging and trying to play with another dog. A good dog training class puts the commands into context—it offers ways to use the dog's new tricks to improve his overall behavior and manners. Some class time should be devoted to household manners and helping you apply the training to real life situations.

Walk out of a class in which a dog is being strangled or hung in the air by his collar and leash. (There is only one incredibly rare instance where hanging a dog this way is called for, and it is not part of training or teaching the dog anything. The only time it can be excused is if the trainer is doing it in self-defense—and the dog is literally trying to kill someone. If there is a dog in a group class trying to kill someone, you don't belong in that class. No one does. Dog training classes are for teaching dogs basic skills; they are not for aggres-sive or dangerous dogs of any size.)

A good dog training class does not depend on equipment. What kind of collar and leash your dog is wearing should have little bearing on any com-mand, except for walking on leash. There is no one type of collar that works for all dogs. A good instructor will help you find the right equipment for you and your dog, and will explain its pros and cons.

A good dog training class should be fun for both you and your dog. Your dog should start to look forward to going to class. You should see improvement in your dog's overall behavior when you practice and do the homework expected of you during the week. A good dog training class should inspire you to work with your dog, and motivate both of you to practice the exercises. Training your dog is something you will do every day for the rest of his life, so it might as well be fun and exciting.

HOUSEBREAKING FOR PUPPIES AND ADULT DOGS

The only real difference between housebreaking adopted puppies and adopted adult shelter dogs is that you know for sure the puppies are not yet fully house-broken, and the adult dogs may already be. Don't worry too much if the adolescent or adult dog you've adopted is not completely housebroken. Any dog can learn to eliminate where you want him to.

You will want to choose an outdoor potty area that's about 20 feet long and a few feet wide. The potty area should be close to your door. If you live in an apartment, the area you choose should be within a few feet from the main entrance or exit, in the gutter (if there is one), or in an appropriate area close to the main entrance. This way, when it rains or snows or you have the flu or sprain an ankle, your dog will be trained to eliminate within a few feet from your door, and you won't have to walk all the way to the park or all the way down the block. You'll appreciate this feature when you need it.

Whether you live in the country, suburbs or city, *leash* your dog (yes, even you country folks with those huge fenced yards—get that leash out in the beginning). You'll want your dog to eliminate while you watch from close by, not only so you can be right there to praise and reward, but so your dog feels comfortable eliminating in front of you. What you don't want is a dog who is afraid to go the bathroom in front of you. If he is, he'll sneak away and hide his accidents. You'll find them the hard way—in the middle of the night, with your bare feet.

As soon as you get home from the shelter, with the leash on, walk your dog around your home, through each room, letting him familiarize himself with everything. As you do this, your dog will sniff and examine his new home. The very act of sniffing will trigger a cascade of responses in him and he will automatically feel like eliminating.

After going through the house, walk him directly outside to his chosen bathroom area, and walk slowly back and forth and back and forth, pacing and chanting an encouraging phrase over and over again (such as "Do your business, do your business . . .").

Keep your dog out there for a maximum of two minutes. If he eliminates within those two minutes, give *huge* praise, then spend some time playing or running with your dog outside, then bring him in to investigate the house— *still on leash.* If the two minutes are up and your dog has not eliminated (a much more likely scenario), simply say nothing and walk your dog back inside. *Keep the leash on.*

Keep him on leash and tethered to you until you are ready to take him outside to his bathroom area again. This can be in 10 minutes or two hours. Or you can wait to take him back out when and if he gets antsy. Repeat the two-minute performance.

If and when he finally eliminates in his bathroom spot, praise him heartily and reward him with some treats. He then has 15 minutes of freedom. You can use that 15 minutes to take him on a long walk outside, or if you go right back inside after rewarding him, he then has 15 minutes of off-leash, minimally supervised freedom in the house. Set a kitchen timer for this, so you don't lose track of the time. After 15 minutes, hook him back up on the leash and don't take him out again for another two hours (if he is under four months); you can wait longer if he is older.

The general rule for how many hours your puppy can hold his bladder and bowels is his age in months, plus one. So a three-month-old puppy can hold it for four hours, a five-month-old puppy can hold it for six hours, and so on. From seven months through adulthood, he should be able to hold it for nine hours total during the day, if necessary, and a maximum of 10 hours every once in a great while.

For every three straight days of clean success, you can add another 15 minutes of freedom to his successful moments, until at last he is housebroken.

Many people want their dog to tell them when they need to go out and go the bathroom. Very few dogs actually do, and even fewer actually tell you only when they really and truly have to go, and not when they just want to go out and have fun. It is better to have a dog who doesn't tell you at all, but rather just assumes that you will let him out often enough, and the rest of the time he should just hold it.

MALE DOG URINE MARKING

Male dogs, even neutered ones, sometimes lift their leg inside your home. This is not the same as a housebreaking accident. Many male dogs are completely housebroken, but occasionally, especially just upon entering a new home or new room, they will lift their leg and squirt some urine to mark their territory and leave their scent.

Following the protocol I've just described for housebreaking will also help prevent your male dog from marking. Another thing that may help is to learn to anticipate when your dog is *thinking* of urine marking, so you can tell him "No!" right before he does it. Telling him "No!" after he does it will not help at all—in fact, it can backfire and teach him to sneak off and mark when you're not looking.

How do you know what he's thinking? Your dog will always sniff before he marks, and the sniffing is different from other, regular sniffing. Urine marking sniffing is on objects up high, about the height of his shoulder. The dog will usually arch his neck and point his nose downward to reach the sniff spot, and he may sniff tentatively, as if he does not want to accidentally touch the surface with his nose. Then sometimes the dog will sniff and walk a step away from the spot, then turn back in the opposite direction.

CLEANING UP THE SPOTS

With all accidents, for any reason, clean up the spots with an odor-neutralizing enzymatic product. Soak the spot thoroughly, especially if it is a urine-marking stain, since one of the reasons for urine marking or eliminating is to mark over previously marked territory. The better you clean, the less likely your dog is to return and eliminate there again. It is helpful to put the odor neutralizing solution into a plant mister or empty spray bottle so you can squirt it onto vertical surfaces.

THE BASIC SIT

Your new dog may already know how to sit on command, or you may have taught your previous dog to sit. The method I am outlining here is worth using, even if your dog already seems to know the "sit" command, because it teaches the dog not only to sit, but also to offer this position to get your attention or to have his needs met. So instead of getting your attention by other obnoxious means (such as barking at you, by nipping at your clothes or hands, pawing at you, and so on) the dog trained to sit using this method will sit to be noticed.

It is quick and easy to train, and within this training lesson your dog will learn *how to learn*. So everything that comes after will be easier and quicker for him to pick up. From this one behavior comes many different uses.

By far the quickest and easiest way to teach a dog to do anything is with food treats. That doesn't mean your dog is only working for food, nor does it mean you will always need to have food with you to get him to behave. Using food treats to *teach* a behavior, but using food treats, praise, petting, games, play, leash walks, rides in the car, meal times, etc., to *reward* the dog for complying, is by far the most efficient, effective and fun way to train a dog.

Teaching the Sit

1. Hold a fistful of yummy, soft, tiny treats in one hand.

2. Bring your hand down to your dog's nose, because you are going to use the food as a lure. If you hold your hand high, or draw it away quickly to avoid the dog going after it, you will simply lure the dog to jump up, so keep your hand (with the food) right at the height of your dog's.

3. Slowly move your fistful of treats from the dog's nose to a spot in the air directly above his head and between his ears.

4. As he lifts his nose up to follow the food, his rear end will touch the ground and he will end up in a sitting position.

5. As soon as his rear end hits the ground, open your fist and feed your dog a treat. Then, without losing his attention, lure him directly forward using another treat, until he is standing again.

6. Do not feed your dog for standing up; you are only luring him into a stand so that you can quickly lure him into a sit again for another repetition.

7. Feed only when the dog ends up in the sitting position.

8. Repeat several times in a row, without interruptions and without losing your dog's attention, until it gets easier and easier to lure him into the sit.

9. When the luring is smooth and easy, you are ready to test your dog.

Test Your Dog

1. Show your dog a jackpot (a fist full of treats), but keep your fist at your dog's nose and do not lure him into the sitting position. Just wait.

2. Ignore your dog as he jumps up, licks at your fist and tries everything in his power to get you to open your fist and give him a treat.

3. Suddenly, he will pause with a fairly intelligent look in his eye and start thinking. He will think about how he was able to access those treats by having his rear end on the ground.

4. When your dog places himself in the sitting position, reward your dog with an entire handful—the jackpot—and end your training session.

When You Resume Training

1. When you resume training, do not lure your dog into the sitting position. Merely show him the food and wait him out. Let your dog figure this out for himself. Not only is it great fun to watch the wheels and cogs of a dog's mind at work, but your dog enjoys the challenge and mental stimulation.

2. When he offers you a sit, feed him one food treat.

3. Walk a few steps so that the dog gets up out of position, and repeat, until your dog is sitting *ad nauseam*, to get any and all attention from you.

Using the Sit

1. Wait for your dog to offer a sit before going out the door to the back-yard or out the front door for his walk.

2. Wait for your dog to offer a sit before placing his food bowl down during mealtimes.

3. Wait for your dog to offer a sit before you clip his leash on.

4. Wait for that sit any time your dog wants something, then reward him with whatever he wanted.

5. The more and varied rewards a dog will work for, the stronger the behavior, and the more reliable.

COMING WHEN CALLED

This is probably the most important command your dog will ever have to follow. All members of your household should be using the same command, and your command should be just that—a command. If you casually call your dog to come when he's in the yard by blowing kissing sounds and saying, "Come here, sweetheart," I guarantee that is *not* how you will sound when you stop at a rest area on the thruway and your dog accidentally leaps out of the car and is running down the highway.

You will need a consistent command that will be there for you in an emergency: "(Dog's Name), come! Gooood dog, yay, gooooooood, wonderful." Say his name first, then the command: "come."

Then praise and coach him in. Let him know that the entire process of coming toward you is just as great as getting to you, and you appreciate that the travel is the hard part. This also lets your dog know that you aren't angry at him for being away in the first place (even if you are angry!), and it also motivates your dog to see you as a good target to go to.

To start with, model what you want your dog to do: Go right up to his nose with your hands filled with goodies. Command him "(Dog's Name), come," and use the treats to lure him to turn around and come just a few steps toward you.

Remember, he must *tag* you. Your treats/hands should be touching your pants or skirt at your dog's height, so that you're assured he will always come in close enough to be grabbed by his collar in an emergency.

When he gets to you, praise, pet and hug him, and give him anywhere from one to a handful of treats. Tell him "OK" and release him to go back to what he was doing. Repeat. Let your dog see that calling him is merely a delightful interruption of his fun, not an end to it.

Gradually get further and further away before you call him. Always run backward a few steps so that you are enticing and fun, and your dog always learns to turn around, leave what he was doing and come to you.

This is the one command I never stop giving my dogs food treats for. It is so important, so hard to maintain control of, and the off-lead world is so alluring, I want to be able to have something equally enticing to offer my dog. Forever. It is worth it to me, and I am sure it is worth it for my dogs. Let the only time you don't have a reward be the one time you are unprepared in an emergency. Then it won't matter to your dog that you don't have a food treat, because he won't find this out until he gets to you—and then he is safe anyway.

Always praise, reward and appreciate your dog for coming. Vary the type of food treat and how generous you are. Keep it exciting. Introduce the concept of a jackpot: something huge and excellent and unexpected for coming when called, like an entire pile of goodies, or a huge slab of liver, or a rawhide bone, or pull out his food dish and pour in his kibble, and right then and there let him have his adored meal.

When you are calling him away from something distracting, like a squirrel, or to come indoors from playing in the yard or a park, let your dog believe that coming when called is merely an interruption: praise, treat, then release with "OK" and send your dog back away to play. Then, when you really do need your dog to come in and stop having fun, he won't mind as much.

This is one command that can never be taken for granted. You must be willing to continue training and rewarding and motivating and jackpotting your dog from now until the day he dies—so he won't die early from running away and being hit by a car.

WHAT TO DO IF YOUR NEW DOG GETS CARSICK

Many dogs start out being nervous in cars. Some salivate heavily; some drool and vomit. Many people worry that car sickness is a permanent condition in a dog. It is not. The fastest and most effective way to cure carsickness is to pack up your car for a weekend camping trip, at least four hours away from home. Bring your dog and spend the weekend hiking, enjoying the outdoors, camping and living out of your vehicle. Feed your dog once a day at the end of the day.

Bring lots of paper towels and plenty of blankets to cover the car seats. But you won't need them for very long. The more you live out of your car and persist in spending lots of time driving to fun places and hiking and walking and swimming and other things, the faster your dog will acclimate. Since the car will feel like his home, he will simply get used to it.

This seems like the last thing owners of carsick dogs want to do or are willing to try, but it is basically foolproof. And you'll have a great weekend.

HELPING YOUR DOG STAY HOME ALONE

Teaching your dog that you are not abandoning him when you leave him home alone is not always easy. Dogs who have come from the shelter are very ready to bond with you, and they usually form instant, very strong, deep bonds. The same holds true for most people adopting a dog from the shelter. People who choose to save a life by adopting a shelter dog usually form bonds with their dogs that are just as intense. Both you and your dog can feel devastated the first time you have to leave the dog alone. The earlier in the relationship you set things straight and start practicing this, the better your dog will feel, the better you will feel, and the better the relationship will be.

The most important way to make sure you have a confident, relaxed dog when he is left alone is to give your dog strong and strict guidance, especially in the first few weeks after the adoption. Just when you feel sorry for him and want to overpamper him, the kindest thing you can do is set firm, clear limits. If you run the household and provide good leadership, your dog will follow directions and will feel more confident overall. A dog who feels confident because of your good leadership will feel equally confident and comfortable when you leave him alone.

Here are some recommendations to prepare you and your dog for separation:

- Be very casual about departures and arrivals, including leaving your dog when you take a shower, use the toilet, run upstairs to get something, etc.

- The best way to prepare your dog for separation is to implement dozens of teeny tiny departures in the house. Close doors behind you, and move about the house doing little jobs by yourself sometimes. Your dog needs to learn that it is not necessary to follow you everywhere, especially if he is not comfortable or unfamiliar with being left alone.

- Don't look back.

- Start all these recommendations as soon as you bring your dog home. That very day. It is never too soon to help you and your dog feel comfortable being apart.

- Depart the house frequently—walk out the front door, closing it behind you, then turn right around and walk back in. Do this until it becomes commonplace for your dog. Ignore your dog completely while heading out and returning back. Pretend he is invisible during departures and arrivals.

- If your television is usually on when you're home, leave it on when you go. Don't just turn it on when you are ready to leave (that's like announcing on a bullhorn that you're leaving). Turn it on well before you leave, then leave it on as background comfort. Same for radios. Recent studies have shown that dogs are calmed by classical music. So change your own taste in music, if necessary, at least half an hour before leaving, and 20 minutes before *preparing* to leave as well.

- You must feel OK about leaving, and then your dog will, too. So much of the anxiety about separation comes from both owner and dog. If one feels confident, so will the other.

DON'T BE A SPECTATOR

Although your dog may be very entertaining, no dog needs you to be a mere spectator in his life. In particular, when your dog alerts to noises outside the home, alerts to the arrival of a guest or visitor at the door, or approaches or is approached by a stranger or an unfamiliar dog on the street, you need to intervene and arrange for a good ending.

The events I've just listed are the most common ones in which dogs can develop serious behavior problems. Standing by and watching as your dog alerts, barks, erupts and rushes the front door when he hears someone arrive ensures that your dog will direct his own action, rehearse his own behavioral sequence, and perform his own ending. At first, nothing may happen other than barking. You might even be pleased that your dog alerts you to the presence of a stranger. But each time your dog rehearses this sequence, he can move incrementally toward a potentially serious behavior problem. Left to his own direction, a dog may ultimately end up nipping at or biting the visitor who arrives at the door. Not because your dog is mean, but simply because he will have practiced this same sequence over and over again, enjoying himself immensely. With each sequence, your dog improves his skills, increasing his bark, his speed and his desire to chase away or scare off the intruder. He has the leading role in this performance; each time he adds more to his role, until, ultimately, he may change the ending.

So many people just watch as their dog rehearses his own actions, and they don't intervene because nothing bad ever happens. Your dog isn't mean; your dog doesn't nip or bite. Your dog would never bite, you think. But the truth is that all dogs can bite, and no one ever really thinks their own dog could. Young dogs usually don't bite. But month after month, year after year, until your dog reaches maturity at three or four years of age, your dog can develop into a biter, if he is allowed to rehearse his own sequence of events.

Really, really good dogs don't ever have a problem. Really, really bad dogs will have a problem no matter how much you intervene or try to change them. But the majority of dogs are somewhere in the middle, and could develop either way—into a mature good dog or a mature bad dog. The more you intervene and direct your dog's actions, the more you can steer him into becoming or remaining a good dog.

The same holds true for owners whose dogs get along with *most* other dogs (or kids or cats or people), but every once in awhile, for no apparent reason, their dog growls, nips or attempts to bite. These owners become spectators—they wait and see what the dog is going to do. They watch his behavior unfold, waiting to see if he'll be OK with this dog (or kid or cat or person)—or not. Owners put themselves in the audience and wait to see if the play ends happily or tragically. Will your dog get along with this approaching dog, or will he fight with him?

The best role to take is that of director. Make happy endings by directing your dog's life. Make sure your dog rehearses an act you approve of. Break into the scene early on, when your dog hasn't finished his actions, and make the story end the way you want it to. Redirect your dog's attention, change his emotions, alter the final performance, so that each time your dog starts barking, you call him over to you, make him sit and interrupt his behavior chain of charging the front door. You direct what you want to happen at the front door.

The simple rule is to interrupt your dog early on in the sequence—call his name, call him over, reward him for coming over, give him new directives (sit, lie down, stay, look at you, sit again, give paw, whatever . . .), and then release him to go off on his own after he has forgotten what he was doing and is thinking only of what you and he just practiced.

Stop your dog from barking at the first bark, or the first hint of a bark. Don't wait for him to bark for two minutes, run to the source of the noise and ratchet up the intensity. You'll never really train that first bark out of him, so don't worry about stifling his protectiveness. Your goal is to try to predict when he is thinking of barking, so you can easily interrupt him or even thwart the behavior. If you don't get right on your dog for barking, you're likely to end up with a barker. It is a very self-reinforcing behavior. You'll never be able to shut him up entirely (most dogs will still get out that first alarm bark) but you can learn to cut him off. For the one actual burglar he might identify in your lifetime, he will bark at thousands of visitors and noises, and that will not be helpful. In fact, you'll find that because of that one time in your life you may actually need your dog to bark to alert you to harm, you (and others) will need to just put up with the irritation of his barking all the rest of the time. At the first hint of a bark, interrupt your dog and give him something better to do. Interrupt your dog and then call him over to you. Reward him for coming to you. Have him sit in front of you and reward him for sitting in front of you. Keep him sitting in front of you until he can forget about whatever he was barking at. That is usually at least 20 seconds. The more often you intervene and direct the scenes, the better you can ensure the ultimate outcomes.

EXTRACURRICULAR ACTIVITIES

Most parents wouldn't dream of not enrolling their child in at least one extracurricular activity, and dog owners should feel the same. A dog, too, needs at least one hobby or class or extracurricular activity to maintain his mind and instincts, and to give him an outlet to be a dog. When a dog has no outlet to be a dog, his "doggy" part will come out in unwanted ways and at unwanted times. Your terrier mix may hunt for imaginary (you hope) rats by digging in and gutting your couch and cushions. Your herding dog mix may run ahead of you and your family when going up or down the stairs, trying to turn the flock around, or try to bolt through doorways first, to turn you around and control you. Your retriever mix may take your clothes in his mouth (while you or your children are still wearing them) and fetch you or them somewhere, or take your guests by their hand (in the dog's mouth) and try to pull them inside. When dogs are dogs, they do natural things like dig, chew, bark, run, howl, jump, chase, pounce and more. You can inhibit and suppress just so much. Plain old aerobic exercise is good, but it doesn't satisfy a dog's instincts and natural urges.

Before Embarking on a Physical Activity With Your Dog

Don't try any strenuous physical activity or sport with your dog without first consulting your veterinarian for a full workup and exam. Your veterinarian can ascertain how fit and orthopedically sound your dog is, and whether he is ready for strenuous activity.

The same holds true for you. Before attempting a new physical activity or sport, make sure your own health is checked out. See your doctor; see your veterinarian. Then have fun.

The following sections discuss just a few of the hobbies and activities available for you and your new dog.

Dog Agility

Dog agility is a sport you have may have seen on cable television, on Animal Planet or even ESPN. In agility, the dog and his handler run an obstacle course consisting of jumps, tunnels, A-frames, cat-walks (called dog-walks in agility), weave poles and more. This is a very popular activity, and many dog clubs and dog training schools offer classes. There are no special requirements, but your dog should be the proper weight before asking him to jump or be athletic.

Dog agility is fun and enhances the bond between dog and owner. It is also an excellent way to train a dog to come when called, even when off leash and outdoors, and to come reliably even when the dog is having fun and is a little out of control, since that is how agility feels to a dog. The wonderful thing about agility training is that it is intensely fun for both you and the dog, and yet he cannot do it or enjoy it without you.

Agility is the universal instinct sport for breeds and mixes that do not have a true instinct for a particular job. A Border Collie was bred to herd, and that is his instinct, but a Pomeranian/Labrador/American Eskimo Dog mix does not have a true instinct and job he was bred to do. Still, this individual dog needs to satisfy his natural, mixed-up urges to gather a flock, retrieve a bird, chase his prey, look for direction from an owner and all the rest, and agility is the grand, one-for-all satisfying sport for all dogs.

The nice thing about dog agility training is that, except for teaching your dog not to pull on leash, it covers all other helpful training commands: sit, down, stay, come and pay attention. Agility is a sport for all dogs—mixed breeds and purebreds.

Tracking

Tracking is a sport in which a dog uses his nose to sniff out the path a human has taken from start to finish, and to be able to locate any lost or dropped articles. The dog is taught to follow the ground scent (crushed vegetation and body scent that has settled into the footprints along the path the person he is tracking has taken). Tracking is something all dogs know how to do, and the training is to get us to communicate to them how we want them to do it, and exactly which scent to follow.

Tracking is also a wonderful activity for dogs who may not be able to cope in a group setting with other dogs or strangers—some dogs are too fearful with people, or maybe too aggressive with other dogs, to concentrate in a traditional group dog training class. Tracking is often done one on one, and once an instructor gets you and your dog started, you can practice on your own.

There are competitions where dogs can gain titles in this sport, but it is just plain fun and awe-inspiring to watch your dog use his unbelievable sense of smell, not to mention the fact that training for tracking is usually done in the most beautiful scenic areas.

Even more amazing, although a lot less scenic, is urban tracking, sometimes called variable surface tracking, which is the art of teaching your dog to track the scent of someone who has walked in an urban area, such as on pavement, across a parking lot, across an abandoned, overgrown asphalt lot and across streets.

If you love the outdoors, this activity is for you. All breeds and breed mixes can do this, any size, any shape nose. Bloodhounds may have the Hollywood reputation for having a good sense of smell, but the most squashed Bulldog and the tiniest Chihuahua mix can do it equally well.

Herding

For every herding breed there is a different style of herding—Corgis are bred to do one thing, Border Collies another, German Shepherd Dogs yet another. The instinct to work a flock is so strong that many herding dog mixes are capable of doing the work their ancestors were bred to do.

The herding instinct is a sequence of inherited behaviors that are selected for and shaped to enhance the dog's ability to naturally work livestock in ways that are helpful. The sequence of behaviors is common to all dogs of any breed, so many nonherding breeds may still have a strong ability to gather and bring in a flock. At a vacation dog camp where I teach each summer, all dogs of any breed type are allowed to get into the sheep pen and try herding. Often the most unexpected breeds are the most capable—one year a Basset Hound and a Maltese showed the most promising herding instincts. So no matter what kind of mixed breed or purebred you have, it is worth trying to find a working sheepdog farm with a trainer who offers herding instinct testing. If your dog shows enough instincts, it may be worthwhile to sign up for some lessons. While you probably don't need a dog capable of doing the work, there is nothing as impressive and moving as watching a dog do what his ancient instincts are telling him to do. It can put the hair up on the back of your neck to watch your dog's instincts take over and see him doing what he was bred to do, with skill and knowledge greater than anything you could teach him.

Years ago, I took my then-wild-and-crazy young German Shepherd Dog for a herding instinct test. Every behavior I had thought was neurotic, uncontrollable, lunatic and difficult was in one moment transformed into the most exquisite natural herding ability. For over an hour I watched, entranced, as he began patrolling the flock, knowing instinctively what to do and how and when to do it. All this from a dog found as a stray in Queens, New York, who had certainly never seen a sheep before! I signed him up for lessons, and took him weekly for the next two years. It was an absolute joy to give him this work. I never did learn to read the flock well myself, or ever really learn what I should do to help my dog, but he worked away, ever patient with me, taking over the care and movement of the stock when I was completely incompetent. It transformed my crazy German Shepherd Dog from a seemingly unfocused and out of control dog into a focused and intense working companion. The training and outlet he received each week satisfied his natural urges, exhausted him physically and emotionally, and he came out a better trained, much better behaved pet dog. In fact, I sort of ended up worshipping his talents and abilities. I saw him in a whole new way. I was able to experience some of the best a dog has to offer—a rare, intimate peek into the world of animals and instincts.

Musical Freestyle

This activity involves less instinct and athletic ability than many of the other canine sports. Canine musical freestyle takes ordinary obedience commands and pairs them with tricks, and then sets it all to music for a moving and entertaining way for handlers and dogs to work and train together.

Musical freestyle actually requires absolutely no musical ability or even a sense of rhythm—unless your goal is national competition. Your dog doesn't care how many left feet you have, he just appreciates the training.

This performance sport is popular as a challenging activity for people and smart, underused dogs. There are two main organizations that support it. One is little more serious and rigid, including very specialized moves similar to dressage in horses. The other is a bit more wild and creative, incorporating tricks and very stylized routines. The choice of music is up to the individual.

Frisbee or Disc Dog

Once you can learn to throw properly, the world of disc and Frisbee play opens up for your dog. Many dogs don't actually even seem to care if you cannot throw the Frisbee very well. A dog will run out and scoop up the disc as it rolls upside down along the grass.

There are competitive events for freestyle Frisbee and also toss 'n fetch. In freestyle Frisbee, a handler and their dog work a routine to music that includes fancy Frisbee throws, dance moves, classy tricks and athletic prowess, often including maneuvers where the dog leaps off the handler's back and catches a Frisbee in midair, or weaves through the handler's legs and suddenly cartwheels, catching the Frisbee in mid-cartwheel. There are no breed restrictions.

The dogs best suited for Frisbee are the ones who like to retrieve, or at least chase moving objects. But any dog can enjoy playing fetch with a Frisbee in the backyard or at the park. Craig Rogers, one of the country's current top Frisbee competitors, teaches classes on how to get your dog interested in the Frisbee. If your dog seems like a dud at catching on, Craig suggests starting by rolling the Frisbee along the ground and encouraging him to chase after it. If your dog seems to forget the part where he is supposed to bring the Frisbee back, try running backward and calling him when he picks it up. With some dogs who initially don't seem interested at all, a Frisbee switch seems to get flipped on, and all of a sudden one day your dog loves to and can competently catch the Frisbee.

Rally-Obedience

Rally-Obedience, or Rally-O as it is more casually known, is one of the newest dog sports to become popular. Rally-O is a combination of standard obedience training and agility moves. The sport involves the handler and dog following a predetermined course consisting of a series of signs that indicate what commands to perform.

The training for Rally-O is a great combination of traditional obedience and more spontaneous creative additions. It is appropriate for all dogs, all ages, all sizes, all physical capabilities; any dog would benefit from the mental energy spent in learning so many behaviors and combinations of commands.

More and more dog training clubs are offering Rally-Obedience classes, so finding a convenient class to fit your schedule should not be difficult.

Trick Training

Tricks are not an official sport (although many great dog trainers offer extra classes and workshops in tricks), but an endless list of behaviors to teach your dog. There are the classics: sit pretty, take a bow, play dead, roll over, shake hands and speak (not recommended unless you really like barking . . .). For some challenging ideas, watch *Late Night With David Letterman*. His "Stupid Pet Tricks" segment is a goldmine of creative and intriguing tricks.

A number of excellent trick training books have recently been published, and many of the current and popular dog training techniques involving positive reinforcement instead of punishment lend themselves to some pretty amazing behaviors.

There is nothing silly or stupid about tricks. Tricks are to dogs what books are to humans. We challenge and expand our minds and imaginations when we read, we enjoy a good book, we look forward to a good book and we don't want it to end. Good reading makes our brains work harder and exercises our minds. Tricks are like that for dogs.

Pet-Assisted Therapy

If your dog has a gregarious and sweet nature and can't seem to get enough petting and attention, and you are the sort of person who likes helping other people, then pet-assisted therapy work may be for you. On the human side of things, it requires no specialized training or degrees on the part of the owner, just good people skills and a time commitment. Besides a good, solid temperament and a true joy at meeting new people, a therapy dog needs little extra training after his foundation of basic obedience and manners.

There are many different venues to consider visiting with your dog. There are therapy dogs visiting nursing homes, homeless shelters, school programs, cancer centers, pediatric cancer wards, hospices, head injury rehabilitation centers, and therapy dogs who work with the developmentally disabled and autistic people, just to name a few. Many dogs prefer different populations over others. Many owners feel more comfortable with one type of facility over another. Even with as little as one visit a month, you and your dog can make a difference to other people in your community.

Once you have trained your dog (or perhaps your adopted dog came to you well trained), you can have him evaluated and officially certified as a therapy dog with one of the two main organizations: the Delta Society and Therapy Dogs International. Owners of registered therapy dogs are covered by insurance through the certification agency. Also, many institutions will only allow registered therapy dogs on the premises. The organization you register with can help you find facilities in your area. And what a great way to show the world how wonderful your shelter dog is!

Earthdog

For terriers and terrier mixes, Dachshunds and Dachshund mixes who are bred to "go to ground" (hunt and dig out vermin from underground tunnels), earthdog training offers the opportunity to go hunting without the risk or bloodshed of actual hunting. Bales of hay are used to create a burrow and a den, and dogs take turns doing what their genes are telling them to do. It is a far better thing to let them dig it out of their systems at an earthdog event than to watch a terrier mix destroy your garden.

Skijoring

Both skijoring and dog sledding require at least a few inches of snow. So they are dependent on both the weather and your geography. Nonetheless, it is worth mentioning these sports since they are so much fun and require no specific breed or mix, or any special training. Skijoring is cross-country skiing with a special elastic waistband to which your dog is attached by harness and gang-line. Your dog whisks you forward while you cross-country ski. Not being a very expert skier myself, I consider it "extreme" cross-country skiing.

It is a wonderful thing to be moving as fast as your dog for mile after mile. And I find any sport or outdoor activity I include my dog in becomes so much more enjoyable than it would be alone. Outdoor dog sports keep me fit and committed to my exercise routines; they keep my dog healthy and active outdoors, and healthy and tired indoors. The perfect dog!

There is, amazingly, no real size or weight minimum necessary to have fun skijoring. In fact, there are times I wish I had a smaller and lighter dog than my 21-pound herding mix, Bea, because it still sometimes feels too fast for my two left skis.

Dog Sledding

Imagine standing on the back of a wicker kick-sled, being pulled along a path in a snowy wilderness, the only sound the whoosh of the sled runners and the running of the dogs. The dogs are joyous doing this, which is one of the reasons the sport is so enjoyable. The enthusiasm and pure joy the dogs experience is inspiring.

You do not need a Husky or any sort of northern breed to have fun dogsledding. If you want to try the sport without your dog first, to see if you enjoy it, there are many dog-sledding vacation tours where they teach you about the sport and then take you out on some rides, ranging from a few hours to a few days.

If you enjoy the sport, you can give it a whirl with your dog. The most promising candidate for this sport is simply a dog who pulls strongly on leash. The perfect dog has nothing to do with breed type, and not much to do with size, although if your dog weighs less than 35 pounds, it is helpful to have more than one dog pulling you (see Chapter 9 for tips on adopting a second dog). Small, lightweight kick-sleds are inexpensive, and the only further equipment needed is a padded dog-sledding harness and gang-line. If you do cross-country skijoring already, you will only need to purchase the sled.

Backpacking

Often, having a dog can motivate you to try things you have not yet tried. Backpacking or day hiking with your dog is one of those activities that is one thing without a dog, and a whole other experience with a dog. A dog is great company in the backcountry, and he helps you feel safe as well. And dogs are the kind of companions who can keep you company and at the same time respect your need to be alone, since they never interrupt with conversation or opinions.

There are even little dog packs that rest on your dog's back like saddlebags and enable him to carry his own food, water and supplies. There really is not much extra training needed before you can drive out into the country and hike: just a reliable "come" command (see pages 160–161) and/or good on-leash skills—although even without that, getting pulled on the trails isn't the worst thing, especially going uphill.

Mountain Biking

Again, to enjoy the trails on your bike with your new dog requires no special training other than a reliable "come" command. In the absence of reliability, a padded sled dog harness and a line attached to the front of your bike afford you a thrilling time on the trails. The harness and line was my solution to the puzzle of how to enjoy the great outdoors with a hound mix who wasn't reliable off leash, and loves pulling on leash (a lot more than I do).

Road Bicycling

There is an attachment you can purchase for your bike that comes off the side and has a hook for your dog's leash. Because it has a spring in it, it has lots of give, and it is pretty easy to stay upright and balanced on your bike even with the sometimes erratic running of your dog. You'll need to be careful when pedaling with your dog on pavement, because in just a short while the concrete or asphalt can wear down your dog's paw pads. You need to take special care and watch out for this, since most dogs will not limp or give any indication while out on the road (they're usually having too much fun), but will come up lame and with bloody pads when you arrive home or at the car.

If you haven't ridden a bike since you were a child, get back on, take a few practice rides, and then, when you're comfortable, try attaching your dog. Just do short rides to start; starting on more remote and less trafficked roads is a good idea. Remember your helmet.

Mountain Scootering

A mountain scooter is a relatively new thing—a hybrid of a mountain bike and a scooter. It looks essentially like a mountain bike, but instead of a seat and pedals, it has a skateboard or scooter platform on which to stand. They're fun all by themselves, but incredibly fun when you hook up your dog on his sledding harness and attach a line to the front of the scooter. You can stop even the strongest of dogs when you need to, even without a command, just by squeezing the hand brakes.

This activity can also border on the extreme, as you can get some serious speed going. It is great exercise for you and your dog, and it gets you both out on the trails. I cannot recommend it highly enough.

Other Activities

There are many other sports and events you and your dog can participate in. Some events are like the snooty (if not racist) country clubs of the past and do not allow mixed breeds, but the world of dogs is changing; most instinct sports and dog activities are now open to all breeds and mixes.

Your local dog training club or dog training instructor can probably introduce you to more.

When in Public With Your Dog

Remember, always bring baggies to scoop your dog's poop, or, if you're in the backcountry or out on the trails—use two sticks as chopsticks and pluck up each bit of poop and hurl it deep into the woods and off the trail. Every time another hiker comes upon a pile of dog poop, it gives all dogs a bad reputation and threatens to destroy our freedom to take our dogs on the trails. No one likes to step in dog poop—not on a city sidewalk, not deep in the woods on the trails.

Trail and Sidewalk Etiquette

Whether you are walking, hiking, biking, skiing or dogsledding, proper trail etiquette applies to all. When you come across other trail walkers or sidewalk pedestrians, no matter what they say about how much they love dogs, always reel in your dog (if he's on leash or harness) or call over and leash your dog (if he's off leash); get off your equipment; walk; and keep your dog in a heel position (at either side of you, walking at your pace aligned with your hip). Many people are seriously afraid of dogs, and even if you know your dog will just run past, the other person does not, and it can be frightening to have a large, speeding dog coming at you. Certainly, if the oncoming hiker or pedestrian has a dog, you must gather in your dog to walk past them.

Flexi-leashes have their place in giving leashed dogs extra room for exploration, but are like chainsaws when the dog is given too much line in a crowded environment. Courtesy means reeling in your dog and locking your Flexi-leash at its shortest length when you are anywhere near other people or dogs.

If you don't have absolute control of your dog and cannot call your dog instantly off an oncoming, loose dog, then your dog does not belong off leash in an area where there is any chance of running into other pet owners and their dogs.

Letting a long-line or an extra long leash drag behind a dog who is unreliable or still in training can afford the same freedom as being off leash, but enables you to quickly step on the end of the leash and physically reel the dog in when others approach. The critical elements in all of this are maintaining proper trail manners and keeping a good image of dogs in the public eye.

If you have a dog who occasionally barks or displays (lunges, leaps up and down, acts aggressive or out of control) at the end of his leash, or accidentally gets loose and runs over to another dog, *always always always* apologize profusely for your own dog's behavior—*even if you know or believe it was not your dog's fault*. It does absolutely no good to find fault (deserved or not) in the other dog or owner; it does improve relations for all future encounters to apologize and continue on. More important than being "right" is the fact that you will, in all likelihood, encounter the same dogs and owners again in your lifetime, and it serves everyone well to try to get along.

Chapter 8

When All Else Fails

There may be any number of reasons why you reach the point where you feel you can no longer keep a dog. Most reasons have their roots in problem behaviors, or mismatches between the dog and other animals in the home. Almost nobody who started out wanting and then adopted a dog decides to bail for frivolous or petty reasons. Sometimes the reason we give may sound trivial (the dog needs more room to run, the dog got too big, the dog needs someone who is home more), but they are shadows of the real reasons, which remain elusive unless you understand dog behavior. No one should judge you if you feel you do not have the right home for a dog. Any shelter that cares about its dogs will welcome back (or *should* welcome back) an adoptee.

One of the real reasons it is so hard to come up with accurate and valid descriptions of the behaviors that cause a dog to be returned is that if the behavior problem is serious, or cannot be corrected by training, then ultimately the dog could get euthanized, and nobody wants that. In fact, we'd practically go to any lengths to avoid that. So we say of a dog who tears up the house, howls, salivates and has panic attacks whenever left alone, "He just needs someone who is home more." Of the dominant aggressive dog who makes us uncomfortable at times, or sometimes even frightens us, we say, "He needs more room to run."

PROBLEM BEHAVIORS AND WHAT TO DO

The following is a simplified breakdown of problem behaviors or questionable behaviors, and suggestions for dealing with them.

House Training

If your dog is peeing or pooping in the house when you are home, or when you are not looking, or when you are in another room—you are probably experiencing a house-training problem. This is not a cause for alarm, although it can feel extremely frustrating, as this behavior problem tends to confront you several times a day. But if you enlist the advice of a professional dog trainer, this is a problem likely to be solved in a short amount of time. Stick with this problem until it is resolved.

There are many instances of puppies who reportedly house-train themselves: owners who declare that within three days, or one day, or one week, their puppy was completely house-trained. I would almost rather hear that someone is experiencing house-training problems, because I have seen a link between puppies (eight to 14 weeks old) who house-train readily and almost immediately, and serious dominance issues—sometimes dominance aggression. But fear not—this is not to say that every house-trained puppy, or every puppy that was easy to house-train, is aggressive. It's just an informal link I have noticed with some puppies. It makes me feel some relief when an owner calls with a puppy who is having many accidents.

If your dog is lifting his (or sometimes her) leg or leaving small spots of pee on or near vertical surfaces, and this is done either when you're home or when you're not home, it's a urine marking problem. This is also solvable, and sometimes all the dog needs is more time for his neutering to kick in. With the help of a professional trainer, this problem is likely to be easily resolved.

If your dog is peeing or pooping only when (or primarily when) left alone, you are more likely to have some separation problems and less likely to have a house-training accident. This problem is also very solvable, and you should seek the advice of a professional dog trainer.

Destructiveness

If your dog is chewing on or destroying items in your home (pillows, books, TV remote, shoes, table legs, furniture, bedding, etc.) mostly when you're not home, and often starts to gnaw on things when you are home (but you can stop him), this is likely a simple destructiveness problem. It's sometimes due to boredom, lack of exercise or mental or physical stimulation, or just because the dog is still an adolescent (they like to crush, kill, destroy things . . .). This is very fixable. This dog can benefit from group dog training classes, or a hobby, as well as a session with a dog training professional for personalized suggestions for help.

If your dog is destroying your personal items and tearing up carpets or flooring near exits and/or windows, or destroying doorways, windows, escape routes and exits when he is left alone, he is probably experiencing serious separation problems, and is not just being destructive because he is bored. This type of destructiveness can often be accompanied by vocalizations (howling, whining, nonrhythmic barking or combinations of these), and sometimes also pooping or peeing when the dog is alone. These can indicate a serious separation problem.

While this is usually a pretty serious behavior problem, it is well worth putting every effort into resolving it, since dogs likely to exhibit this problem are also typically extra sweet, loving and highly social, so their good points are as extreme as their problem behavior. The sad truth is also that dogs with severe separation problems do not re-home well. This is one behavior problem that tends to get much worse in the next home, since each abandonment further aggravates the problem. This is not to say that you should stick it out or live with the problem just because the alternative might be euthanasia. This is a serious problem, and one that causes tremendous distress, not just to the owner; a dog with serious separation problems is not just a nuisance; he is a very anxious and suffering dog unless the problem can be resolved (and it cannot always be successfully resolved).

Usually, regular dog obedience training (while it cannot hurt) does not improve this problem. Your first choice for help may be with a veterinary behaviorist (a veterinarian who is also board certified in behavior) or a dog trainer who is well versed in dealing with severe separation problems. Your dog will need an immediate program of behavior modification and sometimes short-term adjunct medications, especially for the immediate future.

Mouthing

If your dog is very mouthy—that is, he uses his mouth and teeth (even if the pressure is very gentle) in play, during greeting, when he jumps up, when you take him by the collar to guide him or move him or hold him back from something—these are all potential signs of a behavior problem rather than simply a training problem. Puppies are all mouthy, but a dog over four months old who does a lot of mouthing/teething/gnawing of your hands, feet or arms, especially when jumping up, when excited or when playing, can be a rambunctious type who needs more training and exercise and stimulation. He can also have a more serious dominance issue, bordering on dominance aggression. Either way, this dog needs both a private behavioral evaluation by someone who is experienced in understanding and evaluating temperament, and an adjunct group dog training class.

If your dog does any mounting or humping of humans, whether the humans are in his household or are guests, this should be evaluated by a dog training professional. If your dog humps pillows or other dogs, or "air humps," it is not a concern (maybe a little embarrassing for you) unless the dog finds self-pleasure and begins to increase the frequency and intensity of his object humping (masturbation). Mounting humans can be anything from a benign state of arousal to a symptom of serious dominance problems, and the diagnosis should be left to a professional.

Pulling

If your dog pulls you mercilessly when on leash, this is usually very easily solved with a change in collar or equipment. In addition, you and your dog should sign up immediately for a fun group dog training class. Or, you can do what I did after five years of struggling with a big, strong dog who pulled relentlessly on leash: Fit her with a sled dog harness and take up the sport of mushing.

Growling

If you have heard your dog growl at you or a family member, no matter what the reason (except in the midst of play, and then the growl should not have been accompanied by direct eye contact), you need to contact a dog training professional for an evaluation into the meaning of the growl(s). A growl can be a fairly meaningless one-time event, or it can indicate a serious threat. Growling is not what a dog does *instead* of biting; growling is always a warning that the dog is *thinking* of biting. Many people believe that when a dog growls but doesn't bite, he is telling them he won't bite. The opposite is true. He is telling you, in as nice a way as a dog can, that his growling is a precursor to biting unless you understand what he is saying. To do this, you will need a professional evaluation.

If your dog has growled at a guest, stranger or visitor at the door, or at an approaching stranger or friend in the street or out in the neighborhood, he should also be evaluated by a professional, although the dog's motivations for growling are usually different than for growling at familiar people. In this case, the dog may be growling more out of a fear of unfamiliar people, or out of a territorial sense. This is best nipped in the bud, and should immediately be evaluated by a dog training professional. It is not something huge to worry about; it can be worked on easily when addressed early on—can quickly develop into something more stubborn or dangerous if left alone.

If your dog has growled at an object, or at something new or changed in his environment (for example, a garbage bag placed in the street at nighttime, or a homeless person approaching with many coats on, wheeling a supermarket cart and talking loudly to himself), or because he hears a noise in the hallway or out on the street—this is usually not serious enough to warrant a call to a professional. But you should be aware that the best way to respond to the growling dog in these circumstances is to either ignore him and continue heartily on with whatever you were doing—thereby setting a confident and carefree example—or ignore your dog and march boldly up to whatever object your dog growled at (perhaps not the homeless person) and squat down and investigate it yourself, or touch and talk confidently and happily to the object—thereby setting a confident, carefree and curious example. What you *don't* want to do is to try to soothe or calm your dog, or tell him, "It's OK." That strategy can work better with a child, who has the gift of intellect and verbal language, which a dog doesn't. A dog only picks up your tone of voice and timing of attention, so a dog who growls at a strange object because he is afraid of it and gets soothed by his owner will interpret that as a reward for and encouragement of his fear and growling.

Lots of Energy

If your dog seems hyper and very active, as if he needs more exercise than you feel you can give him, but he has no other behavior problems, then you need to get off your own butt and exercise with him, fulfilling his needs while making yourself healthier. If you cannot join in on the exercise because of physical or medical limitations, there are still plenty of ways to give your dog the exercise, and to enjoy it vicariously. Dogs who don't naturally retrieve things can be taught to. Other people in your neighborhood can be enlisted or hired to help exercise your dog.

If all your dog needs to be happy and calm and better behaved is to have more exercise, then you *do* have the time, and you *can* and *will* provide this for him. That is your commitment and responsibility to this dog, and you owe it to him and to yourself. You need to make the time in your crowded life for exercise anyway; it's good for you, and something you need to do to keep healthy in every way. You know this, you have always known this, and now here is your chance to make a lifestyle change and keep your promise to this dog.

Don't think that there is someone out there with more time who would do better with the dog. No one in this day and age has time. There are people who simply create the time and space to get out and move, and those who lament that they have no time. Make time. It's what your physician wants for you, it's what will make you feel better about yourself, it will make you healthier, and here is your actual excuse to get it done.

Join a dog training class for your dog's mental health, then spend a half hour every day, either in the morning or in the evening or whenever—get outside, and walk briskly, run, hike, bike or play Frisbee with your dog. There is nothing as good for your own physical health as a good dog. Dogs make exercise fun. Seeing the joy they get out of it will keep you on track.

Time

If you feel like you just don't have enough time for the dog, or you feel like someone else would do a better job of training him, or you feel that someone with a different schedule than yours could better handle the dog, then you need to first seek the advice of a dog training professional. Chances are, your reasoning is not just about the logistics, but rather that your dog may have an underlying, more serious, temperament or behavior problem that is hard to recognize. Your dog may have some serious issues that have not been uncovered, but are enough to give you a vague, uneasy feeling that manifests itself by convincing you that yours is just not the right home for this dog. Chances are, there is a more serious temperament issue lurking just below the surface that you are sensing, but do not want to consciously acknowledge. Acknowledging it might mean he is more of a problem dog than most people could handle. Ask yourself the following three questions:

1. How often does this dog approach me (not when I cajole or call him over) or initiate, on his own, an affectionate interaction (nuzzling, licking, coming over and sitting and wagging his tail while making soft, squinty eye contact, and so on)? Almost never, Infrequently, Sometimes, Often, or All the time?

2. If I were to look over at my dog and smile at him, how often would he put his ears back; make soft, squinty eye contact; and begin wagging

his tail? Almost never, Infrequently, Sometimes, Often, or All the time?

3. Does my dog's tail get lower when I talk to him, touch him, pet him, discipline him and hold him? Almost never, Infrequently, Sometimes, Often, or All the time?

Your answers to all of these should be either "often" or "all the time." If your answer to any of the three questions was anything else, then it's worth calling a professional dog trainer for an evaluation or a consultation before making any placement, surrender or return decisions. It may very well be that your dog has a serious underlying behavioral issue that should be fully understood before you make any decisions.

IF IT JUST DOESN'T WORK OUT

What are your options if you feel you cannot keep the dog you've adopted, or find out he's the wrong dog for you after you bring him home? Or perhaps you are reading this chapter because you already have a dog you can no longer keep. Either way, there are options available.

If You Cannot Keep Your Dog Due to Growling, Snapping, Biting or (You Think) Aggression

One option is to return your dog to the original shelter. Before you do, consider the following:

- Will the shelter listen carefully to the behavioral history of your dog, and either make an appropriate future placement (very rare and difficult to do with aggression) or take responsibility and euthanize the dog? If not, it may not be in the best interest of your dog or any future unsuspecting adopter to do so.

- Will the shelter simply re-home the dog no matter what, without either fully disclosing the dog's liabilities or even caring about the dog's aggressiveness? If the shelter is likely to do this, it may not be in the best interest of your dog or any future adopter to do so.

- Will the shelter just keep adopting him out, until finally one person keeps him or surrenders him to a different shelter, or euthanizes the dog privately? If so, it is not in the best interest of your dog to do so.

- Will the shelter keep him alive until he dies naturally (a strict no-kill policy), and if so, will the dog be housed in humane conditions for the rest of his life? If humane conditions are not being met for every dog, every day in that shelter, then it is not in your dog's best interest to return him to that shelter. If the shelter has a policy of sending unadoptable dogs out to a "sanctuary" (another no-kill facility that takes unadoptable dogs), then you need to make sure that either you or at least three staff members of that shelter have personally gone to the sanctuary and investigated and explored every nook and cranny and have seen where the dog is going to spend the rest of his life. If you wouldn't put your dog there, or if anyone at that shelter wouldn't personally place their own beloved dog in that sanctuary, then it is unconscionable to send a shelter dog there. It is equally hideous to send a dog to a sanctuary based on hearsay about the conditions at that facility, no matter how many people the shelter knows who have been to visit it or check it out. Each person responsible for the dog must personally go and investigate.

Another option is to re-home the dog yourself privately. You may be forced to if the shelter will not take back your dog. There are many risks associated with this choice.

- A dog with aggression problems should not be adopted out unless it is under the direct supervision of a professional dog trainer or behavior expert who is highly experienced with aggression, **plus** the counsel of a qualified attorney.

- Most people, even if you fully disclose and describe in detail when and where and to what extent the dog will be aggressive, do not understand what aggression really means. It is therefore irresponsible to re-home the dog, since the only person likely to adopt is someone you are duping; anyone who truly knows what aggression means would not take on the responsibility, liability and ultimate heartbreak of adopting an aggressive dog.

As you can probably tell, I am very opposed to re-homing an aggressive dog. If it is to be done at all, it should be done by responsible, experienced professionals.

Another humane option is to euthanize the dog. Certainly, there are many things to think about when it comes to this choice:

- This can be terribly painful and difficult to do, even if you know it is the right or only possible option. You may want to work with the shelter to provide the euthanasia (either with or without you being present). If you adopted the aggressive dog from a shelter, I believe it is the responsibility of that shelter to euthanize the dog (and to have screened him well enough the first time, so a person doesn't have to go through what you are going through now).

- The shelter may not work with you, in which case you will have to handle it yourself. Make sure you have a sympathetic veterinarian, one who understands euthanizing for serious behavior problems and agrees with it. There is nothing worse than coming to that final, excruciating decision, only to be treated with doubt and contempt—or worse yet, refusal when you are ready to make the appointment. It is perfectly understandable if you know it is the right decision, but cannot bring yourself to do it or to be there when it is done. There are people who cannot bring themselves to be present when a dog is euthanized, and people who feel it is necessary to be there. Neither person is better than the other. Your dog will understand and be forgiving either way.

If You Cannot Keep Your Dog but Don't Think He's Aggressive

You have a few options. The first is to privately re-home the dog. Here are a few things to consider:

- Are you equipped to properly assess this dog in order to find just the right placement for him?

- Are you equipped to properly screen callers and potential adopters?

- Are you willing to follow up for a few years, and remain committed to taking the dog back into your home if the dog is no longer wanted?

- Are you willing to take on the financial and emotional liability of re-homing the dog if he bites someone in his new home?

If the answer to any of the questions above is no, return him to the shelter where you got him (they absolutely should accept returns!) or surrender him to a shelter that is adept at re-homing and can assess your dog objectively and make the right placement or euthanasia decision. In either case, consider the following:

- If you want a "no kill" shelter, understand that almost always they will have a waiting list, sometimes months long.

- If you need an open-admission shelter that can take your dog right away, you must ask yourself: Are the conditions in which the dog will be housed humane? Will care be taken to maintain his behavioral, emotional and mental health until he finds a home? Could you find an open-admission shelter that has a very high adoption success rate? If the dog is behaviorally sound and adoptable, is it fair to surrender him to a shelter with limited resources where he may be euthanized due to lack of space or time? Is it fair to put that responsibility and stress on that shelter? Would you feel more comfortable taking responsibility for placing the dog rather than risking possible euthanasia?

When your dog is in a shelter, whether your dog lives or dies, whether your dog is ultimately adopted out or ultimately euthanized, he deserves—*it is his right*—to be cared for in humane conditions. Humane conditions are not just a given in any shelter. Just because a shelter is called a "humane society" or a "Society for the Prevention of Cruelty to Animals" does not ensure the dog will be housed in humane conditions.

Humane conditions have more to do with the type of care a dog will get and less to do with the physical setup. Cruelty to animals is not just physical abuse. Cruelty to animals comes in many forms. The shelter environment is extremely stressful for any dog: loud, echoing kennels, barking 24 hours a day, a dog to his right, a dog to his left, a dog across the aisle from him, dogs being walked and passing in front of his own kennel many times a day. The shelter dog usually lives in a constant state of arousal and overstimulation. Dogs in kennels simply do not get the same amount of human contact, touch and comforts that a house pet gets. A sociable dog deprived of sufficient human interaction is one who is truly suffering.

Dogs live in the moment. They can no more dwell on a traumatic past, worry about something they did, than they can dream of a better future. Therefore, the conditions the dog lives in day to day in the shelter, and the emotional, behavioral and mental care he gets, is critical. Even if you cannot keep your dog, or it was a mismatch in the first place, it is your responsibility to make sure your dog is going to be cared for humanely. In the ideal world, it would not be your responsibility to assess the conditions your dog would be kept in at an animal shelter; all animal shelters would provide the minimum standards for not just physical, but behavioral, emotional and mental health of the dogs in their care. But we do not live in the ideal world.

WHAT TO EXPECT WHEN CALLING THE SHELTER

You may be treated with understanding and encouraged to bring the dog back, or you may be asked to first speak with a behavioral counselor.

You may be treated with venom, and the shelter workers may believe you are a bad person who gave up on a perfectly reasonable dog because you are uncommitted and basically irresponsible and uncaring. A part of you may doubt yourself as well, and a good part of you will feel bad either way. Still, you should not be abused by the shelter staff. You are making a very difficult decision, and you did not come to it lightly. You deserve to be treated humanely.

What Sometimes Happens When You Try to Return a Dog

When asked for a one-line reason why they are surrendering their dog, people will give a one-line reason. When the shelter asks more about the dog's behavior, owners will describe their dog's problem behavior in more detail. In other words, people will reveal their dog's problems (often aggressiveness) when a shelter takes the time to ask owners meaningful questions about their dog, and to ask in a nonjudgmental and nonconfrontational way.

Shelters have spent too many years blaming owners for behaviors and circumstances that are beyond their control. Many shelter workers believe that all dogs will be fine if given enough training, time and love. When an owner returns a dog for a serious behavior problem, the shelter staff often knows that the ultimate outcome for the returned dog could be euthanasia, and this is the last thing anyone wants for a dog. So often, shelter staff will be blaming, confrontational or harsh with adopters who need or want to return a dog. Although you deserve to be treated humanely and with compassion and understanding, or at least with respect, you can expect that at many shelters you will not be treated well. And again, this is not to excuse the behavior of some shelter people, but the bad attitude is ultimately because of a huge love and caring for the dog, and concern for the dog's fate. Still, being humane is being humane; there should be as much caring and compassion for humans as there is for dogs.

Even if you signed a contract during the adoption stipulating that if you can no longer keep or care for the dog, you must give the dog back to the shelter, the truth is that many shelters will still give owners a hard time for doing so. Many owners choose not to return their dog to the original shelter for fear of a confrontation, and usually owners are feeling guilty anyway and cannot handle a confrontation.

It is far better to adopt a dog from a shelter that will readily and compassionately take back their dogs for any reason than it is to need to return a dog and have no place to take him, or no place to take him without being yelled at and blamed for doing so.

With a 50 percent divorce rate among humans (and that's when people date, live together and then marry), is it any wonder that some dog adoptions don't work out? Even with a thorough temperament evaluation, there are always behaviors that only come out in the home. A shelter can evaluate a dog forever, but still not be able to accurately predict whether that shelter dog will get along with your cat, your dog, your ferret, your rabbit or your children.

SPECIAL CONSIDERATIONS FOR FAMILIES WITH YOUNG CHILDREN

With the help of this book, you have tried to fully assess the dog's behavior and temperament with children. You have tried to screen for all potential problems, especially aggression toward children. But it is important to understand that if a dog is alive, he is capable of aggression. The only dog incapable of biting is a dead dog. What you have looked for in a dog who will be living with young children is a dog who has very high thresholds for all types of aggression; you want a dog who is going to live with young children to have a long, long fuse.

You are not just looking for a dog who is merely *tolerant* of young children. You are trying to find a dog who *adores* children—in fact, almost *prefers* them to adults. This is because all children, even very well-behaved and well-supervised children, will eventually do something to the dog, relentlessly, invasively, past the point of what may be considered fair or tolerable, and you desperately want to make sure the child does not get bitten or hurt at that moment. You want the dog to be as happy with a family as the family is with the dog.

Positive, loving relationships with dogs at a young age promote responsible, respectful, humane and caring adults. Children who are bitten by dogs are scarred not just physically, but emotionally as well, often for life.

In the evaluation process, you have looked at the dog's thresholds and responses to normal, everyday circumstances, such as how tense he may get when petted, nudged or approached while eating; and how tense he may get when petted, nudged or approached when chewing on a bone or pig's ear. You have observed how tolerant he is of having his body handled, or being hugged, and then being hugged for a longer period of time than he may want; how tolerant he is of being restrained, or being made to do something he doesn't want to do, or being held back from doing something he really wants to do. You have studied how brutal or gentle and respectful of his own size and the size of humans he is; and how affectionate, loving, congenial and social he is (since the more social he is, the more tolerant he will be of any of the above average discomforts). Bear in mind that you are trying to evaluate how the dog may behave in a home while he is living in a kennel. The task is difficult, and the ability to accurately predict future home environment isn't foolproof. But it is necessary to handle and work with the dog, and put him through the most complete assessment you can before placing him in a home with young children.

While temperament testing can lower the risk for new adopters, it is by no means a guarantee that you will never encounter aggression. You need to follow up with the shelter or a professional to make sure the dog is settling in well and not heading for an aggressive episode.

What to Watch Out For

- Watch out if your dog uses his mouth in play or to move or control the child. Any dog over five months of age should not be using his mouth to play, and is indeed probably not playing. The dog is probably trying to control or dominate humans with his teeth. No matter how gentle your dog appears to be, this is a cause for concern.

- Watch out if your dog cuts in between you and your child when you are hugging or engaging in any affectionate interactions. This can indicate jealousy, or rank/status aggression, or guarding of you, the adult, as a resource.

- "Let sleeping dogs lie" is a saying written by someone who really knew dogs. Teach it to your children (and keep an eye on visiting children), and **never** allow them to startle, awaken or hug a sleeping dog. Also, dogs by nature are grouchier and testier at night, or in the evening, and if your dog drops off into a heavy sleep in the evening, put him away in a private room or encourage him to get into his crate, so that you can prevent the possibility of a child startling or waking the dog.

- Watch for any growling, even in play. Dogs never growl for any reason other than to warn us they are thinking of biting. Growling is never a vocalization a dog makes just to "talk," although some breeders of certain breeds have mythology that their breed "talks" this way (commonly Rottweilers). Dogs don't talk by growling. They growl to let us know they need help and they are warning us that the next time they might bite.

- Watch for combinations of events. For example, your dog might be fine if approached by a child while chewing on a piece of rawhide, and your dog might be fine when approached and hugged while resting on your couch, but your dog may growl or even bite when approached by a child and hugged while resting on the couch chewing a bone. Your dog may be fine being hugged by a child in general, and the dog may be fine when held by the collar and restrained from chasing the cat, but your dog may growl, snap or bite when hugged while being restrained from something he wants to chase.

- Watch for signs of physical, rough play from the dog towards the child, or from the child towards the dog.

- Watch for any displays of rough, physical strength from the dog toward the child.

- Watch for any snapping, nipping or mouthing, even during play.

- Watch for any mounting or humping of the child (or an adult) by the dog.

- Watch for any signs of resentment or avoidance of physical contact from the dog toward the child (the dog backs off or leaves the room when the child approaches, gets close to or hugs the dog).

- Watch for any signs that the dog is afraid of the child (the dog backs away or tries to escape when the child appears or approaches).

- Watch for any signs that the dog seems "jealous" of intimacy or physical affection between parents, or especially between child and parents (for instance, the dog barks or cuts in between people during intimacy).

- Watch for any signs that the dog might be guarding his food bowl, his bones, his toys or a stolen item. (The dog may tense up, show the whites of his eyes, freeze or hunker down over the object, whip the object further away from the approaching child, or give the hairy eye-ball to anyone nearing him and his object.)

- Watch out if your dog is chained out, tied up, penned in or fenced in where he can see children playing, squealing, running or riding their bikes. This frustration and rehearsal of real chase-predation-play behavior can lead to actual attacks when and if the dog ever gets loose while aroused.

- Watch out if your dog ever seems out of control, disobedient or wild with children, especially when the children are running around or playing.

"He Got Too Big"

My shelter got a phone call from a mother who wanted to surrender her 10-month-old shepherd mix because, she said, "He got too big." She had adopted him from another shelter when he was just four months old.

When I first started working at a shelter 22 years ago, these "excuses" people gave for wanting to "get rid of" their dogs would infuriate us. They showed us just how irresponsible and uncommitted people really were. We would say (mostly in private, but sometimes, just to vent, directly to the callers), "What did you think? You knew when he was a puppy that he was part German Shepherd Dog. Did you not think he was going to grow up to be big?"

So when this mother on the telephone said that her family no longer wanted their dog because "he got too big," I remembered how it *used* to make me want to react. I have learned from experience that most pet owners are rarely uncommitted, irresponsible people giving up their dogs for trivial reasons. The one-line reasons often seem trivial, but that is only because we either ask them to sum up all their reasons for surrender in one line, or they come up with one sort of benign reason that masks the real reason (which they might not even be aware they know) why they can no longer keep their dog.

People who surrender their dogs are not necessarily bad people. In fact, they never want to think their dog might not be adopted out and will then be euthanized. They hope and believe whatever problems they are having with their dog are the result of something they are doing wrong, or they lack the proper time, space or training ability to provide the right home for the dog. Sometimes this is true, and sometimes the dog is actually quite aggressive and needs far more than "room to run" could offer.

The first thing I asked this woman was where she had gotten the dog. She said it was from another local shelter. I knew that the shelter she mentioned insists in its adoption contract that all adopted dogs are returned to them if things don't work out. So I asked if she had called the original shelter to tell them she could no longer keep the dog. She said she had, but had been asked by the shelter manager if she had done any obedience training with her dog. She hadn't. He told her it was her responsibility to have trained her dog, and that the shelter would not take her dog back until she had done her part and tried training. Still not wanting the dog, she called our shelter.

Obedience training, or any kind of training, is a great thing. It enhances the bond between person and dog, improves the relationship, stimulates the dog and helps keep the dog under better control. But obedience training cannot change basic temperament, and it does not address serious aggression. Theodore Kaszinski, the Unibomber, was educated: he went to school, learned to read and write and learned to build bombs. None of that schooling made him less violent or disturbed.

When talking with this woman about her 10-month-old dog that had gotten "too big," I realized what she meant was that the dog was *behaviorally* too big. It was not about physical size; she knew the four-month-old shepherd mix puppy she adopted was going to grow into a big dog. A big dog was fine with her. There was something more to the problem.

The dog was well cared for, was neutered and up to date on his vaccinations and was healthy, but apparently he was just too big for them. So I asked her when her dog seemed so big, and what exactly he did when he seemed so big.

And what she said next horrified me.

She said when her dog was out in the yard with her two young sons, he would play "kind of roughly." I asked her what the dog did when he seemed so rough. She said, "Like when the dog would grab my two-year-old son by the arm and drag him across the yard."

And that is "big." I told her to bring her dog to my shelter immediately. I didn't want her to have that dog around her children another minute.

DON'T GO IT ALONE

When all else fails and it comes time to return or re-home your dog, don't do it alone. You should have the counsel and coaching and company of a skilled dog trainer or behavior professional. The decision is a very difficult one, an emotional one, and not one you should have to go through alone. It is hard enough trying to explain and qualify your reasons to your friends (some of whom will be supportive and others of whom will not), let alone to strangers at a shelter. It is as important to find someone with excellent dog-behavior skills as it is to find someone who will treat you humanely and supportively.

Chapter 9

Adding Another Dog

Having a wonderful dog is wonderful; having two wonderful dogs is even more wonderful. I am someone with *five* wonderful dogs, and that's a lot. But I am a dog professional with the time, energy, and hobbies to meet all their needs. There is something to be said for having one dog on which to shower all your love, praise, devotion and attention.

There is equally as much to be said for having two dogs to complete your family. There is nothing easy about having two dogs, let alone *easier*. Some people think two dogs will keep each other company and entertain each other when the owners are not around, but the truth is that having more than one is usually more work. With many added benefits. But usually more work as well. Almost no dog will teach another dog his good habits; dogs teach each other their less-than-pleasant habits. The quiet dog rarely teaches another dog to be quiet, but the barking dog readily encourages his friends to bark with him.

But having two can add to the joy and fun of their lives and our own lives. Life is less lonely with a dog, and even less lonely with two dogs. That goes for your dog(s), too—life is less lonely for them. Dogs don't necessarily play together while you are away at work—in fact you usually have two dogs pining away for you. But when you do come home, two dogs make for an even bigger and better homecoming event. And whether or not dogs play together during the long hours you leave them for during your work schedule doesn't mean they aren't keeping each other good company.

It's important, when deciding to add another dog, to base the decision upon your own personal desire for a second dog, and not solely on the possibility that your resident dog would enjoy a companion. This chapter will help you select the most compatible companion, but the first hurdle is to make sure you are the one who really wants to add another dog. After all, if the pleasure of an added dog belongs only to your resident dog and all the chores belong to you, you will not likely be one big, happy family. Make this decision for yourself first, and then for your dog to share.

No matter how much you want to adopt a second dog, no matter how much you are ready to bring home a second dog, no matter how much you know your resident dog likes to play with other dogs and would really appreciate a dog-mate (not the procreating kind), no matter that you are basing your decision upon your resident dog's needs and wants, *you will feel guilty*.

You may feel like you are displacing your resident dog. You may feel like you are dividing your heart. You may feel like you are betraying your resident dog. It's OK.

These feelings are common to a lot of adopters, and luckily, they're fleeting. You (or your resident dog) will not feel this way for very long. I only mention this so that when and if you have these feelings, you will realize other people have felt this way, it is normal to feel this way, and there is no need to return your new dog because of these feelings. They will pass.

One dog is never enough!

CHOOSING A COMPATIBLE COMPANION FOR YOUR RESIDENT DOG

There are some basic formulas for achieving the most harmonious household. For instance, for whatever reason, female dogs make the best dog leaders in a household with more than one dog. They also fight the fiercest battles, and have been known (although it's very rare) to fight to the death.

The generalizations in the boxes below are not based on statistical percentages of dog-dog relationships most likely to fail, but rather on the most common and difficult-to-fix behavior problems dog trainers encounter in their private practice.

The dog-dog problems that are most common and difficult to resolve are not necessarily representative of the rate of problems within that particular matchup. In other words, just because two fighting female dogs of the same age, same size, and same breed or breed type is the most difficult in-home dog-dog problem to resolve doesn't mean that *most* pairs of female dogs of the same age, same size, and same breed or breed type are the most likely combination to fight. It's just that when they do, it's usually bloody, serious and difficult to fix.

Combinations With the Best Chance for Harmony

Resident dog female, older, larger + New dog male, smaller, younger
Resident dog female, larger + New dog male, smaller, younger
Resident dog female + New dog male, smaller, younger
Resident dog male + New dog female

If Both Dogs Are the Same Gender

Resident dog should be older, larger
Resident dog should be older
Resident dog should be larger

Most Risky Combination

Resident dog female + New dog female
Both dogs same age, same size, same breed type, same personality with people

So the information in these boxes is really just a way to reduce your likelihood of an in-home dog-dog problem. So much depends on the individual dogs.

Doggy Bitches and Bitchy Dogs

If your instinct is to call a male dog "she," then likely the dog is what we would call a "bitchy dog"—a feminine looking and acting male dog. In dogs this a fine thing. In all likelihood, he will simply not be a macho kind of dog, either with people or with other dogs. And this is great if you have children in the household or the neighborhood, or a top dog type at home. (Of course, it simply might be a mistake, and you tend to call all dogs "she" since all your own dogs or your childhood dog were female.)

The same holds true for a female dog you automatically call "he." She may be what we call a "doggy bitch." She may have big, thick, powerful thigh muscles. She'll look tough. And she may be a very macho female dog, both with people and other dogs. Doggy bitches sometimes go so far as to lift their legs when they pee, and they sometimes urine-mark many times on a walk, just like a male. Sometimes doggy bitches don't get along well with other female dogs, but do quite well with males. They are not necessarily dominant with people. If you already have a female dog at home and she is set in her ways or can get a little testy with visiting dogs, a doggy bitch may not be the best choice for your second dog. If you have a doggy bitch at home, try to choose a male dog as a companion.

WHY DOG-DOG AGGRESSION MATTERS FOR EVERYONE

Dog-dog behaviors are as important to observe in placing shelter dogs as are dog-human behaviors. You want to select a dog who will be a compatible playmate for your resident dog, but you also want to see what the new dog is like with dogs in general. There are very few places in this world where you can have a dog who will not end up meeting another dog. While your dog doesn't have to be able to play in a dog park or at a dog day care center, he should not want to cause harm to another dog. It is no fun to live with a dog who lunges, barking and growling, at every unfamiliar dog that passes by. And it is dangerous to live with a dog who might seriously cause damage to another dog. A friend of mine, while walking her dogs on a leash in a suburban neighborhood, watched in horror as her 13-year-old Shetland Sheepdog was attacked, killed and then *eaten* by a loose and unattended Pit Bull mix. The Pit Bull mix had been adopted from a shelter a few days before the attack.

In urban areas, shelters have to place dogs who will meet multiple new dogs on leash (often the most difficult way for dogs to meet and get along) every day. In many urban areas, dog parks are the only off-leash play and exercise opportunity for dogs. In suburban areas, shelters have to place dogs who will encounter other dogs while being walked on a leash, and also (more frequently than urban owners) meet unsupervised, off-leash dogs while they are on a leash. Also in suburban homes, dogs often spend time in small backyards, abutting other fenced yards, often with neighboring dogs to meet behind a barrier (another very difficult way for dogs to meet and get along). Even in rural areas, many owners have no fences and dogs run free more often. In rural areas, all hiking and biking routes are frequented by other people, usually with off-leash dogs.

All shelter dog placements need to be done with as much information as possible on the dog-dog aggressiveness and manageability of each dog. It is just as important for your new dog to get along with unfamiliar dogs in the neighborhood as it is for him to get along with your resident dog. There really is no adopter who can guarantee his dog will never meet another dog. You want your new dog to be safe and appropriate with all dogs.

Dogs who lunge at other dogs while on leash (whether it's true aggression or just a ferocious display) are nightmares for owners to deal with. Walks become more and more unpleasant, and thus more and more restricted and infrequent. One of the great pleasures of dog ownership is taking your dog for a walk. One of the most important things you can do with a dog to maintain good mental health and increase your odds of keeping your dog is to take him off territory for a walk on-leash each day. Imagine a child who is only allowed in his home and backyard, and never goes out or sees anything else.

Dogs who lunge at other dogs while on leash are feared by other people in the community. Dogs who lunge at other dogs while on leash are pegged as "aggressive" or "vicious" by neighbors, since it's the display that impresses and frightens people.

THE DOG-DOG AGGRESSION TEST

Dog-dog behaviors are perhaps the most complicated to figure out and interpret. Most of the signals, signs and actions a dog sends to another dog are conflicted, dynamic and have many possible meanings. But don't despair! You will learn something from each dog-dog interaction, and there are certain concrete observations you can make that will greatly enhance your chances of selecting a compatible second dog.

There are three categories of dog-dog information you will want before adopting a dog:

1. How does this dog behave when meeting and greeting other dogs while on leash?

   - Can he pass by other leashed dogs without lunging or barking?

   - Does he get so aroused and worked up that he redirects his frustration and would bite his owner?

2. Can this dog live with another dog in his household?

   - If so, what sex? What age? What size?

3. Is this dog aggressive with other dogs?

   - Is this dog likely to injure, maul or kill another dog? (Keep in mind that dogs who have killed other dogs will often play or be neutral with half of all dogs they meet.)

The Testing Procedure

This test can be done outdoors, if you have the time and space, or indoors in the biggest room you can find. Whether indoors or out, the testing area must be away from barking kennel dogs.

You may be evaluating the dog twice, since at first you will go to the shelter to select a dog *you* like; then you'll return to the shelter with your own resident dog to evaluate how the two *dogs* get along.

There are five main parts to the test:

1. **First Glimpse:** This is when you evaluate how the dog responds when he first sees another dog and is restrained from approaching. This test enables you to evaluate how obsessed or nonchalant the dog is with strange dogs. It also enables you to evaluate how the dog behaves when he's frustrated around another dog, and how he copes with his frustration. This test also flushes out a dog who might be a bit of a nightmare on leash—the type of dog who lunges and barks and strains at the end of the leash whenever he sees another dog. Dogs like this, while not always truly dog-dog aggressive, are difficult to control when out on leash and unpleasant to take for a walk, to say the least. This might matter less to you if you live in a remote area or have a secluded, fenced-in yard.

2. **Approach:** This is when you evaluate how the dog behaves when approaching another dog while he is on leash. Dogs behave the worst with each other when on leash. There are a few reasons for this, the primary one being that the leash changes the posture of a dog. When a dog strains at the end of the leash as he's approaching another dog, his front end gets thrust forward, his eyes bug out and everything about his body is saying to the other dog, "I am very bold and aggressive and I would like to challenge you." This can cause many a dog to respond aggressively.

3. **Nose to Nose:** This is the first time the dogs you are testing actually get to greet and touch each other. A growl, snarl, hackles up or bark here is not necessarily a bad sign. There are many possible responses to this particular test, and it can be the point where the dogs either fight or play.

The Health Risks

You may encounter shelters that do not allow you to have two dogs meet, for fear of disease transmission or some other regulation. Is there a risk of disease transmission when you introduce your own dog to the shelter dog? Absolutely. But you will be exposing your own dog anyway if you end up adopting. Furthermore, as long as your own dog is up to date on vaccinations and in relatively good health, there are very few life-threatening illnesses your dog can catch. The most potentially dangerous diseases your dog might be exposed to are distemper and parvovirus. Distemper is fairly rare in most areas of the country, except the very rural Midwest, some parts of the Southwest and some South Central Plains areas, and even there, it's not all that common.

Parvovirus is a viral diarrhea that is most potentially lethal for puppies under six months, and less life-threatening for adult dogs. Adult dogs rarely end up with parvovirus. Dogs with either of these diseases are usually very sick, and look and act very sick. By the time these dogs are contagious, it should be obvious to the shelter staff that they are not feeling well.

The most likely illness your dog will contract from a shelter dog is an upper respiratory infection, or a kennel cough. Like the common cold, these diseases are rarely life threatening to the otherwise healthy animal. The importance of evaluating both dogs together far outweighs the risks for a snotty nose and a dry, hacking cough.

4. **Loose Lead Contact:** The dog who makes it to this test is a dog who has not shown any true aggression so far. In this test, there will be a moment where the dogs will either spark a squabble or engage in play.

5. **After a Minute:** In this test you can evaluate how the two dogs play, how hard, with which play style, and how intense they might get.

The Test

Your own dog should come into the testing room first and be there for a few minutes before the testing begins. I want your own dog to feel as settled and as comfortable as possible before the other dog is brought in. You are trying to set up the situation where your own dog is the first one in the room/territory and is fairly comfortable and rooted, so that the test simulates the situation in your home: The shelter dog would be moving into a home where the resident dog is comfortable, first in the territory and has control of the resources. I acknowledge that your own dog will not feel too comfortable in the shelter, whether you are conducting the test indoors or outdoors. But setting the situation up this way at least tips the accuracy of the test in your favor.

Trainers and behaviorists know the worst way to introduce two dogs is indoors, in a small space, on leash. With that said, that is the way this test will be conducted. With a limited amount of time and space, you still need to try to ascertain how the two dogs might get along, as well as whether the shelter dog being tested is seriously aggressive with other dogs. The test does keep the safety of both dogs in mind. Each part of the test builds on the previous part, so if the dog doesn't pass one test, it is unsafe to continue on to the next.

1. First Glimpse

1. Have your own dog settled into the testing space (indoors or outdoors for a few minutes at least) and on leash. Hold the leash so there is only four feet of slack.

2. Have a helper (either a shelter staff member, a volunteer, a family member or a friend) bring the other dog into view, at least 10 feet away from your own dog.

3. Allow the dogs to see each other, but they should not be able to reach each other.

4. Time 60 seconds.

5. Observe both dogs' responses when allowed to see each other but not allowed to approach. This can frustrate some dogs and cause the dogs to strain on the leash. Hold your ground, and do not allow an approach. Do not yank on the leash or correct, discipline or influence either dog. This is not a training session; it is a test to determine their natural responses.

If either dog is straining on leash, let them, and don't try to yank or pull them upright. Straining on leash is okay for the testing process, since it is often the way real dogs will meet in real life. In testing dogs, we have only a few minutes to ascertain information that will last a lifetime. It's okay to use the worst-case scenario in which to assess dogs, as long as the worst-case scenario is commonplace and likely to actually happen.

Dogs who strain on leash usually do not have good greeting skills and/or are not well liked by other dogs. This seems to be not only because they are aroused, but also because their body posture ends up contorting.

Pass Responses for the Shelter Dog

- The shelter dog looks at your dog with only mild interest.

- The shelter dog looks away from your dog and engages with a human at least twice (makes soft eye contact, puts his ears back, and begins wagging his tail or wags harder when looking at the human).

- The shelter dog play bows and wide wags, with his tail level or just above level.

- The shelter dog barks once or twice rhythmically, but not more than four barks in a row.

- The shelter dog looks at your dog, but then completely ignores him and engages with humans.

Pass Responses for Your Own Dog

- Your dog looks at the shelter dog with only mild interest.

- Your dog looks away from the shelter dog and engages with a human at least twice (makes soft eye contact, puts his ears back, and begins wagging his tail or wags harder when looking at the human).

- Your dog play bows and wide wags, with his tail level or just above level.

- Your dog barks once or twice rhythmically, but not more than four barks in a row.

- Your dog looks at the shelter dog, but then completely ignores him and engages with humans.

Your dog may hard-stare, glare, growl or bark at the shelter dog, or stiffen or put his hackles up. If your own dog does these things, the shelter dog's Pass responses should include:

- The shelter dog looks away, breaks eye contact and lies down facing away.

- The shelter dog play bows and then loses interest within five seconds.

- The shelter dog looks or acts frightened by your dog's reactions.

Gray Area Responses for the Shelter Dog

- The shelter dog shows moderate interest (tail up high over his back, ears pricked forward, standing up on his toes, leaning forward toward your dog, straining at the end of the leash) . . .

- **But** also disengages from your dog *on his own*, at least twice, to engage in contact with a human.

Gray Area Responses for Your Own Dog

- Your dog shows moderate interest (tail up high over his back, ears pricked forward, standing up on his toes, leaning forward toward the shelter dog, straining at the end of the leash) . . .

- **But** also disengages from the shelter dog *on his own*, at least twice, to engage in contact with a human.

If your own dog lunges at the shelter dog, strains forcefully at the end of the leash, growls, barks, doesn't calm down in 60 seconds and does not disengage from the shelter dog at all during 60 seconds, you may need to have a professional evaluation done on your own dog, to test for serious dog-dog aggression problems.

If your own dog has played with many dogs in his lifetime, without a puncturing of the skin or shaking or thrashing the other dog, then proceed with caution. If you know your own dog well and he has a stellar history with other dogs, then the shelter dog's Pass responses should include:

- The shelter dog looks away, breaks eye contact and lies down facing away.

- The shelter dog play bows and then loses interest within five seconds.

- The shelter dog looks or acts frightened by your dog's reactions.

- The shelter dog growls back without straining forcefully at the end of the leash.

- The shelter dog lunges back at your dog a few times.

- The shelter dog hides behind the tester.

Fail Responses for Both Dogs

- Instant growling.

- Instant lunging.

- Instant hysteria—leaping, lunging, snarling, growling, etc.

- High-pitched whining and straining.

- Intense, silent straining.

- Either dog trembling with brow furrowed, ears upright and forward.

- Eye-stalking the other dog.

These Fail responses can indicate some serious dog-dog aggressiveness, and may indicate that your own dog might not be a good companion for another dog in his household. It may also indicate the shelter dog is not a safe candidate for adoption.

2. Approach

1. Let both dogs approach each other, nose to nose.

2. Keep the leashes taut as they approach.

3. Prevent contact if either or both dogs begin lunging and snarling and growling and straining hard. Terminate the test. Either nix the adoption of this particular dog or contact a dog behavior professional for further evaluation.

Pass Responses for the Shelter Dog

- The shelter dog looks at your dog with only mild interest.

- The shelter dog looks away from your dog and engages with a human at least twice (makes soft eye contact, puts his ears back, begins wagging his tail or wags harder when looking at a human).

- The shelter dog strains forward and sniffs the air, but does not drag your helper across the area to get at your dog.

- The shelter dog play bows and wide wags, with his tail level or just above level.

- The shelter dog barks once or twice rhythmically, but not more than four barks in a row.

- The shelter dog looks at your dog but then completely ignores, engaging with humans.

Pass Responses for Your Own Dog

- Your dog looks at the shelter dog with only mild interest.

- Your dog looks away from the shelter dog and engages with a human at least twice (makes soft eye contact, puts ears back, begins wagging tail or wags harder when looking at human).

- Your dog strains forward and sniffs the air, but does not drag you across the area to get at shelter dog.

- Your dog play bows and wide wags, with his tail level or just above level.

- Your dog barks once or twice rhythmically, but not more than four barks in a row.

- Your dog looks at other dog, but then completely ignores, engaging with humans.

Your dog may hard-stare, glare, growl or bark at the shelter dog, or stiffen or put his hackles up. If your own dog does these things, the shelter dog's Pass responses would be:

- The shelter dog looks away, breaks eye contact and lies down facing away.

- The shelter dog play bows and then loses interest within five seconds.

- The shelter dog looks or acts frightened by your dog's reactions.

Gray Area Responses for the Shelter Dog

- The shelter dog shows moderate interest (tail up high over his back, ears pricked forward, standing up on his toes, leaning forward toward your dog, straining at the end of his leash) . . .

- **But** also disengages from your dog *on his own*, at least twice, to engage in contact with a human.

Gray Area Responses for Your Own Dog

- Your dog shows moderate interest (tail up high over his back, ears pricked forward, standing up on his toes, leaning forward toward the shelter dog, straining at the end of his leash) . . .

- **But** also disengages from shelter dog *on his own*, at least twice, to engage in contact with a human.

If your own dog lunges at the shelter dog, strains forcefully at the end of the leash, growls, barks, doesn't calm down in 60 seconds and does not disengage from the shelter dog at all during 60 seconds, you may need to have a professional evaluation done on your own dog to test for serious dog-dog aggression problems. If your own dog has played with many dogs in his lifetime, without puncturing the skin or shaking or thrashing the other dog, then proceed with caution. If you know your own dog well and he has a stellar history with other dogs, the shelter dog's Pass responses would be:

- The shelter dog looks away, breaks eye contact and lies down facing away.

- The shelter dog play-bows and then loses interest within five seconds.

- The shelter dog looks or acts frightened by your dog's reactions.

- The shelter dog growls back without straining forcefully at the end of his leash.

- The shelter dog lunges back at your dog a few times.

- The shelter dog hides behind the tester.

Fail Responses for Both Dogs

- Instant growling.

- Instant lunging.

- Instant hysteria—leaping lunging, snarling, growling, etc.

- High-pitched whining and straining.

- Intense, silent straining.

- Either dog trembling with his brow furrowed, ears upright and forward.

- Eye-stalking the other dog.

These responses can indicate some serious dog-dog aggressiveness, and may indicate that your own dog might not be a good companion for another dog in his household.

3. Nose to Nose

1. Allow dogs to reach one another.

2. Leashes can be taut if the dogs are straining or leaning into them, or can be slack if the dogs are relaxed.

3. Observe how the dogs react when they first touch and get access to one another.

Pass Responses for the Shelter Dog

- The shelter dog looks at your dog with only mild interest.

- The shelter dog looks away from your dog and engages with a human at least twice (makes soft eye contact, puts his ears back, begins wagging his tail or wags harder when looking at a human).

- The shelter dog play-bows and wags wide, with his tail level or just above level.

- The shelter dog barks once or twice rhythmically, but not more than four barks in a row.

- The shelter dog looks at your dog but then completely ignores, engaging with humans.

Pass Responses for Your Own Dog

- Your dog looks at the shelter dog with only mild interest.

- Your dog looks away from the shelter dog and engages with a human at least twice (makes soft eye contact, puts ears back, begins wagging his tail or wags harder when looking at a human).

- Your dog play bows and wide wags, with his tail level or just above level.

- Your dog barks once or twice rhythmically, but not more than four barks in a row.

- Your dog looks at the shelter dog but then completely ignores, engaging with humans.

Your dog may hard-stare, glare, growl or bark at the shelter dog, or stiffen or put his hackles up. If your dog does these things, the shelter dog's Pass responses would be:

- The shelter dog looks away, breaks eye contact and lies down facing away.

- The shelter dog play bows and then loses interest within five seconds.

- The shelter dog looks or acts frightened by your dog's reactions.

Gray Area Responses for the Shelter Dog

- The shelter dog shows moderate interest (tail up high over his back, ears pricked forward, standing up on his toes, leaning forward toward your dog, straining at the end of his leash) . . .

- **But** also disengages from your dog *on his own*, at least twice, to engage in contact with a human

Gray Area Responses for Your Own Dog

- Your dog shows moderate interest (tail up high over his back, ears pricked forward, standing up on his toes, leaning forward toward the shelter dog, straining at the end of his leash) . . .

- **But** also disengages from the shelter dog *on his own*, at least twice, to engage in contact with a human.

If your own dog lunges at the shelter dog, strains forcefully at the end of his leash, growls, barks, doesn't calm down in 60 seconds and does not disengage from the shelter dog at all during 60 seconds, you may need to have a professional evaluation done on your own dog, to test for serious dog-dog aggression problems.

If your own dog has played with many dogs in his lifetime without puncturing the skin or shaking or thrashing the other dog, then proceed with caution. If you know your own dog well and he has a stellar history with other dogs, the shelter dog's Pass responses would be:

- The shelter dog looks away, breaks eye contact and lies down facing away.

- The shelter dog play-bows and then loses interest within five seconds.

- The shelter dog looks or acts frightened by your dog's reactions.

- The shelter dog growls back without straining forcefully at the end of his leash.

- The shelter dog lunges back at your dog a few times.

- The shelter dog hides behind the tester.

Fail Responses for Both Dogs

- Instant growling.

- Instant lunging.

- Instant hysteria—leaping lunging, snarling, growling, etc.

- High-pitched whining and straining.

- Intense, silent straining.

- Either dog trembling with his brow furrowed, ears upright and forward.

- Eye-stalking the other dog.

These responses can indicate some serious dog-dog aggressiveness, and may indicate that your own dog might not be a good companion for another dog in his household.

4. Loose Lead Contact

1. As soon as the dogs make contact, their handlers should immediately loosen the leashes and begin "the dance"—the handlers anticipate the entanglement of the leashes as the dogs circle or weave, so the handlers move in larger circles, *ahead* of the dogs, thereby preventing the leashes from getting tangled. It should look like the handlers are going around a canine Maypole.

2. If the leashes become tangled, have one appointed handler reach swiftly down to the collar of one dog and grab the base of the leash there, then drop the handle and quickly pull the leash up from the base. Do not pick up the dog's feet or reach underneath the dog, as the dog may be aroused from meeting the other dog and could unload on the handler with a bite.

Pass Responses for Both Dogs

- The dogs play bow.

- The dogs wag their tails tail low and wide while wriggling their butts.

- The dogs keep their heads slightly averted or perked, with necks stretched upward and arched.

- Their bodies are not posed frontally.

- There is no sustained, direct eye contact.

- The dogs sniff nose to nose with upright tails; tails are wagging stiffly but rapidly, like a rattlesnake.

- The dogs poke after a sniff.

- The dogs sniff the anus or genitals of the other dog.

- Play erupts within 30 seconds.

- The dogs make brief but benign contact and then separate and explore the environment.

Your own dog may growl, snap or lunge briefly toward the shelter dog. If that happens, an acceptable response from the shelter dog is to back off immediately, avert his eyes and retreat from your dog.

Gray Area Responses for Both Dogs

- The dogs remain stiff and their tails wag stiffly.

- Eye contact is sustained and direct.

- Either dog has his hackles up from the base of his tail to his neckline the whole time.

- Either dog has his hackles up from his mid-back to the base of his tail, or anywhere in between, for the entire time.

- Instant, rough play.

Fail Responses for Both Dogs

- Intense straining or lunging.

- Instant growling.

- Instant lunging.

- Instant hysteria—leaping lunging, snarling, growling, etc.

- High-pitched whining and straining.

- Intense, silent straining.

- Either dog trembles with brow furrowed, ears upright and forward.

- Either dog eye-stalks the other dog.

- Either dog orients repeatedly to the other dog's belly.

- Either dog snaps, growls, snarls, nips or bites.

- Either dog chomps, clacks or chatters his jaw.

In addition, the shelter dog fails if he jumps up or comes over your dog's shoulders and tries to bite your dog on the back of the neck, or if he snaps, growls, snarls or bites.

5. After a Minute

1. Follow the dogs around with loose leashes, and allow them to do whatever they want and go wherever they want.

2. If the dogs are playing, allow play for 60 seconds and then, without pulling or tugging on leashes, you call your own dog and have your helper call the shelter dog.

3. Handlers can use the dogs' names, make kissy sounds, clap their hands sharply or cajole the dogs to them in any way except physically manipulating them with their leashes.

4. Release the dogs to continue playing for another two minutes.

Pass Responses for Both Dogs

- The dogs play with mild to moderate intensity and, when called, separate and go to their handlers readily.

- The dogs play for awhile, then disengage on their own and explore the environment or go to a human.

- The dogs ignore each other but remain relaxed; they may or may not follow each other around and explore the same things.

Gray Area Responses for Both Dogs

- The dogs play roughly and intensely, but separate and go to their handlers readily.

- Either dog wants to play way more than the other; one is persistent in pursuit of play with the other.

- One dog is afraid of the other (he trembles, hides from the other dog, is tense, not freely moving, and may lick his lips a lot), but the other dog (who is not afraid) gently tries to cajole the fearful one to play, or cajoles and then ignores him, exploring the environment.

Fail Responses for Both Dogs

- The dogs play roughly and intensely and cannot be interrupted.

- Your own dog separates readily, but the shelter dog cannot be interrupted.

- A fight breaks out, and when the handlers try to separate them, neither dog can stop straining and trying to get to the other dog.

- Either dog immediately jumps up or comes over the other dog's shoulders with snapping, growling, snarling or biting.

- Either dog orients repeatedly to other dog's belly and snaps, growls, snarls, nips or bites.

- Either dog has to be physically hauled away from the other dog to get them to stop playing.

- One dog is afraid of the other; the dog who is not afraid spends a lot of time staring at the one who is afraid; the dog who is not afraid stalks the frightened one with his eyes; the dog who is not afraid walks around the perimeter of the area and urine marks, or sniffs and urinates more than three times.

Beware

Beware the silent or whining dog—one who is straining on the leash, aroused, ears up, brow furrowed, eyes big and round.

Beware the dog with a razor thin line of hackles between the shoulder blades.

Beware the dog who is obsessed with playing—plays instantly and constantly, is difficult to interrupt.

Beware the "eye-stalk" dog. This is when the dog instantly makes direct eye contact, gets very still, may or may not lower his head slightly, may or may not stalk forward, and often freezes in his posture in relation to the other dog.

Beware the dog who is on leash and is so hysterical in the presence of other dogs that he is lunging, growling, barking, leaping, straining. This dog is likely to unload all that stress on you—with a bite. Don't "correct" or jerk the collar of this dog, because that can very likely trigger a bite.

THE FOUR PLAY STYLES

Dogs play with one another in four basic styles. Some of the different styles blend well for nice, compatible play, while others do not combine well. While it is not the worst thing if your own dog and the dog you adopt have vastly different play styles, it is good to be aware of this before you bring a dog into your household. It is especially important if you live in an urban or suburban area and your dog(s) will be going to a dog park or dog day care for exercise, and will need to play compatibly with lots of other dogs (and play styles) to get his aerobic or off-leash exercise.

1. **Rough and highly physical body contact:** These dogs play by pushing into one another's space. They run hard, clash, rear up on their hind legs and then clash like rutting elk. There are lots of body slams and hip checks, all done with a fair amount of brutality. You'll see lots of hard impact and physical contact. (This style is common to the bully breeds, Pit Bulls, Boxers, some Labrador Retrievers and sometimes Doberman Pinschers.)

2. **Chase or be chased:** These dogs play by instigating a chase by running and egging another dog on. They usually like to both chase others and also be chased. These dogs like to run, and enjoy the excitement of

The dog on the right is a rough and highly physical playing dog, and the dog on the left is a gentle mouth-wrestler. What has happened is the dog on the right has repeatedly slammed into the dog on the left, who became frightened and then defensive, and finally snarled and snapped at the other dog to stop the game.

being chased. (This style is common to herding breeds and mixes, and sometimes sighthounds.)

3. **Mouth wrestlers:** These dogs play with their mouths. Usually one dog lies down with his butt in the air while the other dog dances around his head, their mouths engaged: There is the lazy, lying down role and the agile, leap up and over role. There is often vocalizing. (Various breeds and breed mixes seem to play in this style.)

4. **Scare and be scared:** These dogs play in the same way that children watch a scary movie: They can't help but thrill themselves by peeking through their fingers during the scary part. These dogs are not frightened or scared of other dogs—they just like to play by poking and jabbing at the other dog. Then they both freeze and then suddenly burst out in play. Often these dogs keep their ears pinned back, don't look directly at each other, and one will parry forward and poke and prod to get the other one to play. Both dogs get equally thrilled by play and the sudden explosions of activity. (Various breeds and breed mixes seem to play in this style.)

The play styles that combine best:

- Chase and be chased plays well with mouth wrestlers

- Mouth wrestlers play well with scare and be scared

- Scare and be scared plays well with chase and be chased

The one play style that doesn't seem to blend well with others is rough and highly physical body contact. These dogs play wonderfully with each other. But what tends to happen when a rough and highly physical body-contact player meets a dog with a different play style is that the not-rough player is unaccustomed to the brutality of the other dog, and often misinterprets that physical contact as an act of aggression. Or he will feel pain or shock from the contact and then become defensive. When he becomes defensive he may lash out—which the rough and physical dog tends to interpret as aggression. A squabble or fight may ensue. Here's a typical scenario:

A chase and be chased dog meets a rough and highly physical body contact dog. The chase dog runs and entices the rough dog to chase him. The rough dog gives chase, catches up and then plows hard into the dog being chased. He stuns the chased dog. The stunned chased dog yelps, then gets snarly and defensive (and certainly doesn't feel like playing anymore). He may snap, growl or lunge at the rough dog. The rough dog is merely playing and cannot figure out why the other dog got so nasty. The rough dog assumes the chase dog is spontaneously and unpredictably starting a fight, so he fights back. Each dog ends up thinking the other dog unpredictably started the fight.

Hurt, scare, hurt, squabble. When this scenario repeats itself enough times, some dogs (of any play style) can begin to believe all other unfamiliar dogs are unpredictable and aggressive, and therefore best greeted with offensive aggression. In other words, the best defense is a good offense.

Some Thoughts About Free Play

No matter what the play style, very compatible or not very compatible at all, I do not recommend allowing dogs to play for more than a minute or two without interrupting them. In this day and age we in the dog world seem to be encouraging lots of dog-to-dog play. There are a lot of dog day care centers and dog play parks; there is a lot of free play encouraged in group puppy classes, as well as in some adolescent or adult classes.

While it is hugely important that a puppy grows up knowing how to meet, greet and play appropriately (neither too afraid nor too bold) with other dogs, I believe significant damage can be done by too much free play. A dog simply needs to not *fight* with another dog. He does not need to want to *play* with other dogs. In fact, the older a dog gets, the less he may want to meet, let alone *play* with lots of new dogs.

If you cannot verbally call your dog away from playing with another dog, your dog is what I would consider out of control. A lot of very bad habits can develop with a dog who is out of control with other dogs. This applies to two-dog families as well as dogs playing with their dog friends. The bad habits that can develop over time include dog-dog aggressiveness, general lack of control, over-exuberant greetings with other dogs and with people, the dog stops listening to or obeying you, especially when he's off-leash or out of reach, and more.

Control and compliance come with consistent training and a strong history of rewards for complying. When a dog plays obsessively and uninterrupted with other dogs, he can begin to believe *that* is the most fun, and perhaps far more rewarding than what *you* have to offer. When you want him to follow your lead, the dog may feel you are no longer worth listening to—that what you have to offer is not as much fun as what other dogs have to offer—and begin to ignore you. Getting control back means becoming a good leader, and a good leader is one who provides the access to the most fun things.

Granted, nothing tires out a dog like free play with another dog, but your dog could get tired out by playing with *you*—a bike ride, a brisk walk in stimulating new territory, a run through the woods, a session of Frisbee or fetch. Good bonding, good and gentle leadership, good mutual enjoyment are what create the strongest and most lasting relationships and the best behaved dogs. You don't want to be in the bleachers watching your dog; you want to be in the game.

WELCOMING A SECOND DOG INTO YOUR HOME AND YOUR HEART

I would not change the house much to welcome the new dog. Leave dog possessions and toys as they are, if you have them already lying around the house, since I think the best time for dogs to learn whose possessions belong to whom is right at the very beginning—when your resident dog will be testier and more selfish, and your new dog will be most unsure and most apt to accept all your resident dog's rules. I think it's best to get these rules out in the open right from the start, when tensions might be higher, since this is when there will be the greatest difference between the status of the two dogs. Letting them settle the rules will set both dogs up for a compatible and unambiguous existence together.

If you have toys lying around, I would add to the toys—make sure if rawhide chews or bones lie about, that there are enough for each dog to have one (even though no matter how many duplicates of one item you provide, both dogs will always want the one toy the other dog has).

If you normally keep a full bowl of dry food out 24 hours a day for your resident dog, you'll have to pick this up and start feeding both dogs twice a day on a regular schedule. Even if you are one of the rare, lucky ones able to leave food out all the time and actually have your dog maintain a proper weight, it is extremely unlikely to work out with two dogs. Two dogs make for competition, and competition usually increases the appetite and speed at which a dog will eat. Also, a dog just coming out of a shelter is likely to feel a more intense desire for food and toys, since the shelter environment tends to be quite competitive (so many dogs kenneled side by side) and deprives dogs of resources.

While you'll want to shower your new dog with love and attention and assure him his new home is permanent and he can feel safe and sound, it is best to shower your resident dog with the most attention during this time. You don't want your resident dog to feel that whenever the new dog is around, *he* gets all the attention and your resident dog gets ignored. You want your resident dog to learn that whenever that new dog is close by, the resident dog gets showered with attention. He will quickly look forward to having the new dog come closer, since it predicts extra love and attention for himself. The new dog will also see that the resident dog is most important in your household, and that helps the two dogs establish a clear status hierarchy. You can use two hands and pet them both, but it is best at the beginning of the relationship to let your resident dog know clearly that he is still the most important—top dog in your heart.

If you have a family, make sure the kids don't shower all their attention on the new and novel dog (which is the temptation), to the exclusion of the resident dog. If you have more than one child, have each child pick a dog to shower attention on, then call a switch and have each child trade dogs and repeat the attention.

If you have adopted a second dog particularly to belong more to one member of the family than the others, it is still important to help both dogs figure out their role with each other first, and then have the new dog learn that one person will be his primary caretaker. It's hard for two dogs to live in the same household and each be the apple of someone's eye, and then understand that with each other they are not two equal apples. Two equal apples may constantly struggle for position as the big apple. It is easier for the dogs, and will cause less friction in the long run, to let them first work out the details of being two dogs in the same house (with your resident dog maintaining the big apple status and the new dog accepting a lowlier apple status), and then to part ways after a few days or a week and each become the most special dog for a different family member.

First Things First

The best *first* thing to do when bringing home a new dog is to take both dogs on a long, fun, side-by-side, off-territory walk. This will enable both dogs to scrutinize each other, fully sniff each other, blow off some steam, tire themselves out and have fun on neutral territory together, before working out the details of living together in one home.

It can be a good idea to take your resident dog with you to the shelter to pick up the new dog. Make sure your car is equipped with either two crates or that you can safely tether each dog to a different seat (one in the front seat, one in the back). If you can, have a different family member sit with each dog in the car. If you live alone, bring a friend along to help out.

Drive to a good area for walking or hiking, leash both dogs and march out for at least half an hour. Allow the dogs to alternate between sniffing the earth and each other, and then trotting briskly with just aerobic exercise as the goal. Then when you arrive home, both dogs will be tired out, familiar with each other, more relaxed and better able to gently work out how they are going to live together and share their new family.

WHAT DO DOGS FIGHT ABOUT?

Most fights occur when the owner is home. That's because fights between two dogs in a home are not usually fights for higher status among the dogs, but for higher or different ranking in relation to you. We tend to be our dogs' most prized resource.

Most fights occur in competitive places—like doorways and thresholds. Most fights are aggravated inadvertently by the influence we have with the dogs. One dog may growl at the other, and we just naturally yell at the growling dog to stop it. But by doing that, we side with the dog being growled at and send a message to the dog who growled that we will not support him as the one with power in that situation. We send a message to the dog being growled at that he, with us on his side, is more powerful than he thinks, and he ends up with a falsely inflated sense of status—while the growler ends up with a confused idea of his own position. When one dog growls at the other, it is usually because the dog getting growled at did something inappropriate and bold or pushy, or didn't respect the growler's warning eye, or status, and subtly challenged the growler.

Status, rank, hierarchy in a multidog household is not necessarily set in stone, but there is usually one dog who is the leader in most situations. Behaviorists call this top dog "alpha." The best dog leader will readily relinquish control of resources and share resources with the other dogs, and sometimes it can be hard to tell who is the true and predominant leader. The less adept dog leader will covet and desire control of all resources, all the time, and make huge, gross displays to obtain or keep them. Some dogs aren't alpha with other dogs by nature, but end up as the leader in a multidog household because they are obsessed with material things—in other words, they are Lord of the Possessions.

How Fights Get Started

Most in-home fights between dogs are the result of a possession problem. And, as I said, the possession most often squabbled and fought over is you. Here's an example of a common scenario when a new dog is brought into a household with a resident dog:

The resident dog is cuddling or snuggling with the owner, and the new dog approaches. The resident dog hard-stares and growls at the approaching new dog. The owner is horrified that the resident dog growled, thinks that's aggression and yells at the resident dog to stop growling. The new dog assumes the owner disagrees with the resident dog's assertion of superiority, and supports the new dog as the all-important dog in the household. The new dog continues to approach the owner. The owner ousts the resident dog from cuddle/snuggle area and invites the new dog closer. The owner showers the new dog with attention, especially because the owner thinks the new dog was treated so rudely by the resident dog. The resident dog is confused: He always believed himself to be the owner's most special and most important dog, and therefore assumed he had the right to respond to the new dog's intrusiveness with a hard stare and a growl. The resident dog assumed the owner would agree that his position is alpha dog. Now the resident dog is confused about what his place is. Does the owner love him best? Does the owner want the new dog to get the top spot?

When the owner hears the resident dog growl, and then yells at that dog for growling, it confuses both dogs. If the owner hadn't interfered, the resident dog would most likely have taken care of the whole situation on his own with the hard stare and growl, and the new dog would have immediately understood that he had behaved too casually, too soon. He would have backed off, averted his eyes, curled his body away and waited until the resident dog gave him permission to approach. But now, the resident dog has to growl even harder to maintain his status, because the owner did not back him up. This situation usually progresses over time; next time the resident dog will have to hard-stare, growl louder and lunge. And the next time, hard-stare, growl, lunge and snarl. And the next time, hard-stare, growl, lunge, snarl and snap. And so on, until very soon a fight starts.

The entire progression could have been avoided if the owner had just let the dogs work out that initial interaction between resident dog and approaching new dog. Assume that, under the rules of canine etiquette, the new dog deserved a hard stare and a growl (he wouldn't have received any discipline had he waited farther away for a signal from the resident dog that it was safe to approach and share the owner's attention), and allow the new dog to receive the warning and take heed. If the new dog had not responded appropriately by slowing his approach or waiting out of reach until the restrictions relaxed, then the next most appropriate action for you to take is to support and assist the resident dog by sternly telling the new dog to stay, or by temporarily shooing the new dog away. At the very least, if you can't bring yourself to do anything else, stand up and walk out of the room neutrally, ignoring both dogs.

Of course, this is easier said than done. These types of interactions can break our hearts! We want nothing more than to shower our new dog with attention and welcome him into our home, and to instantly be one big happy family. The thing to understand is that for a dog, one big happy family *is* one where he is growled at, and he has to follow strict rules and guidelines and request and obtain permission to access certain resources. The happiest households with more than one dog are ones in which there is some growling, posturing, hard stares, general grouchiness, some play, and lots of rules from both the owner and the alpha dog.

Some people believe that in a household with more than one dog, the owner is in the top position (which I absolutely agree with), and that absolutely no growling or posturing is tolerated. In this scenario, the owner rules with an iron hand and keeps the peace by suppressing and inhibiting any minor squabbling. This works well for many multidog households. Personally, I am very stern when I need to be. I can stop my dogs in their tracks with just my voice if I need to. But I allow them to posture, hard-stare and growl as they see fit to work out minor issues.

It's easier to support your resident dog as top dog and as the apple of your eye than it is to adopt a new dog and support him in that role, thereby demoting your resident dog a notch or two. Again, it can be heart wrenching to shower your resident dog with attention while somewhat ignoring or offering the loving leftovers to your new dog. But for the dogs, it will be absolutely fine.

Should You Let Them Fight It Out?

I have often heard it suggested that you should just let two dogs fight it out. That way, so the theory goes, they will establish their relative hierarchy once and for all. I don't know what kind of drugs an owner would need to be on to stand by and watch their own dogs fight—whether or not the dogs would be better off for it. Ever since I was eight years old, I have always had more than one dog in my life. I have seen squabbles and minor fights between my own dogs, and some serious fights between my dogs and my parents' dogs, especially when I moved back home for a while. Even if, intellectually, I thought it was best to let two dogs fight it out (which I do not believe), I have never been able to stop myself from screaming or shrieking when a fight breaks out.

Nothing gets your adrenaline going like a dog fight. There is something primal and powerful about it, even among small dogs. The minor squabbles my dogs sometimes have are really over before I have time to get hysterical. There is never bloodshed during these brief events (although sometimes I feel that if I had a weak heart, I would be dead by now...).

Do not allow two dogs to fight it out. They might certainly establish something, but some dogs will fight and cause harm, and some dogs will fight to the death. You don't really know the level of aggression in your dogs. You may be familiar with your resident dog's history with other dogs and know that it is benign, but you are bringing home an unknown dog, and you are creating a new combination of dogs. You don't and won't know what this particular combination of dogs could produce.

Most dogs can live together in peace (or relative peace). If you are confused or concerned about the behavior of your new dog with your resident dog, seek the advice of a professional dog trainer or behaviorist who is familiar with dog-dog issues, and seek this advice as soon as possible. Most dog-dog problems can be resolved, especially if they are caught early on. Most dog-dog issues that occur when you're bringing a new dog into a home with a resident dog are not serious, and can be worked out quite successfully.

How to Break Up a Dog Fight

The most common way for a human to get bitten by a dog is while breaking up a dog fight. It is also the most common way to receive a serious and damaging bite. So how do you break up a dog fight without causing yourself serious harm?

Most of the current recommendations are absurd, and are obviously written by someone who has never been around two dogs in a serious fight. "Spray them with water from a hose." What are the odds your two dogs will pick a fight near a water hose? Mine never have. Two dogs in my shelter once had a fight near a water hose, and by the time I got to them (the shelter staff had been spraying them with water for a few minutes) they were two *wet*, fighting dogs. Another choice bit of advice is "spray them with a fire extinguisher." Again, never have I been around fighting dogs when I have also been anywhere near a fire extinguisher; plus, I don't know what harm the foam could cause. I have seen people break oak chairs across the heads of fighting dogs, and pull one dog apart from the other dog by his hind legs—only to have the dogs still connected by their jaws. Fighting dogs are aroused dogs, and arousal causes more arousal.

The best tool for breaking up a dog fight is a spray can of citronella oil. The product is called Direct Stop, and is sold in portable and convenient small canisters that shoot a long, direct stream of harmless but intrusive citronella oil. If you can't get your hands on a can of Direct Stop during a serious dog fight and you are alone, grab a solid object and try to shove it between the dogs' faces (as opposed to hitting them on their heads). Keep your hands on top of the object, or at the top end, while pushing the object down between the dogs' faces. Throwing a blanket over one dog and trying to work it down between them is another option. If there are two people present, each one grabbing a dog by the hind legs works well—unless the dogs are attached and are not letting go (as often happens in a terrier fight), in which case a solid object jammed down between their faces while one person has one dog by the hind legs can pry them apart and then keep them apart.

A serious dog fight *always* warrants a call to a professional dog trainer or behaviorist.

The best way to avoid conflicts between dogs is to select your second dog wisely. Try **not** to adopt a second dog or puppy that is very similar in nature and personality to your resident dog. By selecting two dogs with very similar temperaments, you are increasing the chances that both dogs will want to fill the same exact place in your heart and in your household. More competitiveness and conflicts are likely in this scenario. If you are falling in love with a dog at the shelter who is very similar in nature to your resident dog, at least go for the opposite sex. This tends to increase your odds of a successful and harmonious long-term relationship.

Index

A

"A" = arousal, Safety SCAN, 79–82
activities
    backpacking, 172
    dog agility, 166
    dog sledding, 171
    earthdog, 170
    Frisbee (disc dog), 168–169
    herding, 167–168
    mountain biking, 172
    mountain scootering, 173
    musical freestyle, 168
    pet-assisted therapy, 170
    Rally-Obedience (Rally-O), 169
    road bicycling, 172
    skijoring, 171
    tracking, 166–167
    trail/sidewalk etiquette, 173–174
    trick training, 169–170
activity areas, locating early, 9
adolescent dogs
    adoption age guidelines, 68–70
    age determination factors, 143–144
adopters
    animal shelter questions/responses,
        18–19
    dealing with shelter refusals, 16, 48–49
    health check before physical activity,
        165
    home visits, 18–19
    lifestyle adjustments, 2
    non-aggression re-homing, 183–185
    overcoming new dog worries, 139–141
    pledge, 151–152
    pre-adoption checklist elements, 3–9
    right time/right dog decision, 2–3
    shelter screening process, 47–49
adoption age, 65–72
adoptions
    age guidelines, 64–72
    allergy issues, 63–64
    animal shelter process, 49–50
    breed generalizations, 74–75
    day pass, 64
    Internet sources, 29–40
    male versus female, 60
    Pit Bulls, 72–74
    puppy issues, 61–63
    rescue groups, 27–29
ads, Internet scenarios, 30–40
adult dogs
    adoption age guidelines, 70
    age determination factors, 144–145
    housebreaking, 155–157
aerobic exercise, socialization, 11
affection (lack of), Bite-o-Meter, 84–85
after a minute, dog-dog aggression, 200,
    210–211
age, determination factors, 141–145

aggression
    animal shelter evaluation, 16–17
    behavior indicators, 54–57
    Bite-o-Meter levels, 82–89
    children's issues, 9–10
    children's warning signals, 187–189
    dog-dog test, 197–212
    human gender factor, 96
    humping behavior, 178
    incurable behavior, 53–54
    mouthing behavior, 178
    multiple dog household, 196–197
    puppies, 61–63
    returning your adopted dog, 181–183
    Safety SCAN observations, 76–82
    self-trained puppy link, 176
    severity scale, 52–53
    small animal compatibility, 10–11
    temperament testing, 10, 51–52
agility training, dog/owner activity, 166
alert barking, owner reaction to, 163–165
allergies, adoption options, 63–64
aloofness, Bite-o-Meter factor, 84–85
animal shelters
    adopter screening process, 47–49
    adopter visit supplies, 93–94
    adoption process, 49–50
    behavioral rehabilitation, 90–91
    behavior response testing, 96–99
    behavior scenarios, 94–95
    breed determination types, 147
    children's visitations, 17–18
    customer service responses, 14–15
    day passes, 64
    dealing with refusals, 16, 48–49
    defined, 21
    disease transmission risk, 199
    dog-dog aggression test, 197–212
    don't judge by the cover, 19–20
    full access facility, 22
    "He Got Too Big" return reason,
        189–190
    home visits, 18–19, 49–50
    limited access facility, 22
    limited admission facility, 22
    locating, 13–19
    low-kill facility, 22
    no-kill, 22–24
    no-kill facility, 20
    open admission, 22–23
    questions/responses, 15–18

regional differences, 25–27
return process, 181–186
rural versus urban, 25–26
sanctuaries, 22
stray animal holding period, 21
temperament testing, 16–17, 51–52,
    99–113
truths about, 1–2
versus rescue groups, 27–29
when to avoid, 16–17
word forms, 21
approach, dog-dog aggression test, 199,
    203–206
arousal, aggression indicators, 79–82
Assess-a-Hand, animal shelter visit
    supply, 94
Assess-A-Pet. See also temperament testing
    attentive handler in chair, 112–113
    back stroke test, 109–111
    food bowl guarding, 121–126
    handler in chair test, 111–112
    hand movements, 106
    hand presentation, 104–105
    leashed dog observations, 106–109
    leash walking tests, 126–128
    noise response, 113
    pig's ear guarding, 116–120
    preliminary observations, 101–103
    professional level tests, 114–137
    resource-guarding tests, 116–126
    stuffed animal cat tests, 134–137
    tail set observations, 101–103
    temperament test, 100–113
    toddler doll tests, 128–133
attention sharing, multiple dogs, 216
attentive handler in chair, 112–113
automobiles, crate uses, 8
avoidance, children's warning signal, 188

B

backpacking, dog/owner activity, 172
back stroking, Assess-A-Pet temperament
    testing, 109–111
barking, owner reaction to, 163–165
basic commands, obedience classes, 153–155
bath mat, animal shelter visit supply, 93
behavior problems
    aggression indicators, 54–57
    children's warning signals, 187–189
    destructiveness, 176–177

growling, 178–179
"He Got Too Big", 189–190
house training, 176
humping, 178
hyperactivity, 179–180
mouthing, 177–178
pulling, 178
severity scale, 53
behavior response testing, 96–99
behaviors
    aggression, 9–10
    alert barking, 163–165
    Bite-o-Meter levels, 82–89
    biting, 54–57
    carsickness, 161–162
    chase-predation-play, 189
    dominance, 55–56
    fear biters, 59–60
    fearfulness, 58–60
    overcoming new dog worries, 139–141
    rehabilitation programs, 90–91
    separation anxiety, 162–163
    severity scale, 52–53
behavior scenarios, 94–96
bicycling, dog/owner activity, 172
bike paths, exercise activity, 9
birds, compatibility issues, 10–11
Bite-o-Meter, aggression observation
    elements, 82–89
biting
    aggression indicator, 54–57
    Bite-o-Meter levels, 82–89
    fear biters, 59–60
blankets, carsickness cure supply, 161
boarding kennels, locating early, 8
body postures
    attentive handler in chair test, 112–113
    back stroke test, 109–111
    handler in chair test, 111–112
    hand movement responses, 106
    hand presentation responses, 105
    leashed dog/inattentive handler,
        106–109
    tail set observations, 101–103
bonding, failure recognition, 180–181
boredom, destructive behavior reason, 177
breed rescue groups, purebreds, 27–29
breeds
    determination factors, 146–149
    generalizations, 74–75
    Pit Bulls, 72–74

C

canned dog food, animal shelter, 93
carsickness, overcoming, 161–162
cats, 10–11, 134–137
cautiousness, aggression indicators, 78–79
"C" = cautious, Safety SCAN, 78–79
chase/being chased, multiple dogs, 212–213
chase-predation-play behavior, children's
    warning signal, 189
chewing, behavior problems, 176–177
children
    adoption rules, 89
    animal shelter visitations, 17–18
    dog adoption issues, 9–10
    multiple dog household, 216
    returning your adopted dog, 186–189
    toddler doll as temperament test
        stand-in, 128–133
    warning signals, 187–189
citronella oil, Direct Stop, 221
cleaners, odor-neutralizers, 8–9, 158
coat length, breed determination factor, 148
coats, allergy issues, 63–64
collars, obedience class uses, 155
Come command, training process, 160–161
commands
    Come, 160–161
    obedience class components, 153–155
    Sit, 5–6, 158–160
community parks, exercise activity, 9
companionship, puppy/time-alone, 11
crates, 7, 8

D

day pass, animal shelters, 64
defecation, 6, 156, 176
destructiveness, 176–177
development traits, age determination,
    141–145
dilated pupils, biting, 85–86
dinner engagements, re-scheduling, 8
Direct Stop, citronella oil, 221
disc dog (Frisbee), 168–169
disinterest, Bite-o-Meter factor, 84–85
dog agility, dog/owner activity, 166
dog-dog aggression test
    after a minute, 200, 210–211
    approach, 199, 203–206
    categories, 198
    first glimpse, 198, 200–203

dog-dog aggression test (continued)
    loose lead contact, 200, 208–210
    nose to nose, 199, 206–208
dog parks (free play), 214–215
dog-sitting services, locating early, 8
dog sledding, dog/owner activity, 171
dog-walking services, locatingearly, 8
dominance, aggression indicator, 55–56
dominant aggressives
    children's warning signals, 187–189
    human gender factor, 96
    humping behavior, 178
    mouthing behavior, 178
    multiple dog households, 196–197
    returning your adopted dog, 181–183

E

ear carriage, breed determination, 148
ear length, breed determination, 148
earthdog, dog/owner activity, 170
enzymatic cleaners, keeping on hand, 8–9
etiquette, trail/sidewalk activities, 173–174
euthanasia, defined, 22
euthanizing, defined, 22
exercise area, 9, 11
exercise, cure for hyperactivity, 179–180
exercise lack, destructive behavior, 177
eyes, 85–87

F

Fail Responses
    attentive handler in chair test, 112–113
    back stroke test, 111
    behavior response testing, 98–99
    dog-dog after a minute test, 211
    dog-dog approach test, 205–206
    dog-dog first glimpse test, 203
    dog-dog loose lead contact test, 210
    dog-dog nose to nose test, 208
    food bowl guarding, 121–126
    hand extension test, 105
    handler in chair test, 112
    hand movement test, 106
    leashed dog/inattentive handler test, 109
    noise test, 113
    on-leash walking test, 127
    pig's ear guarding, 116–120
    stuffed animal cat test, 136–137
    toddler doll test, 129–133

family dogs, temperament, 76
fear biters, strangers, 59–60
fearfulness
    Bite-o-Meter factor, 85
    children's warning signal, 188
    human gender factor, 96
    reasons for, 58
    temperament testing, 58–60
feeding times, household rules, 5
females
    adoption issues, 60
    doggy bitches, 196
    gender determination, 141
    sexually mature/intact, 77–78
fenced yards, aerobic exercise, 11
fights
    Direct Stop, 221
    multiple dog households, 217–219
first glimpse, dog-dog aggression,
    198, 200–203
first-time dog owners, lifestyle, 2
flexi-leash, trail/sidewalk etiquette, 174
food bowl guardingl, 189
food bowls
    multiple dog households, 216
    resource-guarding tests, 121–126
foods, 5, 93, 154
free play (dog parks), 214–215
Frisbee (disc dog), activity, 168–169
frozen (paused) position, Bite-o-Meter
    indicator, 87–88
full access facility, animal shelter type, 22
furniture, 5–7

G

gender, determining, 141
Gray Area Responses
    attentive handler in chair test, 112
    back stroke test, 110–111
    behavior response testing, 97–99
    dog-dog after a minute test, 211
    dog-dog approach test, 205
    dog-dog first glimpse test, 202–203
    dog-dog loose lead contact test, 209
    dog-dog nose to nose test, 207–208
    food bowl guarding, 121–126
    hand extension test, 105
    handler in chair test, 111
    hand movement test, 106
    leashed dog/inattentive handler test, 109

noise test, 113
on-leash walking test, 127–128
pig's ear guarding, 116–120
stuffed animal cat test, 135, 137
toddler doll test, 129–133
growling
behavior problems, 178–179
children's warning signal, 188

H

handler in chair, temperament testing, 111–112
hand movements, Assess-A-Pet, 106
hand presentation, Assess-A-Pet, 104–105
harmony formulas, multiple dogs, 195
health checks, adopter/animal, 165
"He Got Too Big", dog returns, 189–190
herding, dog/owner activity, 167–168
heritage, breed determination, 146–149
hiking trails, exercise activity, 9
home visits, potential adopters, 18–19, 49–50
housebreaking
accident cleanup, 158
behavior problems, 176
crate uses, 7
frequency scale, 53
male urine marking, 157
potty elimination area, 6, 156
puppies/adult dogs, 155–157
household rules, 4–9
How to Breed Dogs (Dr. Leon F. Whitney), 147–148
human females, unknown animal behavior, 95–96
human males, unknown animal behavior, 95–96
humping
children's warning signal, 188
dominant aggressive indicator, 178
hyperactivity, behavior problems, 179–180

I

inattentive handler, 106–109
inattentive handler in chair, 111–112
Internet
ad guidelines, 31–32
ad scenarios, 30–40
adoption source, 29–40

J

jealousy, children's warning signal, 187, 188

K

kill, defined, 22
killing, defined, 22
kitchen timer, housebreaking uses, 157

L

Lab-Boxer mix, animal shelter, 147
Labrador mix, animal shelter, 147
leases, pulling behavior, 178
leashed dog, temperament testing, 106–109
leashes, 155, 156
leftover foods, used as training reward, 5
leg length, breed determination factor, 148
levels, Bite-o-Meter, 82–89
lifestyles, 2, 8–10, 194
limited access facility, shelter type, 22
limited admission facility, shelter type, 22
local police, shelter referral source, 14
loose lead contact, dog-dog aggression test, 200, 208–210
low-kill facility, animal shelter type, 22
lures, leftover food as, 5

M

males
adoption issues, 60
bitchy dogs, 196
gender determination, 141
sexually mature/intact, 77–78
urine marking, 157
mature dogs, adoption age guidelines, 70
mixed breeds, 27, 146–149
mountain biking, dog/owner activity, 172
mountain scootering, 173
mounting, children's warning signal, 188
mouthing, 177–178, 187
mouth wrestlers, multiple dog play, 213
movement, breed determination, 146–147
multiple dog households
aggression considerations, 196–197
attention sharing, 216
benefits/shortcomings, 193
breaking up fights, 220–221
cautions/concerns, 212
conflict avoidance methods, 221

multiple dog households (continued)
Direct Stop, 221
disease transmission risk, 199
dog-dog aggression test, 197–212
fight reasons, 217–219
food bowls, 216
free play (dog park) issues, 214–215
harmony formulas, 195
new home introduction, 215–217
overcoming guilt trip, 194
play styles, 212–214
reasons for, 193–194
toys, 215–216
musical freestyle, dog/owner activity, 168

N

neutering, aggression reduction, 77–78
newborns, age determination, 142
nipping, children's warning signal, 188
"N" = no need for humans, 82
No Bad Dogs (Barbara Woodhouse), 61
noise response, Assess-A-Pet test, 113
noises, fearful dog reason, 58
no-kill facility, 19–20, 22–23
nose to nose, dog-dog aggression test, 199, 206–208

O

obedience classes
advantages, 153
basic commands, 153–155
class size considerations, 154
collar/leash requirements, 155
exercise activity, 154–155
observing before joining, 154
positive reinforcement, 154
reasons for exercises, 155
reasons for leaving, 154–155
teaching you to train your dog, 154
treat uses, 154
observations
Assess-A-Pet temperament test, 101–113
Bite-o-Meter, 82–89
Safety Scan elements, 76–82
odor-neutralizers
housebreaking accident cleanup, 158
keeping on hand, 8–9
off-leash walking, 173–174
on-leash walking, 126–128, 173–174

open admission facility, shelter type, 22–23
outings, exercise activity, 9

P

panic attacks, fearful dogs, 58
paper towels
carsickness cure supply, 161
keeping on hand, 9
parks, exercise activity, 9
Pass Responses
attentive handler in chair test, 112
back stroke test, 110
behavior response testing, 97–99
dog-dog after a minute test, 210–211
dog-dog approach test, 204
dog-dog first glimpse test, 201–202
dog-dog loose lead contact test, 209
dog-dog nose to nose test, 206–207
food bowl guarding, 121–126
hand extension test, 105
handler in chair test, 111
hand movement test, 106
leashed dog/inattentive handler test, 108
noise test, 113
on-leash walking test, 126–127
pig's ear guarding, 116–120
stuffed animal cat test, 135–136
toddler doll test, 129–133
paused (frozen) position, Bite-o-Meter indicator, 87–88
pen/pencil, animal shelter visit supply, 93
pet-assisted therapy, dog/owner activity, 170
physical (rough) play, children, 188
pig's ear
animal shelter visit supply, 93
resource-guarding tests, 116–120
Pit Bulls, adoption considerations, 72–74
play styles, multiple dogs, 212–214
pledge, new dog adopter, 151–152
positive reinforcement, 154, 160–161
Post-It notes, animal shelter visit supply, 93
praise
Come command, 160–161
housebreaking, 156
predation behavior, children, 189
professional behaviorists, 191
professional handlers, Assess-A-Pet temperament tests, 114–137
pulling, behavior problems, 178
pupils, dilated, 85–86

puppies
    adoption age guidelines, 65–68
    adoption issues, 61–63
    adoption questions, 65
    age determination factors, 142–144
    aggressive behavior, 61–63
    housebreaking, 155–157
    mouthing behavior, 177–178
    regional differences, 25–26
    self-imposed housebreaking/aggression
        link, 176
    socialization, 62
    time-alone formula, 11
purebreds, 27–29, 146–149

Q

questions
    adopters, 18–19
    animal shelters, 15–18
    bonding failure, 180–181
    puppy adoption, 65

R

rail trails, exercise activity, 9
Rally-Obedience (Rally-O), activity, 169
rawhide chew, shelter visit supply, 93
rehabilitation, behavior programs, 90–91
relationships, household rules, 4–5
rescued dogs, attitude, 40–45
rescue groups, purebred/mixed, 27–29
resentment, children's warning signal, 188
resource-guarding
    Assess-A-Pet testing, 116–126
    children's warning signal, 189
    pig's ear, 116–120
rewards. See also treats
    housebreaking, 156–157
    leftover food as, 5
    obedience class uses, 154
road bicycling, dog/owner activity, 172
roommates, dog adoption considerations, 9
rough (physical) body contact, 212
rough (physical) play, children 188
rural shelters, common dog types, 25–26

S

Safety SCAN, aggression elements, 76–82
sample ads, Internet adoptions, 32–40
sanctuaries, animal shelter type, 22

scare/be scared, multiple dogs play, 213
scoops, defecation cleanup, 173
scootering, dog/owner activity, 173
senior dogs, 70–72, 145
separation anxiety, 162–163, 177
severity scales, behavior problems, 52–53
sexually mature/intact, 77–78
shedding, allergy issues, 63–64
shepherd mix, shelter determination, 147
shyness, fear biters, 59–60
Sit command, 5–6, 158–160
sitters, locating early, 8
skijoring, dog/owner activity, 171
sledding, dog/owner activity, 171
sleeping dogs, children, 187–188
small animals, 10–11, 134–137
snapping, children's warning signal, 188
sociability (lack of), biting, 84–85
socialization
        exercise area consideration, 11
        free play (dog parks), 214–215
        multiple dog households, 196–197
        puppy aggression considerations, 62
spaying, aggression reduction, 77–78
"S" = sexually mature/intact, 77–78
stallion eye, Bite-o-Meter indicator, 87
startles, children's warning signal, 187–188
state parks, exercise activity, 9
stink eye, Bite-o-Meter indicator, 87
strangers
        alert barking reaction, 163–165
        animal shelter visit behavior, 96–99
        fear biters, 59–60
        growling behavior, 178–179
stuffed animal cat, 94, 134–137
style, breed determination factor, 146–147
supplies
        animal shelter visit, 93–94
        carsickness cure, 161–162
        odor-neutralizers, 8–9, 158
        paper towels, 9
        purchasing guidelines, 8–9
        scoops, 173

T

table scraps, household rules, 5
tail carriage
        Assess-A-Pet observations, 101–103
        attentive handler in chair test, 112–113
        back stroke test, 109–111

tail carriage (continued)
    food bowl guarding test, 121, 122, 125
    handler in chair test, 111–112
    hand presentation responses, 105
    leashed dog/inattentive handler, 108
    toddler doll test, 129
telephones, locating shelter, 13–19
temperament testing. See also Assess-A-Pet
    aggression identifier, 10
    aggression severity scale, 52–53
    animal shelter evaluation, 16–17
    Assess-a-Hand, 94
    attentive handler in chair, 112–113
    back stroking, 109–111
    Bite-o-Meter levels, 82–89
    fearfulness, 58–60
    food bowl guarding, 121–126
    handler in chair test, 111–112
    hand movements, 106
    hand presentation, 104–105
    ideal family dog characteristics, 76
    importance of, 51–52
    leashed dog/inattentive handler,
      106–109
    leash walking tests, 126–128
    noise response, 113
    pig's ear guarding, 116–120
    preliminary observations, 101–103
    professional level tests, 114–137
    resource-guarding tests, 116–126
    Safety SCAN observations, 76–82
    small animal compatibility, 10–11
    stuffed animal cat, 134–137
    tail set observations, 101–103
    toddler doll tests, 128–133
terrier mix, shelter determination, 147
testosterone, aggression element, 77–78
therapy dogs, dog/owner activity, 170
thunderstorms, fearful dog reason, 58
timelines, puppy/time-alone formula, 11
toddler doll, 94, 128–133
town clerks, shelter referral source, 14
toys, multiple dog households, 215–216
tracking, dog/owner activity, 166–167
trail walking, etiquette, 173–174
training
    alert barking reaction, 163–165
    carsickness cure, 161–162

    Come command, 160–161
    housebreaking, 155–157
    organized class advantages, 153
    overcoming new dog worries, 139–141
    separation anxiety, 162–163
    Sit command, 158–160
    when to begin, 153
travel, crate uses, 8
treats. See also rewards
    Come command training, 160–161
    leftover food as, 5
    obedience class uses, 154
    pig's ear, 93
    rawhide chew, 93
    Sit command training, 158–160
trial adoptions, day pass, 64
trick training, dog/owner activity, 169–170

U

undercoats, allergy issues, 63–64
unnatural pause, Bite-o-Meter, 87–88
urban shelters, common dog types, 25–26
urination, 6, 156, 157, 176

V

valuable objects, safeguarding, 6–7
veterinarians, 13, 165
veterinary behaviorist, 177

W

walkers, locating early, 8
walking, 126–128, 173–174
whites of the eyes, biting, 86–87
Whitney, Leon F. Dr. (How to Breed Dogs),
    147–148
Woodhouse, Barbara (No Bad Dogs), 61

Y

yards, exercise area, 11
Yellow Pages, animal shelter referral
    source, 13